SRI LANKA– ETHNIC FRATRICIDE AND THE DISMANTLING OF DEMOCRACY

D0075336

S. J. TAMBIAH

SRI LANKA

ETHNIC FRATRICIDE AND THE DISMANTLING OF DEMOCRACY

The University of Chicago Press
Chicago and London

S. J. Tambiah is professor of anthropology at Harvard University and curator of South Asian Ethnology at the Peabody Musum. His most recent books include *Culture, Thought, and Social Action* and *The Buddhist Saints of the Forest and the Cult of Amulets*.

The University of Chicago Press, Chicago 60637
The University of Chicago Press, Ltd., London
© 1986 by The University of Chicago
All rights reserved. Published 1986
Printed in the United States of America

95 94 93 92 91 90 89 88 87 86   54321

Library of Congress Cataloging-in-Publication Data
Tambiah, Stanley Jeyaraja, 1929–
    Sri Lanka—ethnic fratricide and the dismantling of democracy.

    Includes index.
    1. Sri Lanka—Politics and government.
2. Sri Lanka—Ethnic relations.   I. Title.
DS489.8.T34   1986   305.8′0095493   85-24598
ISBN 0-226-78951-9
ISBN 0-226-78952-7 (pbk.)

Who can protest and does not, is an accomplice to the act.
Babylonian Talmud, Tractate of Abodah Zarah

I shall be asked whether I am a prince or a legislator that I write on politics. I reply that I am not; and that it is for this very reason that I write on politics. If I were a prince or a legislator, I should not waste my time in saying what ought to be done; I should do it or remain silent.
Jean-Jacques Rousseau, *The Social Contract*

CONTENTS

PREFACE

This is an "engaged political tract" rather than a "distanced academic treatise." I am a Sri Lankan; I was born and bred in Sri Lanka, and I am "phenomenologically" involved in the construction of this sketch of the ethnic conflicts there, a sketch that derives both from my lived experience and from my scholarly research and reading. I also want to state that as I labored over this essay I became increasingly confident that I was in fact correctly comprehending, both theoretically and scientifically, the historical movement of Sinhalese-Tamil relations as a whole, and that this understanding necessarily led to certain conclusions that have to be acted upon if the conflict in question is to be resolved. So this essay seeks not only to understand the Sri Lankan problem but also to change it; it intends to be a historical and sociological reading which necessarily suggests a course of political action. It is an exercise in theory and practice attempted in the belief that if educated and liberal Sri Lankans do not express their views now, and do not help shape public opinion now, the government is likely to drag its feet in seeking a viable and just political settlement. This essay was completed more or less in its present form by July 1984, and it does not deal with events thereafter, except in an occasional footnote.

ACKNOWLEDGMENTS

I wish to thank Ms. Radhika Coomaraswamy for permission to reproduce the *Report of the Committee for Rational Development* (1983) as appendix 3; Professor Howard Wriggins and the Princeton University Press for permission to reproduce pp. 268–70 from the former's book *Ceylon: Dilemmas of a New Nation* as appendix 2; and Father Tissa Balasuriya for permission to reprint the report made to the United Religious Organization (1984) as appendix 4.

I have benefited from the comments made on an earlier draft of this essay by my Harvard colleagues, Professors Arthur Kleinman, Sally Falk Moore, Nur Yalman, by Professor Loki Madan of the Institute of Economic Growth, Delhi, by Professor H. L. Seneviratne of the University of Virginia, and by Mr. Devanesan Nesiah, whose firsthand knowledge of local conditions was of great value. I am much obliged to Professor A. J. Wilson, Professor G. Obeyesekere, Professor S. Devarajan, Professor H. L. Seneviratne, Mr. Jehan Perera, and Mrs. S. J. Anandanayagam for making available to me various documents and published sources bearing on the present conflict in Sri Lanka. I want to emphasize that I bear the responsibility for interpretations expressed in this essay.

I am indebted to Susan Rosenburg for undertaking the typing, which also involved the decoding of my scrawl. Small grants given by the Wenner Gren Foundation and the Milton Fund of Harvard University have aided the preparation of this essay.

1
BACKDROP

Sri Lanka is a small island, about 270 miles long and 150 wide as the crow flies, which lies like a pendant at the extreme southern tip of India. Small, with mountains in the center where the tea plantations are situated and a coastline fringed with sandy beaches that today attract tourists from Scandinavia and West Germany, the beautiful island, with its luxuriant vegetation and striking scenery, has rightly been called the "pearl of the Indian Ocean."[1] Almost all visitors to the island wax ecstatic not only over its beauty and the splendor of its ancient ruins and monuments, but also over the warmth, hospitality, and good humor of the Sri Lankans as a people, who, among other things, can laugh at themselves and irreverently retell stories about the foibles of their fellow citizens, especially the politicians. Arguably, no other country in South or Southeast Asia, excepting Thailand, is more open and inviting to tourists, travelers, researchers and field-workers, and seekers of Buddhist truths.

How could such a people and such a blessed island be capable of the horrendous riots that exploded in late July and early August of 1983? The story is a complex one and especially difficult to tell, for the island's chronicles and inscriptions go back to the first centuries A.D. and successive waves of immigrants and generations of descendants can refer back to alleged precedents and paradigms and mythic charters to string together rhetorical accounts as to why and how things were and are as they are.

Notwithstanding their genial qualities, Sri Lankans are also apt to be proud and arrogant abroad: they feel superior to the Indians, the Malays, the Chinese, perhaps even the Japanese.

For their eyes are set on the West, particularly Great Britain, which was their colonial ruler from the early nineteenth century until 1948. They are proud of their British veneer: their elites acculturated more quickly than their Indian counterparts; their island enjoyed a prosperity owing to its plantation economy that was the envy of its Asian neighbors; and the British raj established a school system and a transportation system that, because of the island's size, was more efficient than any could possibly be in the vast subcontinent of India. And therefore, although India is undeniably their parent in many ways, all indigenous Sri Lankans—Sinhalese, Tamil, Muslim—become visibly annoyed, if not outraged, if Sri Lanka is mistaken physically to be part of India (as many people in distant parts of the world innocently do), or if it is thought culturally to be part of "greater India" (as some Indians patronizingly do). But in the post-Independence decades, at a time when new nation states are being founded in Asia and elsewhere, when many new states have initiated modernization and economic development programs, Sri Lankans have tended to rest on their colonial laurels, and to lose their sense of proportion as to their own real situation in South and Southeast Asian politics: that their island is small and of minor stature among much larger entities such as India, Pakistan, Thailand, Malaysia, and Indonesia; that they have little clout in the politics of Asia; that their record of economic development and modernization has been rather poor; and that countries like Thailand and Malaysia, which in the years just after World War II had a lower rate of literacy, a weaker educational system, fewer roads, and less experience in the arts of bureaucratic administration, are outstripping them in most of these areas. Sri Lanka has increasingly become a backwater island, which, however, in turning inward and in becoming preoccupied with its own internal disputes, fuelled by a demographic explosion, a surplus of secondary school graduates, fit mostly for white-collar jobs, and a narrow, straitened economic base, has become a self-destructive pressure chamber. Internal grievances pump up hot air, the pressure increases, and periodic blasts occur. Recent leakages from this smiling but embittered island onto the oil-rich Gulf states of menial, semiskilled, or even skilled workers, and the diaspora of highly educated Tamils as well as Sinhalese men and women of the professions—doctors, engineers, accountants, teachers—to all parts of the globe from the United States and Britain to Zambia and Sierra Leone, do not provide serious relief. They are symptoms of the island's deeper malaise: a small island of many people whose political machinery is running down in an environment of increasing fragmentation and factionalism. The hopes of yesterday—on the part of the left to make it a model neutral socialist state, and on the part of the right to make it an outpost of capitalist affluence and liberal democracy—have become fast-evaporating fantasies. How did these things come about?

The chief question I feel impelled to pose and answer in this essay in terms of the motives and intentions of the actors and the logic of the situation in which they find themselves, is how it is that Sri Lankans—literate, genial, friendly folk—can have come to this sorry pass. Why, on the one side, should an elected majority government committed to liberal democracy have become in its own eyes so righteously authoritarian, an attitude directly or indirectly assented to by large numbers of the Sinhalese populace? And on the other side, why should the Tamil minority, who have by and large considered themselves rightful citizens of Ceylon, have bred terrorist groups, hell-bent on achieving an independent Tamil state, and whose aspirations increasing numbers of Tamils support? Why is it that the Sinhalese, the "lion race," find themselves confronted, till death do them part, by "the tigers"?

The ethnic riots of 1983, when followed in detail, are instructive about the kind of inconsistencies, contradictions, and irrationalities that have free play in the island and which ought to exercise the analytical and interpretive abilities of social scientists and development experts (including economists).

Before I describe the riotous explosion of 1983, which many Sinhalese view as a venting of righteous anger against Tamil "terrorism," and many Tamils as a "holocaust" and attempted "genocide," let me set in place the backdrop of quantitative and distributional facts.

Today most Sri Lankans would think of their population as divided into three "ethnic" categories or communities: the

Sinhalese, who are the majority, constituting about 74% of the population; the Tamils, the beseiged minority, at about 18.2%; and the Muslims, who make up 7.4% (see table 1.1). The Tamils themselves are by general consent divided into two categories: the Sri Lankan Tamils, who comprise 12.6% of the population and consider themselves indigenous and whose migration from South India stretched from the early centuries A.D. to the fifteenth century or thereabouts, and the Indian Tamils, who make up about 5.6%, the majority of whom trace their origins to the waves of South Indian laborers brought by the British from 1825 onwards to work on the coffee, and later, on the tea plantations, which were established in the central highlands around Kandy, Nuwara Eliya, Badulla, Hatton, and Matale. The Muslims, remnants of Arab, Persian, and Malay merchants and seafarers, but in the main composed of people of South Indian origin (Malabar and elsewhere), are distinguished as an ethnic category on account of their religion alone.

The religious affiliations of the people of Sri Lanka, according to the census of 1981, were as follows: Buddhists comprised 67% of the population, Hindus 18%, Muslims 7%, and Christians 8%.

We are here principally concerned with the profiles of the Sinhalese and the Tamils, who today consider themselves as adversaries and antagonists. The mother tongue of the Sinhalese, the Sinhalese language, belongs to the Indo-European family (with subsequent borrowings in vocabulary and syntax from South Indian languages). The mother tongue of the Tamils today (and of many of the Muslims) is Tamil,

Table 1.1: The "Ethnic" Composition of Sri Lanka

Major ethnic group	Percentage	Number
Sinhalese	74.0	10,985,000
Tamil	18.2	2,687,000
Sri Lankan Tamils	12.6	
Indian Tamils	5.6	
Muslim	7.4	1,056,972
Others	0.4	59,400
Total population: 14,850,000		

SOURCE: 1981 Census of Population.

which is a Dravidian language. The majority of the Sinhalese are Buddhists. The remainder are Christians, among whom the Roman Catholics dominate, and are principally to be found among the coastal "fishing" villages and towns of the coast, north of Colombo from Negombo to Puttalam. The majority of Tamils are Hindus, and they too have a Christian minority, the Roman Catholics again predominating, and mainly present among the Tamil "fishing" communities. In actual fact, "fishing" in this context relates to their traditional caste status, which is known as *karāva* among the Sinhalese and *karayār* among the Tamils. These terms are best glossed as referring to people of the coast whose traditional occupations are fishing, boat making, and other ancillary activities.

Although the major identity components of the Sinhalese are their Sinhalese language and their Buddhist religion, and of the Tamils the Tamil language and their Hindu religion, both these populations share many parallel features of traditional caste, kinship, popular religious cults, customs, and so on. But they have come to be divided by their mythic charters and tendentious historical understandings of their pasts. In this Sinhala-Tamil dialogue and confrontation, one contentious claim must quickly be interred by the "objective" historian. Some enthusiastic but misled Sinhalese, and some gullible foreign journalists who do not do their homework, hold that the Sinhalese are (fair) Aryans and the Tamils are (dark) Dravidians, and thereby impose on Sri Lanka the famous divide in India between its "Aryan" north and "Dravidian" south, and thereby also raise the bogey of racist claims. Goonetileke has recently drawn our attention to Voltaire's comment: "If we believe in absurdities, we shall commit atrocities."[2]

In this regard I can do no better than cite *in extenso* as a note the major part of a letter Professor G. Obeyesekere, a Sinhalese anthropologist at Princeton University, who was moved to write on this matter to the *New York Times*.[3] Indeed, it would not be a distortion to say that if it were possible to trace the present-day Sinhalese population's ancestry far enough, all lines would in major part lead back to South India.

As an aside, I cannot resist bringing to the attention of present-day Sinhalese zealots that the dynasty of Tamil kings who ruled the Tamil kingdom of Jaffna in the thirteenth and fourteenth centuries boasted the name *Āriya-cakkaravarti* (Aryan universal monarchs), and that their capital was called Cinkainakar, meaning "Lion City."[4] Thus it would seem South Indians and Sri Lankans share in a Pan-Indian rhetoric of sharing vicariously in noble birth and universal sovereignty.

There is another clarification to be made. The way the ethnic conflict is characterized today, it would appear as if "Sinhalese" and "Tamil" are unambiguous blanket labels that divide persons into separate, bounded collectivities. Moreover, it is made out that Sinhalese and Tamils have always lived in a state of mutual suspicion, competition, and conflict. Some credibility is lent to this chauvinism by the fact that the great Sinhala Buddhist chronicles, principally the *Mahāvamsa,* composed around the fifth century A.D., use the labels Sinhala and Damila to describe the antagonists, the former as the preservers and champions of Buddhism and the latter as the non-Buddhist invaders. Sri Lanka still awaits that breed of imaginative and liberated nonsectarian historians who can accomplish five tasks. The first is to search for as much archeological evidence as is possible, and assess it in regard to the prehistory of Sri Lanka, and to construct the life forms of the autochthonous people who were already there far in the past, long before the Sinhala Buddhist chronicles begin their story. The second is to "deconstruct" these classical Sinhala "texts" and interpret their polemical messages in terms of their original contexts of composition. The third is to illuminate how these same texts have over time been periodically invoked and championed as a legitimating "historical" charter by actors in social and political contexts that are drastically different from those of their original composition. The fourth is to demonstrate that the Sinhalese and Tamil labels are porous sieves through which diverse groups and categories of Indian peoples, intermixed with non-Indians (most notably the Portuguese in the island's period of modern history), have passed through. The fifth is to document the half-forgotten facts that in South India, visibly until the ninth century, there was a strong presence of Buddhism, especially among the mercantile peoples, and that by and large, from the first centuries A.D. until the Cōḷa imperial expansion from the eighth century onwards, and the concurrent Hindu devotional revival and persecution of the Jain and Buddhist communities, the early and classical Buddhism of Sri Lanka during the Anurādhapura and Polonnaruva epochs had more to do with South Indian Buddhism than with the Buddhism of any other Indian region, by way of exchange, reciprocity, transmission of sectarian doctrines, and the granting of refuge to dissident monks during persecutions. Indeed, these exchanges and reciprocities lasted until the fourteenth century. The raising of these matters has as its purpose not the belittling of the Sinhalese civilizational triumphs in the Sri Lankan environment as genuine local achievements and crystallizations, but the debunking of the idea of an age-long and permanent confrontation between two ethnic blocs, the Sinhalese and Tamils.

Indeed, one of the main submissions of this essay is that the Sinhalese-Tamil tensions and conflicts in the form known to us today are of relatively recent manufacture—a truly twentieth-century phenomenon. We can see them as exhibiting over the last three decades a trend toward an increasing "ethnic" mobilization and polarization previously unknown. These regimentations owe more to the ideas and polemics of contemporary "nationalist" ideologues and the politics of nation making and election winning than to earlier concerns and processes.

One has only to go back to the period immediately before the Portuguese and Dutch occupation of the coastal regions of Sri Lanka (ca. 1505–1796) to realize that at that time the island was apportioned and fragmented between the kingdoms of Kōṭṭe, Kandy, and Jaffna, with much no-man's jungle between them. Within these multicentric polities lived peoples, many of whom were recently settled from diverse localities in South India—the Malabar coast, the Coromandel coast, the southern tip of Ramnad, and elsewhere. These peoples lived their lives as components of local or regional sociopolitical complexes rather than as ethnic "Sinhalese" or "Tamils" as they are conceived today. The situation was much the same after the Portuguese and Dutch took control of Kōṭṭe and Jaffna. The coastal peoples, who in the nineteenth century during British times were progressively enumerated and aggregated as the Karāva (fishing) "caste," the Salāgama (the "cinnamon peelers") caste, the Mukkuvār ("matrilineal" Tamil castes), and so on are quintessential examples. The Portuguese conversion to Catholicism of many of the coastal peoples north of Colombo all the way to Puttalan (and in some of the coastal areas of Jaffna) complicated in time the question of the unitary identity of the Karāva as a collectivity. The same problem was compounded when, at the beginning of the nineteenth century, the Karāvas and Salāgamas of the coast south of Colombo, all the way to Matara, presented themselves as born-again Buddhists, and founded their own caste-linked lineages or orders of monks. The rubric Amarapura Nikāya actually harbored a loose confederacy of monastic fraternities sponsored by localities and parochial interests rather than by large-scale unitary castes with communal identity. The Amarapura order of monks stood in opposition to the Siyam Nikāya, the "establishment" Buddhist monastic communities, recruited from that equally fuzzy and diffuse category of persons labeled the Goyigama caste (the "farmers," the "good people," of the interior).[5]

As we shall see later, during these same periods the so-called Sri Lankan Tamils, in contrast to the so-called Indian Tamils, were also not a unitary group or collectivity. They were drawn from diverse localities of origin in South India and settled in the north of Sri Lanka or on its eastern coast over long periods of time in discontinuous waves of migration. This was attested to by internal differences in custom, kinship structure, inheritance practices, ritual cults and so on. Moreover, the eastern portion of the island was in medieval times politically more the outer zone of peripheral control of the Sinhalese Kandyan kingdom rather than the Tamil kingdom of Jaffna.

Thus it seems to me—to make another programmatic statement in the hope of dissolving contemporary fixations—Sri Lanka awaits the blooming of a social historian of the nineteenth and twentieth centuries who will write the story of how different geographical segments (coastal and interior), different caste categories (Karāva, Salāgama, Paravar, Goyigama, and others among the "Sinhalese," and Vellāla, Karaiyār, Mukkuvār, and others among the Tamils), and different communal aggregates (low-country Sinhalese versus

Kandyan Sinhalese versus Jaffna Tamils versus Balticaloa Tamils versus Indian plantation Tamils and so on) have at different times become participants in an increasingly encompassing political process and an expanding colonial-type economy during the time of British rule (1796–1948). And the post-Independence phase of Sri Lanka is necessarily a continuation and transformation of processes set in motion during the critical period of the British raj. While the expansionary and interactional spiral of the last phase of British rule increasingly erased older divisions, the nation-and-state-building activities of the post-Independence decades have, while carrying further the older processes, also stimulated the process of "ethnic mobilization" that has reached its climax in the present Sinhalese-Tamil split.

The Contemporary Distribution of the Tamils vis-à-vis the Sinhalese

The contemporary geographical distribution of the Tamils vis à vis the Sinhalese is relevant for assessing in which parts of the island ethnic conflicts are likely to occur by virtue of the co-presence of the two categories in visible and conspicuous numbers. Figure 1.1 gives the Sinhalese-Tamil distributions by zones.

The Sri Lankan Tamils are the decisive majority in zone 4: much of this area comprises their traditional "homelands" of Jaffna and Vavuniya, Batticaloa, and Trincomalee. Tamils, in this case Indian Tamils mostly, are noticeably present in zone 3, the central highlands of Nuwara Eliya and Badulla districts in particular. They comprise there 15% of the population in contrast to a Sinhalese presence of 79%. It is only in the capital city of Colombo and its surrounding districts that the Tamil presence, both Sri Lankan and Indian, reaches anything like 11% (the Sinhalese proportion here being 78%).

Table 1.2 predicts three sensitive areas where Sinhala-Tamil tensions may be expected to occur. The first sensitive spot is the capital city of Colombo and its suburbs. It is here that large numbers of Sri Lankan Tamils are concentrated as clerical and administrative personnel in government departments and business firms, and as members of professions such

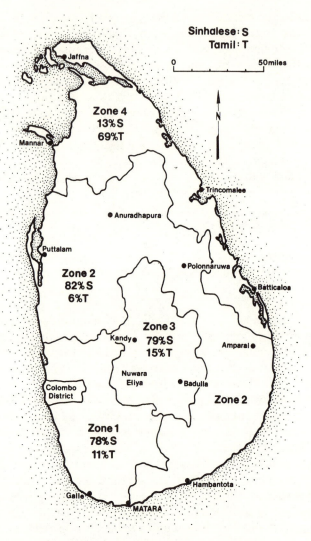

Fig. 1.1: Sri Lankan ethnic distribution by zones.

as medicine, law, and accounting. Indian business and banking interests are also located here, the South Indian representation being visible especially in small retail businesses such as cloth shops, grocery stores, restaurants, and boutiques.

Table 1.2: Vulnerable Areas Where Sinhala-Tamil Clashes
            May Be Expected

| | | Percentage of ethnic groups | | | |
	Sinhala	Sri Lankan Tamil	Indian Tamil	Muslim	Other
1. National capital					
Colombo	77.9	9.8	1.3	8.3	2.7
2. Plantations in Central Provinces by districts[a]					
Kandy	75.0	4.9	9.3	9.9	.9
Matale	79.9	5.9	6.7	7.2	.3
Kegalle	86.3	2.1	6.4	5.1	.1
Badulla	68.5	5.7	21.1	4.2	.5
Ratnapura	84.7	2.3	11.1	1.7	.2
Nuwara Eliya	35.9	13.5	47.3	2.8	.5
3. Contentious: New areas of colonization by districts					
Vavuniya	16.6	56.9	19.4	6.9	.2
Trincomalee	33.6	33.8	2.6	29	1
Amparai	37.6	20.1	.4	41.6	.3

SOURCE: 1981 Census of Population.
[a]Indian Tamil's largest presence in Nuwara Eliya and Badulla.

The second sensitive region, this time fairly extensive, contains the tea plantations in the central provinces, where the Indian laborers are distributed in "coolie lines," and the Sinhalese trading elements are concentrated in the servicing market towns, sometimes cheek by jowl with their Tamil and Muslim competitors. The largest of these towns, such as Kandy, Matale, Badulla, Ratnapura, and Nuwara Eliya, are also government centers and have the usual range of administrative personnel, mostly Sinhalese and some Tamils. The Indian Tamil presence is most conspicuous in Nuwara Eliya and Badulla districts (47% and 21% respectively), and these may therefore be expected to be potentially explosive areas.

The third sensitive area is composed of districts such as Vavuniya, Trincomalee, and Amparai, which were in the past peripheral zones lying between Sinhalese and Sri Lankan Tamil areas of strength, but which in recent decades have been the sites of government-sponsored peasant colonization and other development schemes. They are therefore areas to which poor peasantry from other parts of the island, the majority being Sinhalese, have been transplanted. The Sri Lankan Tamils consider Vavuniya and Trincomalee as parts of their zones, and view the peopling of these areas by Sinhalese migrants as a deliberate and hostile act aimed at weakening them. From the Sinhalese point of view, the reclaiming of the jungle and wasteland of peripheral areas is a much-needed government development activity of which the Sinhalese majority are inevitable beneficiaries.

There is one last set of figures that I must cite that marks another important point about the situation of the Tamils. If one studies their distribution in the country as a whole, one finds that 47% of the entire Tamil population is to be found outside zone 4, which is the zone of their numerical dominance (53% of the Tamils live in this zone). The critical fact is that nearly half the Tamil population lives in areas of Sinhalese dominance, and this dispersion is dictated by the necessity, especially for the Sri Lankan Tamils, of finding employment and earning their livelihood outside the Northern and Eastern provinces because these provinces are peripherally situated in relation to the island's economic and administrative centers and urban formations. Moreover, a concentration of Indian Tamils comprise 15% of the population in the tea plantation districts of zone 3, which lies in the very center of the island and has a preponderant Sinhalese population. These facts have to be borne in mind in assessing how realistic the extremist Tamil demand for a separate state is from the point of view of economic and territorial viability, and in realizing how vulnerable the Tamil "terrorist" activity makes the highly dispersed Tamil population in the Sinhalese provinces to acts of Sinhalese revenge. But from the Tamil separatist point of view, it is precisely this vulnerability that is exposed by their calculated provocation of the Sinhalese, which they hope will increasingly force the Tamils to regroup in areas of Tamil majority as a means of long-term survival.

2
THE RIOTS OF 1983
AND THEIR ORIGINS:
Deep Tensions and Surface Features

In recent times, seven occurrences of mass violence have been unleashed by segments of the Sinhalese population against the Tamils. All these disturbing eruptions have taken place since the achievement of independence by Sri Lanka in 1948. The most destructive of them took place in the years 1958, 1977, 1981, and 1983. (The only other example of ethnic riots in this century—fueled by religious irritations and commercial competition—was the Sinhalese-Muslim riots of 1915, which the British stamped out with severity and some misguided actions.)[1] Thus it is a fair inference that this chain of violent outbursts against the Tamils is very much a phenomenon of the second half of the twentieth century, the worst occurrences exploding in rapid succession after 1977. Thus, whatever the more remote and alleged continuing and deep-rooted sources of ethnic tensions in Sri Lanka, no analyst can do justice to the question without pinpointing critical tensions and pressures at work in the present sociopolitical and economic circumstances of this island, embroiled in the problems and issues of economic development, modernization, cultural and populist revivalism, and political Buddhism.

Indeed, we should take note in this context of another fact that strengthens the foregoing point. The catalog of violent Sinhalese eruptions against the Tamils—eruptions noted as much for unruly mob attacks as for their merciful abatement in a few weeks (a fact equally true of Hindu-Muslim and Hindu-Sikh riots in India)—would be incomplete if we did not allude to the Sinhalese youth insurrection of April 1971, under the political label of Janatā Vimukti Peramuṇa (JVP). This insurrection has been characterized as the "first large-scale revolt against the government by youth in this country," and the JVP has been described as an "ultra-left organization dominated by educated youths, unemployed or disadvantageously employed."[2] The insurgents were, it seems, children of the rural poor, all Sinhalese and mostly Buddhist, and there were among them scarcely any members of other ethnic and religious minorities. This abortive insurrection has some instructive lessons for us as an antecedent event to the ethnic eruptions of the late 1970s and early 1980s. First, the JVP rebellion showed the emergence of a cell-type organization formed for violent action. It was, however, an underground movement formed outside the patronage of the government in power. (What happens when such private cells and mini-armies are organized from within the ranks of the government in defiance of, or parallel with, the official agencies of law and order is the subject of our later analysis.)

Second, the JVP insurrection resulted in the calling out by the government of the army and police, which in fact were tested on this scale for the first time. Their success in dealing with the rebels gave them added prestige and new muscle. (What if these tame armed forces were to condone civil disorder as passive witnesses, or even as collaborators, in the belief that this action was in support of the government interests?) In any case, the insurrection—staged by Sinhala Buddhist youths—showed that there was a malaise of frustrated aspirations among the newly educated youth of a country whose liberal education program was at odds with its insufficient economic expansion. (What if the frustrations in the next round were redirected toward a more defenceless scapegoat, an ethnic minority credited with undue advantages and privileges and manipulations—like the Jews of the European fascist epoch?)

Third, the insurrection invited a most ominous disproportional response from the government of Mrs. Bandaranaike, which was then in power: it proclaimed an emergency shortly before the insurrection in March 1971, and maintained it in force for *six continuous years* until February 1977. During this period thousands of suspects were detained without trial. This precedent has not been lost on the government that succeeded Mrs. Bandaranaike.

Although the riots of 1983 were the last in a series extending from 1956, they were distinctly different from the others in certain respects.

The conventional and agreed-upon story is that the most proximate cause or trigger was the ambush of an army truck and the killing and mutilation of thirteen soldiers at Tinneveli, a place in the Jaffna district in the heart of Sri Lankan Tamil territory, which had been under army occupation for some time. This ambush was made by a group of Sri Lankan Tamil youth who call themselves the "Liberation Tigers" of Tamil Eelam,[3] and whom the government refers to as terrorists. The army of occupation, some 1,200 troops at the time, was composed almost totally of Sinhalese. Indeed, the armed forces (but not the police) in Sri Lanka today are virtually filled by the majority Sinhalese, and the Tamil minority are virtually excluded from serving in them. In 1983, Tamils at best formed only 5% or less of a standing army of around 11,000 regulars and about 2,000–4,000 volunteers. Even more disconcerting is that there has been virtually no recruitment of Tamils into the armed forces, and very little into the police force, for nearly thirty years. Except for the age group close to retirement, Tamils are today virtually unrepresented in the armed forces and heavily underrepresented in the police force if we take their population size as a criterion, a criterion that most Sinhalese automatically invoke in their favor.

On July 23, after the ambush and the killing of the thirteen soldiers, certain outraged army elements brought the corpses in their mangled state to the capital city of Colombo, and publicly displayed them in Colombo's central cemetery of Kanatte (in Borella). It is said by some that these army elements (particularly those who had served with the dead), relatives and friends of the dead who had become emotionally unhinged by grief and the exposure of the corpses, plus some of the local Sinhala populace in the vicinity of the cemetery in Borella, began the actual orgy of killing Tamils in Colombo, burning their homes, businesses, and factories, as well as pillaging and looting them. This outburst paralyzed Colombo for seventy-two hours, during which time the president himself seemed powerless to act, for he himself, for fear of being besieged, was sealed off and protected in his residence by a selected cordon of trusted army personnel. One of the remarkable incidents that, whatever the "beginnings" of the riots, foreshadowed the breakdown of law and order among even those charged with keeping them, was the murder on July 25 and July 27 of some fifty-three Tamil "terrorists" who were at that time incarcerated in Colombo's major prison, Welikade (located in or near Borella). The official version of the incident was that the murders were conducted by outraged Sinhalese prisoners in the same jail. But since the Tamil terrorists were kept apart in maximum security, the murders could not have taken place without the collusion at least of some of the jail guards and prison authorities.

Now a word about the "proximate" cause—the ambush of thirteen Sinhalese troops by the Tamil "Tigers." As we know from elsewhere—Northern Ireland, Lebanon, Israel's West Bank and so on—the combatants usually engage in accusations and counter-accusations, proximate events being preceded by earlier events in a chain of a mutual exchange of mounting insults and violence. If then, in late July, the Sinhalese charged the Tamils with the killing of thirteen soldiers, the Tamils in turn charged the army of occupation in Jaffna with going on punitive expeditions killing innocent civilians and torturing several hundreds without cause. An explosive and as yet unproven allegation was the rape in mid-July of Tamil female students, two of whom subsequently committed suicide. But then the government in turn charged that still earlier in June, the Tigers raided a cement factory in Jaffna that was guarded by troops, and made off with army uniforms and a cache of dynamite. And the Tigers and the TULF (Tamil United Liberation Front) politicians claimed in riposte that on July 3 the government introduced the most draconian measure ever perpetrated in Sri Lanka, namely, Emergency Regulation 15A, which allowed the security forces to bury or cremate the bodies of people shot by them without revealing their identities or carrying out inquests.

Indeed, these mutually escalating recriminations, charges, and outrages are mostly "true" as these things go, but they themselves are symptomatic and indices of a *single web* of insurgency on the one side and ugly repression on the other that has become interwoven to produce a horrifying situation. This above all is Sri Lanka's tragedy.

One strand in this tragic web is that the appearance of the Tamil insurgents, who are dedicated to violent action against the Sinhalese-dominated government, is a recent development of the early 1970s. Indeed, their resistance became militant in 1972 when the government introduced its so-called standardization policy with regard to university admissions, which was realistically seen by the Tamil youth as serious discrimination against them. This militancy became violent when nine accidental deaths occurred in the course of an indefensible police attack on the participants of an International Tamil Conference held in Jaffna in 1974. Previously held in Madras and Kuala Lumpur, the aim of this conference was primarily academic and cultural, both to assess and celebrate the attainments of Tamil civilization in India and elsewhere. The senior police officer (an assistant superintendent of police) who led the attack was promoted for his patriotic act—a response of the government of Mrs. Bandaranaike and one that President Jayawardene was to imitate later—and as if in counteraction the mayor of Jaffna who collaborated with that police officer was killed the following year. This was the first killing staged by the insurgents.

In any case the "terrorist" violence has come at the end of what the Tamil youth and radicals construe to be a persistent, unfair, and sporadically terrorizing campaign of discrimination and domination on the part of the majority Sinhalese that began especially in 1956, with the accession to power of Buddhist Sinhala chauvinism, and against which constitutional, democratic, and lawful action and protests by the Tamils have been to no avail. Whatever we may think of the Tamil contribution to Sinhalese attitudes—and I shall have something to say on this later—yet this much is undeniable: the Sinhalese majority have since 1956 persistently discriminated against the Tamils, especially in the fields of education and job recruitment, and Tamil objections to these injustices have sporadically been rewarded with violence.

And most viciously, it is in the 1980s that violence on the Tamil side and repressive totalitarian measures on the

Sinhalese side (I refer here of course only to segments of the total populations) have fed each other. Remarkably, ever since the United National Party, under the presidency of Jayawardene, attained an invincible majority status with the referendum of December 1982, the Tamil insurgents have stepped up their sporadic guerilla attacks on the security forces stationed in the north, and by July of 1983 killed about forty of them. And the government *pari passu* has retaliated with the imposition of more repressive military rule by virtue of a declaration of emergency in the Tamil districts of Jaffna, Vavuniya and Mannar. This repressive occupation is exemplified by the Prevention of Terrorism Act of 1979, which permitted the government (that is, the army and the police) to hold prisoners incommunicado for up to eighteen months without trial, thus creating classical and diabolical conditions for torture, and by the Emergency Regulation 15A previously mentioned, which simply carried the abuse of human rights to a degree that is difficult to credit to a country that has been considered one of the few countries of the third world to systematically practice democratic principles, to stage relatively orderly elections, and to try to uphold the rule of law.

3
THE HORROR STORY

The 1981 Riots as Prologue

The riots of 1983 that began on the night of July 24 virtually ended in a state of smoldering embers by August 5. As the latest acts in a chain of civilian anti-Tamil violence (one must distinguish civilian attacks from a continuing and intensifying series of army killings—termed "reprisals"—of Tamils) they showed certain features that were as new as they were disturbing. From a retrospective standpoint, it looks as if the riots of 1981 foreshadowed some of the developments that would reach a pathological state in 1983. Therefore I shall refer briefly to the events of 1981 as a prelude.

The Prevention of Terrorism Act had been passed in 1979, and under this provision, in April of 1981, twenty-seven Tamil youths were apprehended and held incommunicado. The insurgents then staged a bank robbery, in the course of which two policemen were killed. In early June, local elections were held in the north to elect members to District Development Councils in a doubly embattled atmosphere of a state of emergency declared there by the government and of an increase in violence. "During the campaign, a candidate and two police officers were killed. Police and security forces, apparently in reaction to the killing of the policemen, went on a rampage in the Tamil City of Jaffna burning the market area, the home of a member of Parliament, the TULF headquarters and the Public Library containing 95,000 volumes."[1] The Public Library in fact contained irreplaceable literary and historical documents, and this book burning by Sinhalese police has come to signify for many a living Tamil the apogean barbarity of Sinhalese vindictiveness that seeks physical as well as cultural obliteration.

Be that as it may, by August 1981, these events had escalated to the second outbreak of communal violence since the election of the new UNP government of Jayawardene in 1977. The clashes began at Amparai, the heart of the Gal Oya multipurpose colonization scheme. A clash between Tamil and Sinhalese students at a sports meet escalated into an attack by Sinhala peasant colonists on Tamil colonists and the burning of a Hindu temple. By August incidents of violence broke out in the gem-mining town of Ratnapura, in Negombo, a coastal town near Colombo, and in several plantation towns in the hill country.

Professor Virginia Leary (of the Faculty of Law and Jurisprudence at the State University of New York, Buffalo), reporting on Sri Lanka on behalf of the International Commission of Jurists, describes the ominous import of these occurrences thus:[2] "Unlike the earlier events of violence in 1958 and 1977 the 1981 attacks of arson, looting and killing appear to have been, in part, the work of organized gangs. The *International Herald Tribune* reported that President Jayawardene, in an interview with a Reuter's correspondent on August 14, stated that the attacks on Tamils in Ratnapura appear to have been organized." Leary further documents that *The Guardian* (London), on August 15, and the *The Hindu* (India), of August 18, also referred to planned violence. It is interesting that the allegations made by "Tamil sources"—that the attacks on passengers on the train from Colombo to Jaffna and on civilians in Negombo were organized by agents close to the government—was more or less given some credibility by the admissions of the president himself: on September 11, the *New York Times* quoted President Jayawardene as saying "I regret that some members of my party have spoken in Parliament and outside words that encourage violence and the murders, rapes and arson that have been comitted." The president then said that he would resign as head of his party if some of its leaders continued to encourage ethnic hostilities. It is more tragic than comic that the president, at critical moments then and later, would sometimes express these statesmanlike evaluations and intentions, only to retreat from and even retract his nobler impulses under pressure from the self-same right-wing elements within his own party.

The 1981 riots also foreshadowed another lapse that would worsen in time: for the most part the police and armed forces did not intervene to prevent Sinhalese mob attacks on the Tamils until the declaration of the state of emergency on August 17, many days after the attacks had begun.

The 1983 Riots: An Orgy of Violence

Let me single out some of the striking features of the 1983 riots, not so much for their shock value as for their revelation of a certain worsening as well as of new developments in Sri Lankan politics.

1. More than any other previous ethnic riot, the 1983 eruption showed *organized mob violence* at work. Gangs armed with weapons such as metal rods and knives and carrying gasoline (frequently confiscated from passing motor vehicles) and, most intriguing of all, because it indicates prior intent and planning, carrying voter lists and addresses of Tamil owners and occupants of houses, shops, and other property, descended in waves to drive out Tamils, loot and burn their property, and sometimes kill them in bestial fashion. These gangs frequently had access to transportation—they traveled in buses or were dropped off at successive locations by the Colombo coastline trains. As *The Times* (London) of 8 August 1983 put it: "This time [unlike in earlier riots] the Government detected plain signs of deliberate organization. The rioters, seeking out Tamil homes and burning them, had a particularly detailed knowledge of who lived where and who owned what." *India Today* (New Delhi) of August 31 confirmed this report: "The mobs were armed with voters' lists, and detailed addresses of every Tamil-owned shop, house, or factory, and their attacks were very precise." Most of Wellawatte, the ward in Colombo where Tamils were concentrated, was burned; so were large portions, and entire lanes, in the wards of Dehiwela and Bambalapitiya.

The communal riots of 1983 began in the capital city of Colombo, although all previous ethnic riots had not begun there. From Colombo, the indiscriminate attacks on Tamils of all varieties spread in ever-widening waves to the towns of Gampaha, Kalutara, Kandy, Matale, Nuwara Eliya, and Trincomalee. This pattern roughly accorded with the largest concentrations of Sri Lankan Tamils (outside their own areas of dominance in the north and east) and of the Indian Tamils in the tea plantations. Following the example of Colombo, but reverting to a well-established pattern, shops and establishments, especially in the market areas of Matale, Kandy, and Nuwara Eliya, were looted and burned.[3] I shall limit myself to the damage in Colombo because the incidents there were reliably reported.

Apart from those killed—the government admitted to a death toll of 350,[4] but the suspected numbers are larger, the Tamil estimates nearing 2,000—the largest immediate tragedy was the number of refugees who had abandoned their homes and their jobs and were crowded in terrified disarray into some fifteen refugee camps in Colombo (called "care and welfare centers"). The estimates of the refugees in the Colombo camps alone ranged from 80,000 to 100,000. In *The Guardian* (9 August 1983) David Beresford wrote: "The Sri Lanka Government told foreign diplomats last night that about 100,000 people needed homes, clothes, household goods, and food for between three and six months, following last month's communal violence." The government also estimated that some 18,000 households were affected.

2. The same newspaper went on to report the second terrifying aspect of these riots: aside from Tamil homes, there was systematic destruction of shops and commercial and industrial establishments, many of which employed Sinhalese labor, and which were an essential arm of the UNP government's policy of economic development. Beresford reported that government officials said in the same briefing session for donor countries: "About 100 industrial plants were severely damaged or destroyed, including 20 garment factories. The cost of industrial reconstruction was estimated at 2,000 million rupees (£55 million). This did not include damaged shops."

Around the same time in early August, the *New York Times* supplemented the information on the scale of the economic destruction: "The shells of [Tamil-owned] businesses line Galle Road, the main waterfront thoroughfare, their scorched signs forlornly advertising the names that marked them for destruction. Lakshmi Mahal, pawnbroker, or Ram Gram stores and florist. . . . Damage estimates are uncertain and incomplete, but the total economic loss has been placed at $300 million or more, and 150,000 are said to have been rendered jobless. . . . About 10,000 foreign tourists were here when the trouble started. All but about 1,500 have left." A significant portion of the jobless included Sinhalese workers, some of whom had participated in the very destruction of their own places of work.

Badly hurt by this conflagration were some of the island's biggest industrialists. Some well-known Sri Lankan Tamil victims were K. Gunaratnam, whose interests spanned textile trade, film distribution, and transportation; A.Y.S. Gnanam, who controlled major manufacturing firms such as St. Anthony's Hardware, Syntex, and Asian Cotton Mills; and R. Maharaja, whose constellation of enterprises included the island's largest cosmetics manufacturing firm, the contractorship for large sections of the island's major development "lead project," namely, the Mahaweli Scheme, and the distribution and retail of imported goods. In sum, textile mills, oil, rubber, and other factories situated in industrial locations such as Ratmalana and Peliyagoda were reduced to ashes.

But this destruction of a good part of the island's commerce and nascent industry was confined not only to Sri Lankan Tamil interests; it did not merely include South Indian Tamil interests; it extended to include *all* Indian enterprises and persons who happened to stand in the explosive and undiscriminating path of the rioting. As *India Today* (August 31) put it: "The most dangerous of all misconceptions abroad that frenzied week was that every Indian is a Tamil, and that every Tamil is a terrorist." This exaggerated perception, if it prevailed was short-lived, but it nevertheless took its toll. Thus the victims included properous and famous Hindu Sindhi and Muslim Bohra businesses owned by the Hirdaramanis and Jafferjees, names familiar in Colombo for some fifty years.

Perhaps even more awesome was the virtual destruction of Colombo's colorful and bustling bazaar of shops, the Pettah, dominated by South Indian retail merchants, but also dotted with the shops of Sinhalese and Sri Lankan Tamil business-men. An unexpected victim in the center of commerce was the Indian Overseas Bank, whose building and records were set ablaze: it was the principal bank used by Indian citizens in Sri Lanka and by many Sri Lankans of Indian origin. "As the looting, arson and massacres continued against the Tamils, it became broadbased to include all Indians, not just Tamils" (*The Week*, Sunday Special Issue, 21–27 August 1983). A Tamil Tiger is reported in the Indian press as ruefully saying that for many Sinhalese India as a whole is populated by Tamils, not merely South India with its fifty million Dravid-ians. Indeed, for them Indira Gandhi and even the great Mahatma Gandhi were Tamils.

I want to make two observations at this point about this blanket reaction to the Indians in Sri Lanka who had been assimilated to "the Tamils." The charitable interpretation—which should not be discounted—is that the anti-Indian reac-tion was an uncontrollable result of the spread of the riots and the cumulative expansion of aggressive emotions. But there are other elements as well. The Tamil dissidents—both the Tamil United Left Front (TULF) politicians and the insur-gents—had in recent times increasingly taken their case to and established links with South India. And this again raised in the Sinhalese minds the specter of (South) Indian intervention. And, as I shall expound later, the Sinhalese in their "collec-tive representations" have in recent decades felt the need to distinguish themselves from their giant neighbor, India, at all levels—cultural, political, and social. This propensity is part of Sri Lanka's entrenched identity problem: a miniscule island that fears being engulfed by the adjacent subcontinent.

3. A third disconcerting feature of the 1983 riots was the complete breakdown of law and order, a breakdown that was caused as much by *the active participation or passive en-couragement of the ultimate guardians of law and order—the police and the army*—as by inflamed criminal excesses of the civilian marauders. There were several instances of the au-thorities' active or passive condoning of the destruction of life and property. I have already referred to the massacres in Welikade jail, which could not have been carried out without

the collusion of prison officers. The *New York Times* (Sunday, 7 August 1983) reported that "Sri Lankan Army troops pulled 20 civilians off a bus and executed them two weeks ago in retaliation for a Tamil guerilla attack that killed 13 soldiers, a government spokesman confirmed today." This was up north in Jaffna.

Elsewhere, in Trincomalee, the beautiful, coveted harbor on the east coast, where Tamils and Sinhalese (the majority of the latter being considered by the Tamils as recent intruders) were poised in equal numbers, sailors from the Sri Lankan navy ran amok, themselves setting a bad example for the civilians to follow. The sailors, later assisted and accompanied by civilians, ran riot, killing and looting and setting houses and shops ablaze. Morawewa, a district of Tamil residential concentration, was reduced to ashes.[5]

But the most disquieting spectacle was the behavior of segments of the armed forces and police right in the capital city itself. We could cite news items from several sources, but let us stick to the *The Times* (of London):

> Army personnel actively encouraged arson and looting of business establishments and homes in Colombo and absolutely no action was taken to apprehend or prevent the criminal elements involved in these activities. In many instances army personnel participated in the looting of shops. [5 August 1983]
>
> President Jayawardene said in a television interview yesterday that troops and police had sometimes encouraged the anti-Tamil violence. The President told a BBC interviewer: "I think there was a big anti-Tamil feeling among the forces, and they felt that shooting the Sinhalese who were rioting would have been anti-Sinhalese; and actually in some cases we saw them encouraging them." [9 August 1983]

This testimony and confession by Mr. Jayawardene was confirmed by *The Guardian* (9 August 1983).

Thus segments of the armed forces that had earned their spurs as protectors of law and order and agents of the SLFP Government in regard to the Sinhalese youth insurrection of 1971 were now in 1983 mutinous breakers of law and order in regard to defenseless Tamil civilians. This indeed was the first *massive breakdown* of law and order among those entrusted with its preservation to occur during Sri Lanka's history as an independent nation-state. It is not surprising, then, that Tamil commentators have perceived this pattern of change in the role of the police and armed forces over the years: in 1958 they saved many Tamil lives and earned their reputation as up-holders of law and order; in 1977 they turned indifferent; but from 1981 onwards they have become a party to the riots, frequently figuring as the prime villains.

Of course, the most proximate cause of the army's degeneration was the sporadic puncturing of their sense of honor and martial invincibility by the ambushes of Tamil guerillas. But there is more to their conduct than outraged vengeance-seeking. What their conduct further signifies is the politicization of the armed forces and their being drawn into the vortex of populist and chauvinist causes to a degree never before known (though previously instances of chauvinist posturing and ethnic aggression on a smaller scale or confined to certain regiments had occurred).

In any case, the degeneration of the armed forces and the police did signify that, at least for a short time, the government—that is the president, the cabinet, and the civilian bureaucrats—were rendered powerless to act. Moreover, during this period the government itself may have lost its hold on the country as illustrated by not implausible stories about its "panicky" appeals for military help to certain countries other than India (such as Pakistan, Bangladesh, Singapore, the United States, and Great Britain). It was public knowledge that the president's house was cordoned off by select and trusted officers and troops in an effort to discourage any attempted marches and sieges by inflamed Sinhalese protestors, who wanted the blood of the thirteen Sinhalese soldiers to be avenged.

It is perhaps a sense of being overwhelmed by the aroused conduct of the Sinhalese *en masse*, a feeling of being crushed and pressured by a massive tide of collective aggression, that we detect in the conduct of a president who delayed imposing a curfew in Colombo for twenty-four hours, until the worst had already been done, and who made no public statement on radio and television for some four days, and when he finally did, could say only that the riots were "not a product of urban mobs but a mass movement of the generality of the Sinhalese people." He then asserted: "The time has come to accede to the clamor and the national respect of the Sinhalese people." Therefore the TULF had to be banned, for there was no other way to "appease" the natural desire and request of the Sinhalese people. Mr. Athulathmudali, who was later to be appointed minister of security, on the same television program in which the president bowed to the action of the generality of the Sinhalese people, nearly wept with ponderous histrionics over a sight he had never dreamed he would see— lines of Sinhalese people waiting to buy food as a result of the riots! He had not a word to say in sympathy for the frightened Tamils crowded in indescribable conditions in refugee camps. In the first days after the holocaust, when the Tamil refugees remained in the camps, neither the president, nor the cabinet, nor even a single prominent Sinhalese politician visited them to commiserate even briefly, or to promise relief and rehabilitation.

In all this we see perhaps not so much a racist indifference and lack of pity as the cowed fear that a tidal wave of Sinhalese mass action had expressed itself and had swept aside the frail crafts of the politicians. The sense of being overwhelmed released dark fears of conspiracy as well. The same president who admitted that some of his armed forces had participated in the riots, and who also claimed that the Sinhalese people as a whole had acted, at the same time pointed his finger at a communist conspiracy (both external and internal), hinted at a naxalite plot, and wagged his finger at India for its alleged expansionist and interfering ambitions. However, at some level the president also knew that the most dangerous tendencies were stirred up by elements within his own ranks; he had to face the unpalatable fact that the strongest threat to any responsible statesman-like action came from hardliners within his government who had encouraged punitive acts against the Tamils as a means of intimidating them.

The question is how we are to understand the mainsprings and trajectory of this short-lived but devastating Sinhalese mob behavior, which shows indisputable signs of manipulation and orchestration by organized factions and interest groups, among whom have to be included elements within the government itself, indeed, within the cabinet and the armed forces, and within their retinues of clients and followers.

On the one hand, the phenomenon goes against the grain of all that the government has tried to accomplish in recent years in the economic sphere. And why would the Sinhalese engage in a war from which they too were bound to emerge as losers of the recent economic gains and expansion of employment? It seems to have been the case that about 100,000 persons were put out of work because of the riots, and that, ironically, is a significant number of jobs the Jayawardene government claims to have provided in the six preceding years. Why would the Sinhalese want to cut off their noses to spite their faces?

To all appearances, the UNP regime in Sri Lanka was firmly in control these last few years. Soon after Jayawardene came to power in 1977, he was able to change the constitution and introduce a presidential form of government somewhat on the French model and a proportional system of representation that was advocated as a means of avoiding the wildly oscillating consequences of landslide electoral victories that had been the result of the British form of majoritarian politics. His own parliamentary five-sixths majority was manipulated not only in the alleged interest of stabilizing politics in the long run, but also to hold a referendum that enabled (by the use of threats and force against opposition parties and at the election booths) the prolongation without elections of the life of the present parliament for six years. Thus the president's power and the UNP's rule seemed assured until 1989 at least. (The feeling of strength and the accompanying slide toward authoritarianism was also reflected by the deployment of an army of occupation in Jaffna [and the Northern Province] and the passing of the draconian Prevention of Terrorism Act in 1979.)

In retrospect, the horrible aspect of the events during the riots, and the government's actions soon afterwards, should not unduly prejudice our assessment of President Jayawardene's positive acts toward settling the Tamil issue and reconciling both the Indian and Sri Lankan Tamils to his regime.

First of all, consider the auspicious deal he had struck with the Indian Tamils. They had voted overwhelmingly for him and the UNP in the landslide 1977 elections; the promises Jaywardene had held out to them had brought the Ceylon Workers' Congress, the largest trade union of the Indian Tamil plantation workers, into the government. Jaywardene did make provision in the constitution for Tamil to be awarded the status of national language together with Sinhalese, although the latter was to continue as the "official" language for purposes of administration. He had negotiated with the TULF over the establishment of District Councils throughout the island. These Councils were to be given certain powers concerning local government, peasant colonization, and primary as well as secondary (but not higher) education. It was hoped that the delegation of such minimal powers would appease Tamil sentiments. In the event, however, there was much foot-dragging and a lack of spirited implementation of the provisions in the face of alleged hostility of the Sinhalese population at large. By a curious twist, the granting of these powers ended up by strengthening the center's, and especially the president's, powers. The central government held all the purse strings, and alienated the Tamils by the appointment of several presiding Sinhalese district ministers invested with overriding powers even in the districts where the Tamils were the majority. President Jayawardene's spirit had been willing up to a point, and no more. He had also tried to mediate the contentious issue of an equitable admissions policy to the universities. For the Sri Lankan Tamils, the application of equal and even-handed criteria of merit and performance at entrance examinations was vital; indeed, it constituted a lifeline for them. The admissions policies were therefore a crucial test of their equal rights as citizens of Sri Lanka. The Sinhalese on the other hand favored an admissions policy based on a quota system that gave the edge to their population ratio, and they defended this curious "affirmative action" on behalf of a majority in power on the grounds of undue privilege enjoyed by the Tamils in this sphere. We shall later test the veracity of this Sinhala signature tune. For the Tamils this Sinhala demand was a lunge at their jugular vein, and the Sinhalese knew this to be a deadly truth. The SLFP, and subsequently Jayawardene, had helped in the formulation of what was called a "standardization policy" that claimed a rise in the number of Tamils admitted.[6] But since university admissions are calculated largely on the basis of district populations, and since the Tamils form a majority in only six of the total of twenty-four districts, the Sinhalese students enjoy a conspicuous advantage over their Tamil counterparts on the basis of demographic rather than meritocratic criteria. All in all, there was just the chance that under Jayawardene's presidential rule and virtual one-party government an accord might be reached on the same lines as the far-seeing but tragically abandoned Bandaranaike-Chelvanayagam Pact of 1957—scotched, incidentally, by a movement led by Jayawardene himself, who was then in the opposition! So one responds with some sympathy to this news item in *The Times* (of London) of 8 August 1983, which describes these petulant and nostalgic words of Jayawardene— words that evidence a missed second chance that many fear might have been the last: "He had prompted action to make Tamil an official language of the country, the devolution of central powers to district councils, and the solution of a bitter dispute over admission to the universities. He would have done more, he says. He was to propose at the round-table conference convened earlier last month that if the TULF would postpone a demand for the independence of Eelam . . . other blessings would follow." Jayawardene had convened an all-parties conference to settle matters, and a popular rumor had it that he was slow to act when the riots broke out in July so as to nudge the beleaguered Tamil leaders into negotiating with him. If there is any truth in this, it is only part of the truth; and the ploy turned out to be a miscalculation, for what was imagined at the beginning to be a camp-fire lit by Sinhala chauvinist boyscouts turned into a raging forest fire that took at least seventy-two hours to put out.

On the economic front, the UNP claimed to have initiated a "liberalization policy" marked by a pro–United States stance, the encouragement of foreign capitalist investment, and a greater reliance on market forces than on state intervention, protection, and subsidization. The UNP had decided on the implementation of four major projects: the Mahāweli scheme, particularly the speeded-up construction of the dams; the housing program; the creation of the Free Trade Zone; and the building of the new administrative capital at Kōṭṭe. (In the event, the last was mercifully scaled down, for it had more to do with fulfilling monarchical fantasies of a new capital named confusingly after a king who bore the same name as the president than with economic development or rational administration). To be sure, the Mahāweli scheme and the housing project had created new employment, especially in the field of construction, but the returns on these projects were expected to be a long time in coming.

Thus the most publicized feature of the government's economic strategy, which it considered its chief means of creating economic growth, was the encouragement of foreign private investors to return to Sri Lanka, after their flight or reluctance to come during the SLFP regime, and invest in and promote export activities, some of which were labor intensive. Cheap Sri Lankan labor would be a major attraction in the context of the establishment of "free trade zones," especially in the immediate vicinity of Colombo, where more infrastructural investments would be provided to supplement the existing facilities. The southwest littoral of Sri Lanka where Colombo is situated, and which incidentally is a heavily populated Sinhalese zone, would be the hub of this industrial development, and also the primary beneficiary of an intensified tourist trade. To achieve these goals the government had established the Greater Colombo Economic Commission.

All in all, by one method of accounting, the UNP government had between the years 1977 and 1983 increased the rate of national economic growth, created significantly more employment, and had relaxed import restrictions, which made available more consumption goods in the market. (It should not be overlooked, however, that a fair part of the reduction of unemployment was caused by immigration abroad.) These features combined to create an air of increased prosperity and activity.

So in the face of all these indications of economic expansion and political aggrandizement, why did the riots occur "against the grain" of events, to undo a great deal of the gains made by the government? Why did the riots occur in a spectacularly virulent form in 1983, when most observers of the scene do not seem to have expected them? Were there portents and cracks in the UNP regime which were invisible then but which we can now identify and interpret *ex post facto*?

First of all, we notice a paradoxical symptom in Jayawardene's seemingly successful assumption of near-total power and his initiation of seeming progress. Although there were Sinhalese shows of aggression against the Tamils under the Bandaranaike and SLFP regimes (1956 and 1958 were memorable years), there were *four* successive punitive actions, including the worst ever, against the Tamils in the seven years of the Jayawardene regime since 1977. How do we explain a spate of anti-Tamil riots in an atmosphere of confident Sinhala domination and progress?

An awful prospect that we should not flinch from considering is the remark made by Neelan Thiruchelvam, a member of Parliament and a member of the TULF, a remark that bears the mark of despair: "This time the Tamil professional and entrepreneurial class has been destroyed" (*India Today*, 31 August 1983). That there was an effort for many years to diminish Tamil participation in the professions and white-collar occupations is well known. A more clouded issue is the reason for the destruction of Tamil—both Sri Lankan and South Indian—commercial interests in Colombo. There were rampant rumors that the "hawks" and "chauvinists" in the UNP cabinet, of the ilk of Industries Minister Cyril Mathew, of whom I shall say more, were thinking of taking punitive actions against the "terrorist" activities of the Tamil insurgents and the intransigence of the TULF politicians in an attempt to make them forswear any intention to secede from the body politic. They were alleged to propose a ruthless crackdown on the Tamils, who they charged with the control of 60% of the wholesale trade and 80% of the retail trade in the capital. Whatever the exaggeration in these numbers, the rumors reveal the deadly strategic efficacy of "punishing" the Tamils in the city of Colombo itself, where most of their professionals, entrepreneurs, and white-collar workers were aggregated. *India Today* (31 August 1983) asserted in print what other sources have also suggested, that Minister Cyril Mathew, who controlled a powerful government labor union (some would say a private army of thugs) called Jātika Sēvaka Saṅgamaya, was implicated in the pinpointing of the Tamil-owned shops and factories to be destroyed. The same jingoist, of whose style of neo-fascist politics I shall have more to say, in a speech made in Parliament on 4 August 1983, at the tail end of the dying riots, defended them with the words: "If the Sinhala are the majority race, why can't they be the majority?"

If, then, the riots were ever intended at any stage by its most organized and chauvinist participants as an attack on the Tamils resident in Colombo at their most vulnerable and exposed front, then the Tamils might be forgiven for wondering whether the perpetrators merely intended the violence to be a coercive twist of the arm (that had later inadvertently maimed their own limbs as well), or, more diabolically, to be a maddened "total solution" that would once and for all pluck out and expel the Tamils from the midst of Sinhala presence. The contemplation of such deeds in itself is symptomatic of the rising tempo of a problematic Sinhala-Buddhist chauvinism that had and still has the potential to incite mass political action. What tendencies within the Sinhalese social and political domain (irrespective of the Tamil irritant) were conducive to generating this volcano? The carrying out of such deeds bespeaks a cataclysmic paroxysm of violence, which was as demented as it was brief in duration. But a volcano temporarily spent can erupt again. How are we to read the future portents and the past evidence?

4
PROBING BELOW
THE SURFACE

I have previously described how, during the riots, the breakdown of law and order, the loss of discipline among the armed forces, and the peculiarly confused behavior of the government indicated that all was not well under the surface. Surveying this sorry unhinging of a government that seemed firmly ensconced in the seat of power, and optimistically implementing a "liberal" economic program of expansion and growth, the analyst is forced to probe beneath the shifting sands in order to discover the not-so-obvious dislocating circumstances that enabled the unleashing of violence and destruction on a scale never before known.

There are three such dislocations that can be detected, and we shall consider each in turn: unevenness of economic development and the pauperization of the lower income groups; the factional competition within the ruling party, combined with a government whose advance towards total power left no space for countervailing opposition groups as checks and balances, thereby encouraging neo-fascist tendencies within its own ranks; and an increasing populism and chauvinism among the urban masses at large, who were attracted to an ideology of "millenarian politicized Buddhism" and a dangerously simplified "racism" that both defined for them an explosive nationalist identity and provided a heady stimulant for aggressive action against the "enemies" of the Sinhalese.

The Economic Imbalances

Agriculture dominates the economy of Sri Lanka. Tea, rubber, and coconut account for 60% of the export earnings and about 17% of the national income. Sri Lanka ranks third after India and China in tea production, and is also a leading rubber grower. Manufacturing contributes about 12% of the national product. There is also some mining of graphite and gems. In 1983, before the riots, Sri Lanka was experiencing an inflation rate of nearly 35%. The rupee had been devalued again on July 4, the exchange rate now being Rs 24.20 for 1 U.S. dollar (in 1977, there were 7.89 rupees to the dollar). The official estimate of unemployed persons was 500,000. The budget deficit in 1983 reached a climactic figure of 23.4 billion rupees, while the trade deficit stood at 21 billion rupees. While it was true that the so-called open "liberalization" economic policy, tourism, and the "lead" projects such as the Mahaweli scheme and the Free Trade Zone had benefited large segments of the Sinhalese populations of the west, south, and southwest most, yet it seems as if this very process of economic growth had also given rise to steeper differences, and therefore a deterioration in income distribution, especially among that same population. While the entrepreneurial, commercial, and tourist-service segments—composed mainly of Sinhalese (despite some prominent Tamil participation)—had enjoyed a degree of affluence, the poorest segments of the working class and the partly to fully unemployed categories, of whom the vast majority were Sinhalese, had experienced a worsening of their living standards since 1977.

From a report written by the Harvard Institute of International Development—which had actively helped the Jayawardene government in an advisory capacity—we learn of these dislocating and disequilibrating developments.[1]

The UNP government had introduced the food stamp program in place of the subsidized rice price policy initiated by the preceding SLFP government. About 56% of the population was covered by the program in 1983.[2] Research by the Harvard group found that inflation reduced the real resource cost of the program and thereby diminished the benefits. In fact "real income for those receiving food stamps had declined by nearly four percent in 1979–80, and by a further 11 percent in 1980–81, despite increases in employment and economic growth." Thus "even allowing for the widespread misuse of the programme, and even after allowing for increases in wages and employment levels," the food stamp program "did *not* compensate for the losses in real income which were imposed on the poorest segments of the population through inflation." In sum, then, the persistent high levels of inflation that heated up the economy during the years 1979–82 actually "reduced real wages and the real value of food stamps to such an extent that the real income of the poorest groups declined."

After a long period of controlled food prices, the UNP government was now moving toward a reliance on market forces for the allocation of food supplies. The HIID researchers limited themselves to a study of rice and wheat alone, and came up with the following conclusions. The current government policy that allowed the world price to be reflected in both the wheat and the rice prices tended "to reduce the caloric intake of the lowest income groups substantially compared to their historical average." The second conclusion, counterintuitive in character, was that higher rice prices, though increasing rural incomes and increasing rice consumption in rural areas, would tend to decrease the demand for rice among the urban working class and poorer segments, thus increasing imports of wheat. "As a result, a high price policy, which restricts consumption and encourages production, nevertheless yields high levels of foodgrain imports." In the face of this, if the government wished to increase the caloric intake of the lowest income groups, it would have to follow a policy of maintaining cheap wheat prices (the market-determined rice prices therefore being left alone since they raised rural incomes). Development economists tell us that such effects that have adverse consequences for the poor are to be expected in "any market-oriented society at a low level of per capita income." But this is cold comfort for the poor. Moreover, certain economists more skeptical of the market process have warned that cheap wheat prices might in fact depress rice prices and therefore rice production as well; this in turn will increasingly divert consumption from rice to wheat to the point of undermining the economy of the Sri Lankan peasantry.

Third, it was discovered that the effective exchange rates prevailing in the early 1980s were unfavorable to the country's exports vis-à-vis its imports: "The real effective exchange rate for exports remains below that for imports, indicating that the trade regime continues to be biased in favour of import substituting developments and gives relatively less emphasis to export promotion." The bias in general then, given current terms of trade, was against exporting and in favor of import substitution.

The final point I want to highlight is perhaps the most disturbing. The high level of inflation was only in part attributable to the world oil crisis and the increase of oil prices in 1978–79. Its more direct cause was the current development projects, which stimulated a rapid price increase that can be ascribed "to the fiscal imbalance of both domestic and foreign resources." Moreover, "there has been little increase in the savings proportion in Sri Lanka so that national savings now finance less than half the total investment, compared to nearly eighty percent in 1978. This means that there has been no shift of resources from consumption to savings to help finance the large increases in investment." Furthermore, although from 1977 through 1979 wages were initially well ahead of price increases, "by 1980 the brakes were applied so that real wages fell for all workers who were at or near the minimum wage level. It was only for those labor sectors that faced a high demand, primarily construction workers, that real wages continued to rise." It was now clearly important to reduce the government deficit.

I think this enumeration of the economic dislocations shows that a liberal capitalist market-oriented policy and certain kind of development program were creating unequal development in the Sri Lankan economy. In real terms the poorer working segments, especially in the urban areas, were experiencing a fall in living standards and in real incomes. Since the greater part of the economic ferment associated with housing, the free trade zones, and tourism was taking place in the southwest sector of Sri Lanka with Colombo as the focal point, it is perhaps logical, in retrospect that the political turmoil should have erupted there. Moreover, since it was the Sinhalese majority who were the primary beneficiaries as well as the victims of the economic "progress," it is the Sinhalese urban poor and working masses who suffered most from relative and worsening income distribution. But our problem is that the riots were not mounted on a class basis—the Sinhalese poor against the Sinhalese rich—but rather were deflected onto a conspicuous and eminently vulnerable segment of the population, the Tamils, who, though a minority of about one-tenth of the population in Colombo, could be pointed to as "privileged" participants in commerce, trade, administration, and the professions. And by their blanket racial logic, the riots wrought their worst havoc on the least privileged—both politically and economically—of the Sri Lankan population, namely the Indian Tamil plantation labor. A final conclusion we may extract from the foregoing economic analysis is that for the Sinhalese urban poor, as far as government-sponsored patronage went, it was in the construction industry and development projects that jobs could be had. Therefore this field of economic activity was a fertile ground for politicians in recruiting and raising their client retinues and private armies to be deployed in an escalating politics of terrorism. It is fashionable to label the Tamil insurgents as terrorists. In fact, "terrorism" has two other manifestations in Sri Lanka: the sort practiced by undisciplined elements in the army and police who go beserk when their kind are ambushed and killed, and the more generalized kind, sponsored by populist politicians and practiced by their private legions of thugs. In some ways it is the last that is the more worrisome because it indicates a cancerous malaise in the body politic at large, and accounts for the most property damage and largest number of human deaths to date.

The Slide to Authoritarianism and the Politics of Terrorism

I have previously referred to the UNP's apparently increasing assumption of total power since 1977. This very process has eroded the country's democratic institutions, procedures, and safeguards. In a remarkable essay, Gananath Obeyesekere[3] argues that the UNP has achieved this by an attempted obliteration of opposition groups, which in turn has set the stage for unrestrained, but organized, political violence sponsored by politicians within the UNP itself.

Let us begin with the UNP's landslide victory in 1977, which decimated the SLFP and Marxist opposition parties, and left the Tamil party (TULF), with only sixteen seats, as the official opposition of the country! This great majority enabled Jayawardene to change the parliamentary rules and, in the alleged interest of a more responsible and stable process of governing, to introduce a presidential system on the Gaullist model together with proportional representation. The new presidential-style constitution of 1978 conferred wide executive powers on the president and gave him immunity from legal proceedings in both his private and official capacities while he holds office. I shall later illustrate how this immunity has been exercised.

The next political act of serious consequences was the passing in 1979 of the Prevention of Terrorism (Temporary Provisions) Act which conferred on the executive, among other things, the power of detention without resort to charge or judicial review and without access to relatives or lawyers. I shall later review the diabolical consequences of this act and its extensions.

In 1982 the Third Amendment to the Constitution was passed (amendments require a two-thirds majority), by which Mr. Jayawardene was reelected for a second six-year term, before the first had expired, by a bare majority of 52.9 percent of the polled votes. This was a close call, especially when we remember that traditionally in Sri Lanka some people vote more than once, and many others are frightened away from voting. It is widely felt by political observers that illegal voting and intimidation have both escalated in recent times to reach a high-water mark in the years since 1977.

The next move, which also came in 1982 in the form of the Fourth Amendment to the Constitution, added to the mounting disconcertion. Citing a conspiracy to undermine the political order—such as an alleged "Naxalite" plot to assassinate cabinet ministers, chiefs of staff, and prominent politicians—the president called for the holding of a referendum to ratify by simple majority a proposal to postpone the holding of parliamentary elections, and to prolong the life of the present parliament by six more years. This referendum was barely won with 54% of the votes polled in the context of mass impersonation and intimidation at the polling booths; it was held at a time when a state of emergency had been declared, some important opposition printing presses had been shut down, and several publications had been banned. It was marked by violence and intimidation on the part of both the principal contenders, the UNP and the SLFP, with the former having a distinct edge on account of its control of the government machinery. During the referendum the police were given wide powers, including the power to incarcerate troublemakers, many of whom turned out to be opposition party organizers. With a five-sixths parliamentary majority (though only 54% of the popular vote), the president, whose term was extended for another six-year period, was now in a position to pass further amendments to the Constitution.

This referendum also enabled the president to stipulate new rules regarding changing sides in Parliament, the resignation of MPs, and by-elections. In effect, it was ruled that MPs can cross over from the opposition to the government but not vice-versa. Moreover, if vacancies occurred, they could be filled by nomination by the respective party leader except when the government itself chose to declare a by-election. Finally, even without an MP proffering his resignation, the government could remove and replace one of its own MPs.

So we are confronted with these astonishing results. The alleged attempt to safeguard a more representative and orderly democracy had by a series of steps—from the introduction of proportional representation, through the change to a presidential form of government, to the staging of the referendum—produced the opposite result of confirming the rule of a five-sixths UNP majority for a long time without the irritant of, and the accountability demanded by, further elections. Moreover, these conquests were near defeats; they were barely won in an atmosphere of political violence. The train of events concluded with a seemingly all-powerful president, who was declared to be immune from court proceedings, and who had in his pocket the letters of resignation of all UNP members of Parliament, whom he could dismiss from office at any time he wished.

All this smacks of an unbridled "oriental despotism" and an absolutist regime, and indeed, the present government has indulged in classes of actions that would amply fit this description. There are two types of actions that I wish to highlight.

1. The first of these has to do with the independence of the judiciary. Paul Sieghart, speaking on behalf of the International Commission of Jurists, accuses the president of Sri Lan... as being guilty of "grossly improper acts," and says that only the immunity enjoyed by the president has saved him from the charge of criminal offence.[4] When he says this he had at least two conspicuous instances in mind. In the course of the referendum campaign of December 1982, a superintendent of police seized pamphlets being distributed by a Buddhist monk. In March 1983, during a protest march to the U.S. embassy the police arrested a press photographer, and subsequently a subinspector of police arrested a senior left politician, Mrs. Vivienne Gunawardene, when she remonstrated at the police station. In both instances, the Supreme Court ruled against the police action and awarded damages and costs to the injured parties. Sieghart reports that the president himself freely admitted to him that he had personally ordered the promotion of the two officers and the payment out of public funds of the damages and costs.

When Sieghart refers to an absolutist "immunity" enjoyed by the president, he has in mind the powers vested in the president by the current Constitution. Under its terms, the president, who is head of state, head of the executive and of the government, and commander-in-chief of the armed forces, who appoints as well as removes ministers, and who appoints judges of the Supreme Court, the Court of Appeal and the High Court, is responsible to Parliament with regard to all acts relating to these powers (Article 42). But the constitution holds that so long as the president holds office, "no proceedings shall be instituted or continued against him in any court or tribunal in respect of anything done or omitted to be done by him, either in his official or private capacity" (Article 35(1)).

2. The second type of action that exemplifies an absolutist regime is the Prevention of Terrorism Act, enacted in 1979,

and whose draconian measures have proliferated rather than shrunken since then. I have at several points mentioned the PTA. It is time now to study it and its workings as exemplifying on the one hand the resort to an indefensible repression by a government allegedly dedicated to democracy, and on the other the resort to murder and torture by an army and police allegedly trained in the best "professional" British tradition. A puzzling feature is that the practice of such violence seems to be "unproblematic" to most of the actors: at least in their public appearances it is not ethical issues of the legitimate use of force and its limits that are discussed, but how "human" the response of the army is when it goes beserk because one of its trucks has been ambushed or hit a road mine. The issues I raise ultimately refer to the question of the internalization of values and standards that are integrally necessary to the existence of institutions such as parliaments, the professions, and so on.

The implications of the Prevention of Terrorism Act, both in its wording and its application, have been the focus of two reports written on behalf of the International Commission of Jurists by two eminent jurists, Professor Virginia Leary, who is American, and Paul Sieghart, who is British.[5] It has also been studied by a delegation of Amnesty International. As this act and its extensions have provided the main legitimation for military and police actions against the Tamil community, it is necessary to study closely its ugly face as a warning to all Sri Lankans, particularly the Sinhalese, as to how a benign people could have allowed a monster to appear and comfortably settle down at their front door and yet mistake it for a watchdog.

The Prevention of Terrorism Act, passed by Parliament allegedly in response to growing political violence in the north, defines certain acts as unlawful, including the speaking or writing of words intended to cause religious, social, or communal disharmony, or feelings of ill will or hostility between communities or racial or religious groups. It also contravenes a law enshrined by the British during their imperial rule, namely, that no confession made in police custody is admissible unless it is made in the presence of a magistrate. The PTA allows confessions made to the police, possibly under duress, as admissible evidence. Moreover, the act declares that any document found in the custody, control, or possession of anyone accused of an offence under the act, or his agent or representative, can be used in evidence against him at his trial without calling its author or maker into account, and the contents of such a document can be construed as evidence of the facts stated in it.

The PTA carries its diabolical measures even further by declaring that it can be retroactive in its implementation. It does so by defining "unlawful activity" as including action taken or committed before the date on which the act came into effect; such action could therefore, if committed before the act's passage, be considered an offence. The act finally provides for prison terms for conviction ranging from five to twenty years or life imprisonment, depending upon the severity of the offence.

These provisions of the PTA have been interpreted and used by the police and army as an open-door policy that permits arrest without warrant of any person; stop and search of any person, vehicle, vessel, train, or aircraft; and seizure of any document or object "connected with or concerned in any unlawful activity" (unlawful activity as I have defined above). A person may be detained for periods up to eighteen months if the minister has reason to suspect him of being associated with unlawful activity. Over the years there have been mounting instances of Tamil civilians being rounded up and detained in camp without access to attorneys or relatives for prolonged periods of time.

Since apologists in Sri Lanka have cited legislation in the United Kingdom enacted in response to the situation in North Ireland as setting a precedent for the PTA, it is necessary to make a comparison. The United Kingdom legislation bearing the same name (that is, "Prevention of Terrorism") was adopted in 1974, repealed, and then reenacted with some amendments in 1978. It is much less far-reaching than its Sri Lankan counterpart in its infringement of human rights. For one thing, the U.K. act defines terrorism more narrowly as "the use of violence for political ends," and includes under this rubric any use of violence for the purpose of frightening any section of the public or the public as a whole. For another, the same act limits the maximum period during which a person may be detained without charge to seven days: there is no way a person can be held incommunicado without trial for a prolonged period, as the Sri Lankan legislation permits. Finally, the act in the United Kingdom remains in force for twelve months, and its continuance must be ratified by Parliament.

Leary makes this comment, which must horrify many Sri Lankans: that in fact "a number of the objectionable features of the Sri Lankan Act are similar to provisions of the widely criticized 1967 Terrorism Act of South Africa. . . . The South African Terrorism Act has been called 'a piece of legislation which must shock the conscience of a lawyer.' Many of the provisions of the Sri Lankan Act are equally contrary to accepted principles of the Rule of Law."[6] Moreover, Leary continues that in addition to these infringements, there was further legislation in place by 1981 that made impossible judicial review by the Supreme Court of the constitutionality of laws considered by the cabinet to be "urgent in the national interest" and passed by the Parliament—impossible because the Supreme Court had to make its determination within twenty-four hours of the passing of the act, unless the president extended the period up to a maximum of three days (Article 124).

Perhaps the most notorious use of this last power by the Government was in the immediate aftermath of the 1983 riots during the period of emergency rule, when it passed the Sixth Amendment to the Constitution, and thereby effectively banned and excluded the TULF members of Parliament—the remaining largest opposition as well as the only political voice of the Tamils—from the Parliament's deliberations, because they were formally committed by their party resolution of 1976 to the establishment of a separate state. The most relevant paragraph in the amendment runs as follows: "No person shall, directly or indirectly, in or outside Sri Lanka, support, espouse, promote, finance, encourage or advocate the establishment of a separate State within the territory of Sri Lanka." Contravention of this law invites such dire penalties as imposition of civic disability for up to seven years, the forfeiture of movable and immovable property in excess of sustenance level, the loss of passport, the right to engage in any trade or profession that requires an authorization, license, or registration, and so on.

The Sixth Amendment also requires that all members of Parliament, officeholders of various kinds, and even every attorney at law shall make an oath to the effect that they "will not, directly or indirectly, in or outside Sri Lanka, support, espouse, promote, finance, encourage or advocate the establishment of a separate State within the territory of Sri Lanka." Refusal entails the loss of the parliamentary seat or of the office or profession concerned.

In being so concerned with the TULF's formal commitment to a separate state, and the Tamil insurgents' determination to achieve it, many Sinhalese who regard the thesis that "the Republic of Sri Lanka is a Unitary State" as a nonnegotiable article of the Constitution have not realized how much the Sixth Amendment puts in jeopardy the Constitution's general guarantees regarding freedom of thought and conscience (Article 10) and freedom of speech and expression (Article 14)—freedoms that necessarily include the freedom to support, encourage, or advocate amendments to the Constitution itself, provided it is done peacefully within the democratic framework. As Sieghart sardonically reminds us: "Were it otherwise, it would have been unlawful for anyone at any time to propose any amendments to the Constitution, including the Sixth Amendment itself. The freedom to express political opinions, to seek to persuade others to their merits, to have them represented in Parliament, and thereafter to seek to persuade Parliament to give effect to them, are all fundamental to democracy itself."[7]

Let us retrace our steps to the fateful year of 1979 when the PTA was passed, and comment on the fact that over the subsequent years it has progressively generated the very militancy and separatist sentiment that it was intended to stem and diminish. As Sieghart observes:

> The power to detain suspects for long periods without the opportunity to access by friends, family, or lawyers, or for regular judicial review, notoriously carries the danger that the detainees will be maltreated while in custody: it provides an open invitation for deprivation, assault and worse—especially if the suspects may be detained by their

interrogators in police stations or army camps, and more especially still if no real control is exercised over the periods for which they are detained.[8]

Since it is Amnesty International that has investigated and reported a number of authenticated allegations of the torture of detainees, let us now let one of its representatives sum up. In the *New York Times* of 24 August 1983, Orville H. Schell reported the chilling turn of events that took place both before and after the 1983 riots.

> The Government has repeatedly denied that its security forces violate fundamental rights. However, as head of an Amnesty International fact-finding mission in January 1982, I received first-hand evidence that incommunicado detention under the Prevention of Terrorism Act was widespread, and that the army and police regularly tortured political suspects and carried out political killings in June 1981, similar to those recently confirmed by President J. R. Jayawardene. I believe that recent killings by security authorities follow a pattern previously set.
>
> President Jayawardene confirmed on Aug. 7 that the armed forces had killed at least 20 innocent Tamils in the north, saying that the army had withheld information from him about the excesses. The Tamils, including an 83-year old teacher, apparently were slain in retaliation by the army, immediately after the killing of the 13 soliders. The authorities are understood to have waived the usual requirement of holding an inquest.
>
> The Government must bear full responsibility for these breaches of the right to life and other violations of human rights, especially in light of the wide powers that in recent years it has given to the security forces, which apparently have interpreted them as a license to act with impunity.
>
> When Amnesty International visited, it learned that prisoners were held incommunicado for long periods and in some cases in solitary confinement for more than eight months. Torture during this period was said to include hanging victims upside down from hooks, beating them with metal bars and driving needles under toenails and fingernails.
>
> Clearly, the Government faces serious internal security problems. It has a responsibility to bring to trial those responsible for violent acts. In addition, it has a responsi-

bility under the International Covenant on Civil and Political Rights, to which Sri Lanka is a party, to make sure that torture and political killings are never used—even in a national emergency."[9]

The overwhelmingly sad thing about the provisions of the PTA and their use is that they are both *disproportionate* and *counterproductive*. They are disproportionate because, as Leary magisterially concludes, the draconian provisions are not strictly required by the exigencies of the situation (as it prevailed at the time of her visit in 1981): "It appears that the situation created by terrorist acts in Sri Lanka is not one threatening the life of the nation and that the provisions of the Act exceed the measures strictly necessary in the circumstances. The violations of human rights resulting from the Act are thus not permissible under the Civil and Political Rights Covenant."[10]

The provisions are counterproductive because they have not only been ineffective in controlling terrorism, but have contributed to its increase since the passage of the act, and to the increased alienation of the Tamil public, which may inexorably be led to the conviction that the "terrorists" are their protectors and that their security lies in the creation of a separate state. In turn, such developments would tempt the Sinhalese public, particularly its middle class, to come under the sway of their own populist extremist politicians. Karl Marx insisted that it is men who make their history; if that is so, then Sri Lankans are making their future of total war and stalemate in a most perverse manner.

Factions and Violence in the Wider Society

Now is the time to cut down the president's seeming absolutism, and to deflate the government's seeming unity of purpose. Despite appearances, Sri Lanka is far from being a monolithic despotism imposed by a government that is solidary, as will be revealed when we probe those factional rivalries within the ruling groups, and the volatile, and at the same time alienating and anomic, social tendencies festering in the society at large. This in turn will lead us to some understanding of the social currents, economic shifts, and psychological eruptions that motivate the ethnic conflicts and civil disturbances we are concerned with.

It is said that at the time of the July 1983 riots there were at least three major factions within the UNP government that were contending for power, and were involved coming up with a successor to a president who had passed the span of four score years. The first group, which is today in charge of the country's security and has close links to the armed forces, consists of Cabinet Secretary G. V. P. Samarasinghe; Presidential Secretary W. M. P. Menikdiwela; Defense Secretary, General S. Attygalle; Lieutenant General Weeratunge, the general officer in charge of operations, the president's own nephew; and Army Commander Major General Nalin Seneviratne, the brother-in-law of Weeratunge.[11] These comprise the group immediately surrounding the president himself and have ready access to him. Next comes the coterie that controls the party machine of the UNP: prominent members of this domain are the UNP chairman, N. G. P. Panditharatne; the UNP secretary, Harsha Abeyawardne; Cyril Mathew, minister of industries, militant Buddhist zealot, and leader of the UNP "trade union,"[12] the J.S.S.; and Ranil Wickremasinghe, the minister of youth affairs and minister of education (excluding higher education, which is controlled by the president). The party machine also controls the country's major English- and Sinhalese- language newspapers printed by the government-controlled and nationalized publishing house (Lake House): these are *The Daily News, The Daily Mirror, Dinamina,* and *Dinakera.*

The third group has coalesced around the prime minister and minister for housing, Ranasinghe Premadasa, who is of lowly family and "caste" origins (he belongs to the Hinna caste) and who has a strong electoral base in Colombo Central, especially Borella, a densely populated area in which working families, urban poor, and slumdwellers predominate. This group contains many MPs who harbor a latent hostility toward the president.

A notorious and archetypal example of a politician-boss, one who has at hand retinues and followers and who engages in organized political violence, is Cyril Mathew, who has also risen from lowly social and caste origins. He has helped to regularize violence as a regular feature of Sri Lankan politics today.

Thuggery and the use of violence are entrenched features of both local and national elections, and of urban (both city and small market town) commercial competition and "trade wars" between entrepreneurs and shopkeepers, who are called *mudalālis*. These latter try to control the retail trade, rice milling, small producers' supplies of cash crops, and local transport services; they are frequently involved in illegal boot-legging and in opium and ganja traffic, illegal felling and trading of forest timber, and so on. There are networks that connect local politicians, local police, and elected MPs to these *mudalālis*. They enjoy government protection and con-tracts which are repaid by bribes and election financing, and most importantly, by their ability during elections to mobilize clients and thugs, unemployed or underemployed rifraff, and to terrorize competitors and adversaries.

Whatever quantitative figures we can assemble about re-cent internal migration trends in Sri Lanka in the context of a population explosion might help us to probe the impulses behind the manifestation of violence at large and thuggery in particular on the island today. Analysis by Kearney and Miller[13] of internal migration based on the 1971 Census estab-lished the following trends. There is evidence of a great deal of interdistrict population movement: a statistic that does not fully estimate the trend but is suggestive is that 16% of all persons born in Sri Lanka, more than two million persons, were residing in districts other than their district of birth. Colombo, the island's metropolis, in which 51.8% of the island's urban population lived in 1971, was the major recip-ient of interdistrict migrants, with a net gain of some 160,000 persons. As an urban magnet Colombo was unrivaled.[14]

The other districts with large net gains from migration present a strong contrast to Colombo, which is perfectly understandable when we realize that they were the sites of the government's peasant resettlement and colonization schemes. These districts are Anurādhapura, Trincomalee, Polonnaruva, Amparai, and Monaragala. They fringe the dry zone of Sri Lanka in an arc extending from the north-central to the southeastern regions. They are not only the most sparingly populated jungle lands being reclaimed for occupation, but are also the border regions between Sinhalese-dominated areas and the Tamil-dominated provinces of the north and east. It is worth noting that the sparsely populated but agriculturally developing district of Vavuniya in the northeast, which is Tamil-dominated and abuts the Sinhala districts of Anurādhapura and Polonnaruva, also had more than one-third of its inhabitants born outside the district and drawn, in this case, from Jaffna.

The potential for ethnic conflict of these border and fringe areas of agricultural and population expansion—particularly Polonnaruva, Trincomalee, Vavuniya and Amparai—is intensified when we take account of the next finding: "The major losses of population through migration appeared in Matara, Galle, Kegalle, and Kalutara districts of the Southwestern Wet Zone, in Kandy in the central highlands, and in Jaffna at the island's northern tip. Aside from Jaffna, with a population density of 728, the other five districts of heavy out-migration all had 1971 population densities of more than 1,000 persons per square mile and ranked after Colombo second through sixth in magnitude of district population density."[15] Thus the most heavily populated southwest and southern districts of Sri Lanka's wet zone, next to Colombo the most urbanized districts and containing the largest proportion of the volatile literate secondary-school leavers, were the major exporters of migrants, not only to urban Colombo but also to the embattled fringe zones of peasant resettlement.[16] Jaffna in turn was a major exporter of its educated to the rest of the country, particularly to the newly developing areas of Vavuniya and Trincomalee, and to the metropolis of Colombo. Kandy, the second biggest city on the island, was also compelled to send out many more migrants than it received.

A last statistic based on the census of 1981 speaks for itself. While the sex ratio (of males in relation to females) for all of Sri Lanka was 103.1 (the urban ratio being 109.1 and the rural 101.6), the sex ratios in the following dry-zone provinces of peasant resettlement, particularly their urban market towns, were disproportionately male: Anurādhapura (total 113.4; urban 127.0, rural 112.4), Vavuniya (total 113.6; urban 124.5, rural 111.1); Polonnaruva (total 129.8; urban 142.4, rural

128.8), Trincomalee (total 115.3; urban 114.4, rural 115.8), Mullaitivu (total 122.8; urban 119.8, rural 123.1). The district of Colombo also reported the next largest imbalance (total sex ratio 110.6; urban 113.6, and rural 102.2). Since Colombo would attract females as well as males for purposes of work and education, one would not expect its sex imbalance to be as large as the new areas of colonization, where those first attracted are usually young adult males (say nineteen to forty years old). If they are married, their female relatives follow them in time, but if they are not, their marriages take place later. In sum, then, these figures point to the probable existence of floating populations of young males either unmarried or living without spouses, concentrated in the growing towns of the remote provinces and in Colombo.

Except for the sex ratios, these demographic trends and migration patterns pertain to a Sri Lanka nearly twelve years removed from the ethnic riots of 1981 and 1983. There is no doubt that in this intervening period the trends delineated would have intensified, not diminished. It is against this backdrop that I want to discuss the phenomenon of thuggery, patronage, and mob violence that has reached cancerous proportions in Sri Lanka today.

In his 1984 report, Paul Sieghart referred to the phenomenon of *goondas*—a word of Indian origin for thugs (another word of Indian origin now incorporated into the vocabulary of the English language), which has found currency in Sri Lanka today. He wrote that *goonda*s

> are essentially, organized gangs of hooligans available for hire by anyone whom it happens to suit to foment trouble in the streets. It is freely admitted that every major political party has its own rented or rentable goonda contingent: there are SLFP goondas, UNP goondas, and doubtless goondas serving other political interests. . . . That they [private armies] exist is not disputed: What is less clear is the extent of the damage they can inflict, and how is it that their paymasters seem to enjoy a surprising degree of immunity from prosecution.[17]

Gananath Obeyesekere has advanced an explanation of why these kind of networks of patronage, brokerage, and violence, which have expanded in recent years, have served as the immediate context for the rise of extreme personages such as Cyril Mathew and his minions.[18]

With the rise in population in recent decades and the corresponding intensification in internal migrations, Sri Lankan villages, especially those in the populous areas near towns, have grown larger as well as more heterogeneous. Furthermore, numbers have swelled in the market towns and the larger urban centers. All in all, then, social stability has eroded, factionalism has increased and, especially in the urban places and market towns, an increasing mass of a largely rootless and marginally employed transient population has congregated in slums and bazaars, constituting a ready pool to be mobilized for instant payoffs. Since trade in the market towns has for some time been distributed among merchants of three ethnic communities—Sinhalese, Tamil, and Muslim—"racial violence has often been directly linked to business competition. Merchants employ the lumpen proletarians of these towns to eliminate business rivals especially during periods of post-election violence."[19] The peasant colonization schemes of the north central dry-zone regions—where thousands of peasants of diverse origins have been transplanted—have become arenas where the same patterns of *mudalāli* control, political patronage by politicians, and resort to violence to settle electoral and economic grievances have become endemic. Thus, "practically all civil disturbances—post election riots endemic after the 60s and race riots—have occurred primarily in these lumpen colonization schemes, in the anomic market towns, and of course in the city of Colombo."[20] In the past these civil disturbances were rarely generated within the agriculturally centered villages. And if the "middle classes," that is, the white-collar and professional segments, were keenly aware of the stakes involved in the competition for jobs among the educated and for clients among the professionals, they did not in the past participate directly in the riots either—although the odd maverick populist leader may have emerged from their ranks, and although for the first time disconcerting accusations have surfaced that in the 1983 riots some Sinhalese lawyers and doctors were implicated in the dispossession and driving out of their Tamil counterparts with long-established and successful practices.

Populist politicians, their party machines, and their private armies of clients and thugs came into their own in these contexts: the established pattern of resorting to violence to settle interpersonal disputes; recent demographic and migration trends that have deposited increasing numbers of the underprivileged in the towns; the reliance on patronage for securing land allotments in colonization schemes, and jobs in development projects and government-controlled departments and corporations; the flourishing of graft in the dispensing of government contracts relating to development projects; and finally, the maneuvering of the UNP into a situation of authoritarian rule.

The Jātika Sēvaka Saṅgamaya (National Workers Organization), led for many years by Cyril Mathew, exploded into a major trade union, overshadowing and eclipsing the leftist unions, at the time of the UNP'a massive return to power in 1977. The sinister and unprecedented feature of this trade union, formed under the ruling party's auspices and led by a man at the center of the party machine and a minister with patronage to distribute, is that it was used to stage protests against legal decisions that went against the government, to invade government corporations or departments where the management had taken disciplinary action against workers who were member of the JSS, to break up public meetings organized by groups or parties that wished to air sincere dissent, and so on. Obeyesekere sums up his scrutiny of the records compiled by the Civil Rights Movement thus: "The pattern in these activities documented by the CRM is clear: the gangs were organized, they came in government vehicles, they were sometimes accompanied by MPs, and for the most part they belonged to the JSS, the trade union of the government in power. This almost certainly accounts for police inaction."[21]

In this series of punitive actions mounted from within the regime in power against the very institutions and norms it is supposed to protect, the worst violation was the attack on the judiciary itself. I have earlier documented at least two such violations. The UNP regime has been no innovator in this matter. The previous SLFP government, especially during the years 1970–77 under the leadership of Mrs. Bandaranaike, did tug and pull and harass the Supreme Court. But the instances of tampering with the justices seem to have reached a new high-water mark, all in an atmosphere of stage-managed blackmail to give the impression that civilian actions support ministerial acts. In this matter I can do no better than refer the reader to an indictment by Michael Hamlyn in *The Times* (of London) of 18 January 1984, entitled "Judges Come Under Attack," which I reproduce in full as appendix 1.

The Economic Correlates of Ethnic Conflicts from 1956 to 1977

We have seen how the UNP's initiation of a "liberalized" market-and-development-oriented economic policy friendly to the capitalist West caused certain unintended displacements which affected the living standards of the poorest sections of the urban and semiurban populations. This has been the story of years 1977-84. But if this change of tack by the UNP produced certain kinds of deterioration that can be correlated with the occurrence of worsening racial riots in 1977, 1979, 1981, and 1983, what are the economic correlates of the racial riots that occurred in 1956 and 1958, when the SLFP, led by S. W. R. D. Bandaranaike and wedded to a "neutralist" socialist and redistributive policy, held sway? And although no riots took place from 1959 to 1977, 1971 saw the explosive insurrection of Sinhalese youth followed by its heavy-handed suppression during the prime ministership of Mrs. Bandaranaike, which was supposedly characterized by the same "socialist" goals. Moreover, this "socialism" did not desist from an oppressive discrimination against the Tamils.

The economic story of Sri Lanka since 1956 contains all the sorry dilemmas and contradictions of a relatively sophisticated ex-colony of Britain, which had been introduced to the promises of welfare policies, attempted to implement and expand them, but was at the same time unable to attain any significant economic growth as an exporter of cash crops in a world of industrial and industrializing countries whose cards were stacked against its type of economy. Sri Lanka's fundamental contradiction has been an achievement of a laudable degree of equity and redistribution in a context of little overall economic growth, and, indeed, at a cost to its economic growth itself. Sri Lanka, since independence, has achieved notable improvements in levels of health and nutrition. Mortality rates have shrunk dramatically and life expectancy increased by 1970 to sixty-six years. The island's population *doubled* between 1946 and 1977. An achievement that received international acclamation was the progressive implementation of universal free education from primary school to university. School enrollment in 1976 was about 80% and literacy stood at 86%. Moreover, successive governments have supported the subsidization of food prices, especially that of rice, and of other costs relating to fuel (kerosene) and transportation, moves aimed at ensuring subsistence to the poor. This policy used up a large portion of the national income. (By 1977 total subsidies equalled over three-quarters of capital expenditure, while food subsidies alone amounted to two-thirds of it.)

So on the one hand in the 1960s and early 1970s Sri Lanka had achieved some progress in income distribution, and by virtue of its expansionary free education scheme, produced a glut of educated youth, trained in the clerical skills of literacy rather than in the technical skills of agriculture and manufacture. A rising tide of expectations regarding jobs, better incomes, and greater access to consumer goods from Japan and the West was frustrated by an economy that failed to grow and to generate the necessary levels of employment. Clearly the gains in equity could not be protected without economic growth, which alone could generate a higher level of employment.

While during the late 1960s Sri Lanka's economic performance compared favorably with that of most South Asian countries, it worsened significantly in the 1970s. The most important reasons behind the decline were on the one hand adverse movements in the country's international terms of trade, and on the other, a steady decline in output from the tea and coconut sectors, and the slow growth of the entire agricultural sector in general.

In the suffocating atmosphere of an economy that refused to take off, the logic of its redistributive ethic drove a government with left-leaning sympathies along the only road that would allow it to continue redistributing: the imposition of a

fifty-acre ceiling on private ownership of land, the nationaliza-
tion of plantations, and their uninspired management as state
corporations or their ruin as peasant cooperatives. The HIID
Final Technical report sums up these trends and their consequences thus:

> Declining commodity prices, a rising effective tax burden,
> and a dual exchange rate that discriminated against tree
> crops depressed producer returns, combined with the long
> drawn-out process of nationalization of the tea estates,
> reduced incentives to take measures to maintain, let alone
> increase yields. In the manufacturing sector growth was
> initially stimulated by an intensive import-substitution
> effort in the 1960s fostered by increasing protectionist poli-
> cies and the expanding role of state enterprises in capital-
> intensive large industries. By the 1970s, however, it had
> become clear that import substitution had run its course
> and that further growth required an outward-looking ex-
> port oriented policy. The introduction of a dual exchange
> rate in 1968, combined with a short-lived import liberaliza-
> tion policy, did lead to some growth in manufactured ex-
> ports but these gains were offset, and eventually brought to
> a halt, by a continued decline in private investment in
> manufacturing. Private investors shied away from expand-
> ing their stake in the economy because of a series of state
> takeovers of industries, the rapid spread of price controls,
> and the reimposition of import controls combined with
> severe import rationing. These policies are reflected in the
> slow growth of exports: 2.5 per anum over the period
> 1960–76 leading to a decline in the share of exports in
> G.D.P. from 30 percent in 1960 to 22 percent in 1977.[22]

At the human level, the consequences of all these vicious
circles and double-binds were reflected in the serious unemployment that has dogged Sri Lanka, and probably been the
single most explosive factor in triggering time and again the
communal riots directed by the have-nots against a nominated
"enemy," the Tamils, who have been stereotyped as privileged, and about whom the Sinhalese man on the street has
been taught to say, "We have already given them too much."
The statistics speak for themselves: in the years 1971–76, the
labor force grew at a rate of about 125,000 persons a year,

while employment rose at just 85,000 jobs a year, thereby adding about 40,000 a year to the ranks of the unemployed. *By 1977 some 20% of the labor force was unemployed.* And if we keep in mind that at least 75% of the population in Sri Lanka is rural, and that agriculture is flexible enough to support numbers of underemployed and dependent persons, we can plausibly suppose that a majority of this unemployed labor force (that is amenable to a quantitative measure) is drifting into the cities and towns and the large congested villages situated on their peripheries, areas which are thus susceptible to be politically manipulated, and to be aroused in protest of their lumpen proletariat condition. Thus the 1980s have indeed inherited the accumulated economic failures of the 1960s and 1970s and a country of dignified peasantry has been held to ransom by populist politicians and their volatile riffraff supplicants.

Chauvinist Ideology, Political Buddhism, and Ecstatic Cults

A major question regarding Sinhalese-Tamil ethnic conflicts is why the periodic expression of Sinhalese mass violence takes the direction it does. We have noted that the level of violence in the society is high, and that there are economic, social, and demographic dislocations that contribute to this expression. But instead of a "class" warfare within the Sinhalese society, or a generalized antagonism between the poor and the rich, why is the aggression directed as Sinhalese punitive action against the Tamils?

The populism, chauvinism, and militant Buddhism among certain segments of the Sinhalese population in the 1980s may be an intensified, and, in some ways, a transformed expression of present-day social tensions. This manifestation, though in large part induced by present circumstances, cannot be fully understood unless it is also seen as a phase in a phenomenon of longer duration. The long-term view enables us to understand not only why there has been a series of anti-Tamil riots since 1956, but also how the seeds of these outbursts were sown in the British colonial era, especially in the nineteenth century. Only the long-term view can also adequately explain how an ideology of the Buddhist religion—an ideology set out in the *Mahāvaṃsa* chronicle by Buddhist monks in the fifth century A.D.—was reactivated and recontextualized to give shape to political aspirations in the twentieth century. Only a long-term account of a "persisting" tendentious Sinhalese collective worldview—the "motivated" view of a beleaguered majority, a majority with a minority complex with regard to India (and South India in particular)—can explain why the Sinhalese in the era of independence, after many years of discriminatory action against the Tamils (who are alleged to be overrepresented in education, employment and so on) that has more than corrected the imbalances in their favor, still persist in making the distorted charge that the Tamils are overprivileged. Why are the Sinhalese still impelled to victimize the Tamils, with the result that, in desperation, increasing numbers of alienated Tamil youths engage in a suicidal mission of violence, which in turn gives the majority the justification for a total extinction or expulsion of the Tamils?

We shall examine in the next chapter the features entailed in the long-term view. There is, however, also something instructive embodied in the short-term view, which focuses on recent developments that suggest the emergence of new components in Buddhism as a nationalist religion and a populist dogma with "racial" claims.

These recently emerging components have to do with the propagation of a Sinhala Buddhist nationalism that, while emptied of most of the substantive contents that make Buddhism a great religion and the source of a rich civilization, has become a slogan that defines a collective identity and an aggressive stance for a mass of urban poor and uprooted migrants and transients deposited in urban slums and marketplaces. This Buddhism of slogans seems to promise a panacea for their frustrations and deprivations.

Increasingly in the 1970s and now in the 1980s we have a formulaic Buddhism which says that to be a Sinhalese is to be automatically a Buddhist and and Aryan, and to be Buddhist is to be able to make a total claim—territorially and politically—over Sri Lanka. Conversely, to be Buddhist is to be Aryan Sinhalese by "race" and "language," and to be

Sinhalese by race gives the right to exclude, perhaps even exterminate, other "races" in Sri Lanka, especially the Dravidians. Such a militant posture and understanding, along with a deadly if tragicomical use of Buddhism and Sinhala identity, go well with another aspect of collective anomic as well as euphoric behavior, namely, the efflorescence of fundamentalist devotion to ecstatic cults.

One such is the Bōdhi Pūjā ceremonies, in which the tree under which the Buddha defeated the threats and enticements of Mara (Death) and then went on unperturbed to achieve enlightenment, is the focus of elaborate propitiation and orchestrated chanting by monks in a rite that Seneviratne and Wickremaratne call a "rite of collective amelioration" which promises relief to the oppressions and frustrated ambitions of "urban educated unemployed youth."[24] The blessings of the Buddha are invoked as wished-for showers of rain to fall upon the parched masses of devotees gathered together in crowd worship and mob anonymity. Another mushrooming cult is the worship of the god Kataragama (of Hindu origin), who it appears, has emerged as the preeminent guardian god of the Sinhalese. In the service of this guardian god, who dispenses favors in return for devotion, shamans (mediums) have mushroomed in a number of new temples in the cities and towns.[25] His central shrine on the southern coast of Sri Lanka is the focus of massive pilgrimages, ecstatic festivals, vow taking, and favor seeking in pursuance of worldly goals. (Be it noted that Kataragama is by Hindu reckoning Skanda or Murukan; the temple of Kataragama previously had Hindu [Tamil] priests under Sinhalese administrative jurisdiction, and was a place of traditional pilgrimage for Hindus, Buddhists, and even Muslims.) For the Sinhalese to take over an ecumenical god and cult and to increasingly claim it as exclusively theirs is seen by Tamils as still another example of unfair and unhistorical monopolistic ambitions.

Indeed, the history and changing significance of the worship of Kataragama is instructive of how there is taking place today in Sri Lanka a profound change from an earlier state of traditional organic social organization, in which castes, subcultures, and specialized groups were held together in their assigned niches and were both ritually and economically articulated with the older medieval galactic politics of Kandy and Kōṭṭe—a pattern and policy that persisted right into British times, when the raj too acted as an umbrella for the pluralistic coexistence of distinct groupings. Today, the credo of the Sinhalese majority is largely that of a collectivity that is experiencing the eroding of the traditional organic structure that stabilized it. It is therefore compulsively seeking a homogenizing "national" identity in terms of a militant and mobilizing religious identity labeled as Buddhism, but a Buddhism shorn of its universalistic ethical message, and in the guise of ecstatic cults, such as that addressed to Kataragama, or even cult objects like the Buddha's tooth relic or the Bodhi tree. In doing so, the Sinhalese are, despite their Buddhist label, approximating in substance the religious complexes and cults of South India, while at the same time repudiating and expelling segments of the Tamil population that either actually brought to Sri Lanka the religious complexes in question or alternatively participated integrally in cults as partners of the Sinhalese from the time of their inception.

My assertion will become understandable when we contemplate these facts. Let us begin with the traditional Kandyan polity, which in the latter half of the eighteenth century under Kīrti Śrī Rājasiṃha (a king of Tamil Nāyakkar extraction) not only was responsible for a revival of Buddhism, its *sangha* and its art and architecture, but also inventively incorporated the cult of the Buddha's tooth relic—the palladium of the kingdom—into the traditional festival of the four guardian gods of the polity, namely, Nātha, Viṣṇu, Skanda (Kataragama), and the goddess Pattini. These guardian gods' cultic centers were distributed throughout the polity, and they were also aggregated in the capital of Kandy as part of the palace complex. On the one hand we note that the daily worship of the tooth relic, conducted by the king, Buddhist monks, and lay officials, was *unmistakably* Hindu in inspiration. Like the great Hindu deities in their temples in India, the tooth relic, in which the Buddha resided as immanent God, was wakened in the morning, subjected to ablutions, then fed throughout the day at set times to music, and finally put to bed. A similar pattern of kingship wedded to a cult of Śiva or Viṣṇu, was a hallmark of the South Indian Vijayanagara and

Cōḷa kingdoms, and the Kandyan cult follows the paradigm. On the other hand, we also note that one of the four guardian gods of Sri Lanka was Skanda (Kataragama), whose priest was always Tamil, but who was nevertheless fully integrated into a Buddhist political ritual that celebrated the integrity of the Kandyan polity. In this respect it is relevant to note that even to this day, the part of the *Perahära* procession that enacts the "water-cutting ceremony" tarries for several hours at the Ganesha Kovil, a Hindu temple patronized by local Tamils of Indian origin.

Now let us address the Kataragama cult and its traditional significance for both Hindu Tamils and Buddhist Sinhalese (and Muslims). Obeyesekere describes the historic change in the significance of the Kataragama cult for the Sinhalese such that Skanda has now become their most popular "national deity."[26] Although Kataragama the site of the cult, and Skanda, the deity propitiated there, were known in earlier times, the popularity of Skanda took a sharp upward turn from the fifteenth to the nineteenth centuries. Relying on the rich evidence provided by Dewaraja, to whose work I shall advert later, Obeyesekere surmises that the cult increased in popularity because of the influx from South India of martial ruling Nāyakkar elements, of non-brahman priests called *pantārams*, and of devotees of Śiva and Skanda called *aňḍi*. Moreover, the endemic internecine warfare between the kingdoms of Kōṭṭe, Sītāvaka, and Kandy inflated the popularity of Skanda as a god of war.

Obeyesekere sees a decline in popularity and public esteem of Skanda during the period 1820–1920, and underscores Skanda's sudden explosive rise as a popular deity from the 1940s onwards, until today we have hundreds of thousands of devotees visiting the cult center during both festival time and off season in order to seek personal and individual favors that draw their salience and intensity from social and marital aspirations, educational and political ambitions, occupational and business uncertainties, and the status frustrations of the people of post-independence Sri Lanka, especially those situated in an urban milieu and exposed to modernization without development. It is noteworthy that Skanda demands from his clients devotion rather than ethical conduct, and in this sense he has "heretical" tendencies. Obeyesekere's documentation focuses its searchlight on the "national" involvement of the Sinhalese in the cult—Sinhala Buddhist devotees are taking to firewalking, previously a Hindu practice, and cult priests and mediums are building Kataragama shrines all over the country, especially in the towns. In the face of all this, Obeyesekere sees in Sri Lanka a decline in Buddhism "as a personal religion." In urban Sri Lanka, Buddhists seem to have taken to a variety of ecstatic cults and show widespread commitment to Hindu-type *bhakti* devotionalism.

It is outside Obeyesekere's chosen framework to describe the significance of the Kataragama cult for the Tamil population. But a communication by Don Handelman[27] is important precisely because it describes how throughout the nineteenth century (despite a seeming decline in the 1870s that was due to restrictions placed on pilgrimage by British colonial authorities who were concerned to stop the spread of disease and epidemics, especially among the Tamil estate population) the annual festival and pilgrimage to Kataragama was a key to the scheduling and coordination of local festivals in honor of the same deity staged by Tamils residing in the southern, western, eastern, and central areas of the island.

For example, the Nāṭṭukoṭṭai Chettiars of Colombo had founded several temples there dedicated to Kadiresan (or Murukan) as their protective deity and their major festival in Colombo, called Ādi-Vēl, was coordinated with the major festival at Kataragama. The *Vēl*, the lance with which the deity destroyed the Asuras (antigods), from each temple was taken to Kataragama to be purified in the water-cutting ceremony that ended the festival. "In point of fact the Adi-Vēl Festival became the single most extensive celebration of the Tamil population of Colombo, one that connected five temples dedicated to Murakan, and one in which numerous Sinhalese Buddhists participated, at least until the riots and the destruction of the summer of 1983."

That this taking of the lances to the Kataragama festival was of widespread significance for the Tamil (as well as Sinhalese) people was attested by Covington in 1893:

The total number thus congregated [at Kataragama] . . . attained its maximum figure on the second week of the festival, only after the arrival of different *Vels* from Colombo [in the Western Province], Kandy [in the Central Province Highlands], Galle [on the southern coast], Ratnapura [in the southwestern foothills of the Western Province Highlands], Gampola [in the Central Province, near Kandy]and Badulla [in the Central Province highlands]. There were altogether seven *Vels* brought to the temple [of Kataragama] by the Chetties and Tamils from the places above-mentioned.[28]

I have purposely dwelt on ethnography in order to make certain nostalgic points. If what Obeyesekere describes is true, as I think it is, that Kataragama has become the major protective and favor-granting deity of the Sinhalese, who have embarked upon the massive worship of him, then this process of "Sinhala modernization" or "Sinhala colonization" of Skanda may obliterate remembrance of the beautiful manner in which, in earlier times, Tamil and Hindu shrines and festival cycles interlocked, how Kataragama, celebrated in Kandy in the Buddhist *Perahära* (whose center piece was the tooth relic), could coexist with the Hindu Ādi-Vēl festival staged in Colombo; how Hindu temples and functionaries traditionally played an integral part in the *Perahära*'s culminating water-cutting ceremonies; and how as even as late as 1980 expectant Sinhalese urbanites of Colombo broke coconuts before Murukan and rubbed shoulders with Tamil devotees. Indeed, I could go so far as to suggest that many Sinhalese have traditionally sought favors from the Hindu Murukan shrines dotted all over the country, and that if Sinhalese mediums and priests are currently establishing their own shrines and cults, they are replicating the patterns of worship of those who have lived in their midst for several centuries, and a number of whom have by now become Sinhalese. At the very moment the Sinhalese intensify their worship of Skanda they deny the heritage of Murukan, and the historian/anthropologist feels he is standing on the shifting sands of ethnic fantasies.

Because features of an organic past exist, the current Sinhala Buddhist racist nationalism that is propagated by extremist politicians is not only mischievous but also violates that past. That past was a rich, complex civilization that celebrated both difference and complementarity. If in Sri Lanka today one had to pick the exemplary propagandist of such destructive militant nationalist "racist" dogma, one would have to pick again someone like Cyril Mathew, who, interestingly, finds support in, and voices his sympathy for, the notorious *bhumiputra* ("sons of the soil") doctrine of the Malaysian nationalist and Islamic extremists, a doctrine that is directed against the alleged Chinese "aliens" in preservation of the interests of "native" Malays, who, it is claimed, have been exploited and robbed by Chinese control of commerce. The doctrine, in short, pleads the cause of corrective affirmative action in favor of the "majority" of Malays.[29] Just as in Malaysia Islam and a claim in favor of "indigenous" Malays (which only nominally includes the tribal forest peoples, who probably have a better claim to being sons of the soil, and excludes the Chinese and Indians who have made the Malay economy what it is) crystallized during a time of populist politics, so in Sri Lanka Sinhala Buddhism has traveled on a parallel path. This is why it makes some comparative sense to say that these "religions" today—in their militant populist incarnations—can be emptied of their traditional ethical and normative substance, and be used as mere diacritics and mnemonics of crowd and mob identity, as rhetorical mobilizers of volatile masses and as instigators of their orgasmic spurts of violence. The indulgence of these frustrations and aggressions requires a designated enemy within their fold, an enemy that is both large and prominent enough to be construed as a threat and as the arch grabber of the wealth, jobs, and influence that so many of the deprived majority feel it their right to claim and enjoy. This is the force behind the Sinhala cry: "We have already given the Tamils too much." It is a cry of collective and dashed hopes. It is difficult to attribute willful intention to such pathos.

5
FROM BRITISH RAJ
TO INDEPENDENCE:
A Sketch of the Antecedents

My account so far has been concerned, first, with the recent riots of 1983, the events immediately preceding them, and their aftermath, and, second, with the political and economic events that sparked the series of riots from 1956 onwards. But these riots were inevitably linked to still re- moter antecedent events. Clearly the most relevant point of entry for reviewing these antecedents is the era of British colonial rule, especially during the nineteenth and twentieth centuries, when the two indigenous ethnic communities, pre- viously separate, were brought together under the umbrella of Imperial rule. The British imposed a single administration, educated an English-speaking elite drawn from Sinhalese and Tamils alike, opened up plantations and imported a new population of South Indian Tamil laborers to work them, and up to a point created a single polity and a plural society.

The political, educational, and economic developments that bear on the Sinhalese-Tamil "ethnic" tensions in the twentieth century during both the colonial and independent eras have been very amply documented,[1] and I shall here merely highlight the most significant features.

The administrative needs of the British raj for a certain number of local English-educated white-collar workers and professionals, along with the activities of the Christian mis- sionaries, who established a great number of schools dis- pensing English and vernacular education, determined the absolute numbers of Sri Lankans who were educated in gov- ernment and mission schools, and, even more importantly, determined which segments of the local population would be the primary beneficiaries. As it turned out, the principal beneficiaries were the low-country Sinhalese (of the southwest), who were engaged in the most vital maritime and commercial developments, and the indigenous Tamils of the north, who, living in a barren area farthest away from both the commercial and plantation developments of the southwest and the central highlands, were eager for education that could open the door of white-collar employment. These circumstances that benefited the Tamils are the source of the recurrent allegation by the Sinhalese that, during the British era, the local Tamils enjoyed an "unfair" educational advantage, and a placement in administrative positions far in excess[2] of their numbers in the total population. The local Tamils in turn have wondered why, when the low-country Sinhalese themselves enjoyed disproportionate educational advantages compared with other segments of the Sinhalese population such as the Kandyans, and when virtually all the entrepreneurial opportunities and huge benefits stemming from tea, coffee, coconut, and rubber plantation industries that became available to Sri Lankans (in the wake of British commercial activity) were monopolized by low-country Sinhalese, that there has been so much resentment through the decades of the Tamil need to concentrate on the white-collar and professional niches as the only way to progress and prosperity.

To the British introduction and development of the plantation economy, especially tea, Sri Lanka owes its last massive wave of immigration of South Indian Tamil "coolie" labor, which was brought in to work in the plantations. This importation of the "Indian Tamil" labor was necessitated by the understandable unwillingness of the Sinhalese rice-farming peasants to turn to wage labor and live in coolie lines. In the event, the Indian Tamil laborers were housed in coolie lines in plantations that were largely established on the mountain slopes, above the Sinhalese valley villages, and came to form distinct social and ecological enclaves within the central zone, where the Sinhalese villagers nevertheless preponderated. It is thus remarkable that an island that has experienced waves of South Indian migrants through the centuries, and in time incorporated them into the local Sinhalese framework or into the indigenous Tamil fold, should have so decisively branded its most recent immigrants as foreign. The separation of the plantations from the villages as physical and ecological spaces and as European-owned enterprises helped to prolong the social distance between Sinhalese peasants and Indian laborers. It is a blot on the Sinhalese conscience that considerations of electoral arithmetic have denied the "Indian Tamils," large numbers of whom have been in the island for several generations, the rights of citizenship and enfranchisement[3]—a blot all the more dark because for many decades now it is this exploited segment of the population that has made the greatest contribution to the island's economy via the tea industry, which earns the greater part of the island's export earnings. But the Sinhalese are not alone in this disgrace. The indigenous Sri Lankan Tamils concentrated in the Northern and Eastern Provinces for quite other reasons of a social nature have traditionally looked down upon the plantation labor as of low caste and/or tribal status, and have not until very recently made an effort to include them within the framework and goals of their politics. The Indian Tamils, therefore, physically and socially removed from Sri Lankan Tamils and united by a common economic condition, have formed their own labor unions, generated their own leadership, and made their own political deals with the Sinhalese majority government.

If then we leave aside the Indian Tamils and return to the indigenous Sinhalese and Tamils, we can say that during the years from around 1880 to 1920 the colonial and missionary educational institutions gave rise to an elite that, whatever its internal caste and ethnic rivalries and differences, did from time to time unite for the common cause of winning for itself a greater representation in the legislative assembly and in the colonial administrative services. The Ceylon National Congress was such a body of the Sinhalese and Tamil English-educated elite, the most conspicuous members of which were drawn from the professions and landed families having plantation and mining interests. But this unity of the Sinhalese and Tamils was already showing cracks when, under the Donoughmore Constitution in the 1930s and 1940s, representation in the Legislative Council on the basis of territorial and demographic criteria became the dominant electoral principle. Territorial representation and manhood suffrage (up-

graded to universal suffrage in 1931) gave a natural advantage
to the majority Sinhalese community in relation to the minorities, among whom the most vocal and politically interested
group was the Sri Lankan Tamils.[4] It should not escape our
notice that the Donoughmore Report was accepted by the
thinnest of margins—the vote was nineteen for and seventeen
against—with all the minority representatives voting against
it. On the eve of independence, the Soulbury Constitution
confirmed the primacy of territorial and demographic criteria
for electoral representation, and rejected "ethnic" minority
pleas for special representation. Despite the bickering among
the professional politicians, they and their colleagues had
common backgrounds, and it was to these loosely associated
elements of the "traditional" English-educated elite that the
British transferred power at independence in 1948. The chief
beneficiary of this transfer of power was that aggregate of
politicians that formed the United National Party, under the
leadership of D. S. Senanayake, which earned the quip from
its critics that it was neither united, nor national, nor a party.

But it was not in the arena of UNP politics or among this
traditional colonial elite to whom the British had transferred
power that lay the seeds of those momentous social and political developments that have turned out to be at once constructive and destructive. Universal franchise, territorial electorates, and majority politics no doubt worked against the
interests of minorities, who would have preferred quotas and
special constitutional protection. But these same phenomena
of democratic politics also eroded traditional bases of leadership and power and produced deep divisions within the
Sinhalese society itself, which had repercussions for the
Sinhalese-Tamil relations.

Although in the British era the main development seemed
to be the growth of that English-educated elite to whom
power was transferred in 1948, there were other developments that were in the long run more explosive but that eluded
the official commentators of the time. The years from 1880
onwards were also the time of two social and religious up-
surges that climaxed in the so-called revolution of 1956. In the
decades preceding 1956, there had emerged and consolidated

a "rural" elite, or at least an elite that would in time speak on behalf of the village fold from whose ranks they had sprung. The members of this new elite were schoolteachers, ayurvedic physicians (who practiced indigenous medicine), traders, and newly rich merchants (*mudalālis*). They were all educated in the Sinhalese language and were therefore spurned by the English educated; and because they wished to conserve "traditional" culture and customs, they were hostile to the spread of a "Western" style of life, exemplified by western clothes, western films, western sex mores, western recreations, and so on. And all through the latter half of the nineteenth century, a resurgent and revivalist Buddhism, self-consciously propagandistic and gaining in organizational strength, began to develop, and was further energized by the Buddhist theosophists (of whom Colonel Olcott and Madame Blavatsky are best known) and by such local leaders as Anagārika Dharmapāla, who, while hostile to Christian missionary activities and influence, borrowed their organizational and proselytizing techniques as well as some of their "Protestant" attitudes toward work and sex. Overall, the most critical development in the Buddhist resurgence was a closing of the ranks, a growing solidarity, and the engagement in a propagandistic activism with political overtones on the part of the Buddhist monks, who since they too had village origins, were natural allies of the new rural elite. In preaching the restoration of Buddhism to its rightful historical place, they were also advocating their own return to prominence in the life of the society and the state.

The ideological package of the Sinhala-Buddhist revival necessarily promoted a multifaceted "nationalism" that, while powerful enough to bring the majority of Sinhalese within its fold, was equally potent in excluding and alienating minority groups speaking a mother tongue other than Sinhalese and adhering to a religion other than Buddhism. The new nationalist cause emphasized and combined, even conflated, three elements: the Sinhalese language, the Buddhist religion, and the Sinhalese "people" as an "Aryan race." To be truly Sinhalese was to be born Sinhalese, speak Sinhalese, and practice the Sinhalese religion, Buddhism.

Among the minorities, the Tamils felt the exclusion most on grounds of both language and religion, and additionally rejected the spurious "Aryan" claims of the Sinhalese.

Since it is in the years immediately after the gaining of independence, and especially in anticipation of the 2,500th anniversary of the inception of the Buddhist religion (Buddha Jayanthi), that the voicing of the nationalist-Sinhalese-Buddhist claims reached a crescendo, it is not surprising that the same years saw the full-scale invocation and manipulation of Sinhalese mythohistory, as set out in the island's foremost chronicle, the *Mahāvamsa*, which was composed by Buddhist monks of the Mahāvihāra fraternity around the fifth century A.D. This text simultaneously presents the dual destiny of the Sinhalese people to conquer, unite, and rule the island of Lanka for the preservation and glory of the Buddhist religion, and the necessary expulsion of the Tamil invaders from South India who had (temporarily) taken possession of the north. The founding legend of Vijaya and his followers, and the story of the violent but valiant career and glorious rule of Duṭṭhagāmaṇi, a culture hero, described in the first chapters of the *Mahāvaṃsa* as having taken place in the first centuries B.C., constitute a most potent ideological charter that unites the themes of people, territory, and religion. Since 1956 Sri Lanka has witnessed the reactivation of this mythohistorical charter at crucial times of political forment as a way of mobilizing the masses and directing their anger and violence against the Tamils. Heinz Bechert has rightly argued that the Sinhalese chronicles—the *Mahāvamsa* and the *Dipavamsa*—in postulating the unity of nation and religion constitute a profound transformation of the Asokan message of the sovereignity of *dharma* (rule by righteousness and nonviolence) in a multireligious society of Buddhist, Jains, adherents of Brahmanical values, and others.

The origination of historical literature in Ceylon in the existing form was an intentional act of political relevance. Its object was the propagation of a concept of national identity clearly connected with a religious tradition, i.e., the identity of the Sinhalese Buddhists . . . without the impact of this idea, the remarkable continuity of the cultural as well as of the political traditions in spite of the vicissitudes in the history of the island would be impossible.[5]

It is not surprising that the post-independence boiling over of the pot of Sinhalese nationalism resulted in the entirely unexpected landslide defeat of the UNP by S. W. R. D. Bandaranaike, who led the opposition groups and championed their nationalist and revivalist demands and aspirations. The same boiling pot also spilled over in the form of the first Sinhalese riots against the Tamils in 1956 and 1958. In the face of the Sinhalese championing of language and religion, the Tamils were now faced with the dire consequences of the dethroning of English as the language of administration and education for higher employment. They in turn rallied to the cause of federalism and regional/district councils, and constitutional protection against discrimination.

Many of my liberal Sinhalese friends were appalled by the scale of the destruction of life and property in the riots of 1983, and have been critical of the government's assumption of near-totalitarian powers, which endangers democracy as a political process. While I agree that 1983 represents a change of scale, I also want to remind them that as early as 1958 a riot took place under the prime-ministership of Bandaranaike and his party, who had been billed as promoting the new aspirations of the Sinhalese masses and as being the very opposite of the UNP in all essentials. The liberal Sinhalese of those years were equally appalled by the violence. I reproduce in appendix 2 a few pages from W. Howard Wriggins's authoritative book, which reports on the 1958 riots, in order to illustrate three things. First to remind my friends of the shape that Sinhalese violence has repeatedly taken over three decades. In 1958 the "aggressors" were not armed Tamil terrorists but leading Tamil politicians mounting a nonviolent Gandhian *satyagraha* campaign to make known their fears. Second, to bemoan the tragic abandonment of the Bandaranaike-Chelvanayagam pact, which constructively proposed a settlement regarding language policy and regional councils. This was a great opportunity, fatefully missed, to settle the Tamil question for all time. (The second missed chance was recently, before the 1983 riots, when a revival by Jayawardene of the previously abandoned agreement was indifferently and inadequately implemented.) Third, to signal the fact that in previous riots, too, the government in power acted tardily to restrain the violence, and that once it acted, its assumption of emergency powers allowed it to push toward autocratic rule, the scotching of opposition groups, and the imposition of press censorship.

In the fateful years of 1983–84 when the Sri Lankan ethnic turmoil seemed hopelessly entangled and almost beyond repair, one cannot but look back on the years 1956–58 as not only a time of promise of a social revolution for the Sinhalese but also a time when a more stiff-backed statesmanship on the part of Bandaranaike might have settled the Tamil question in large part. The aborted promises instead exposed the lack of generosity among the Sinhalese chauvinists, including the activist Buddhist monks banded together as the Eksath Bhikkhu Peramuṇa (EBP), and gave notice of the Sinhalese intransigence towards the Tamils that would progressively drive the latter to a politics of despair. Wriggins, by common consent a reliable witness of those times, tells the story well, and I now recapitulate certain events for those of us who, having lived through them, have forgotten them or, being too young, have never heard of them.

In 1956, by a vote of fifty-six to twenty-nine, the Sinhala Only Bill was passed. The ominous events that accompanied this legislation foreshadowed worse things to come. In the same year the government announced that the leading teacher training college in the country would be reserved for Sinhalese teachers only. Around the same time the Eksath Bhikkhu Peramuṇa demanded that persons educated in English or Tamil be prevented from taking public examinations until the year 1967. (A maverick lecturer in economics, F. R. Jayasuriya, a colleague of mine at the University of Peradeniya, went on a comic fast in support of this demand.) A nonviolent Tamil sit-down demonstration called by the federalist leader Chelvanayagam near the House of Representatives in Colombo to protest such developments led to their forcible ejecture and signaled the first riots of 1956, which flared up in Colombo first, and thereafter in the Gal Oya Valley and the Eastern Province.

And now we come to the missed and lamented opportunity. The Tamil Federal Party had by this time vowed to work toward the achievement of an "autonomous Tamil legislative state within a Federal Union of Ceylon." Toward the end of July, 1956, the prime minister, Bandaranaike, and the leader of the Federal Party, Chelvanayagam, had reached a promising agreement regarding legislation to be submitted to the house. The proposed legislation was to recognize Tamil as a 'language of Ceylon.' Administration in Tamil areas in the Northern and Eastern Provinces was to be in Tamil, although the interests of the Sinhalese-speaking population there were to be fully protected. Legislation then under consideration proposed to establish elected regional councils to correct the overcentralization of Ceylon's administration."[6] While the Tamil leaders called off their *satayagraha* campaign, the Buddhist monks in the EBP, their lay supporters, and a Kandyan political pressure group called the Tri Simhala Peramuṇa, vociferously rejected the agreement as a "complete and abject surrender." The United National Party (UNP), now sensing the direction of the political winds, began to agitate, led by no other than Junius Jayawardene (now president), in support of solely Sinhalese aspirations, and mobilized opposition to what it called unacceptable concessions made to the Tamils. The Buddhist monks capped this agitation by staging a massive sit-down in front of the prime minister's residence, and Bandaranaike felt compelled to abrogate the pact with Chelvanayagam. Thereafter things deteriorated: the Tamils of the north began to deface National Transport buses that had Sinhalese markings, and were deliberating on whether to launch a *satyagraha* campaign when Sinhalese zealots launched the riots of 1958.

It is now time to consider the crucial role of the language issue in Sri Lanka's ethnic conflict. Although the Sinhala conception of nationalism critically related Buddhism to the polity, and although this formula has been taken by the Tamils as evidence of the "intolerant militancy" of Sinhalese politico-religious claims, language has nevertheless been a more important issue than religion in the Sinhalese-Tamil conflicts.

In the immediate years after independence, it became evident that a minority elite of less than 10% of the population practically ruled the country and monopolized the prestigious occupations on the basis of its knowledge of and education in the English language. Moreover, since the country's legal codes and judicial and administrative decisions were also written in English, the majority of the population could comprehend judicial and administrative transactions only through translators and intermediaries. In simple terms, justice, fair play, and efficiency demanded the substitution of the indigenous languages (*swabāsha*)—Sinhalese and Tamil—for English in the conduct of legal and administrative proceedings. And this in turn inevitably required that education itself be conducted primarily in the mother tongues.

But once the principle of replacing English with *swabāsha* was accepted, the next step, which proved to be unexpectedly contentious, concerned the relative status of Sinhalese and Tamil in a country whose majority was Sinhalese speaking. Although Sinhalese has over the centuries borrowed significantly from Tamil, both at the lexical and grammatical levels, Sinhalese and Tamil are mutually unintelligible languages which also employ different scripts. The famous and grossly abused distinction between the Indo-Aryan origins of Sinhalese and the Dravidian origins of Tamil applies at the linguistic level alone.

Language has been the main bone of contention in Sri Lanka since independence because of its relevance for education as a medium of instruction and thereafter for employment. Since there is on the one hand a marked, even excessive, value in Sri Lanka placed on white-collar employment, whose chief provider is the government's administrative departments, and since competition for a limited number of positions—in the administrative services and in the legal, medical, and engineering professions—has been acute among the "middle classes" and the "English-educated" from the 1930s onwards, and since the Tamils, to a greater extent than the Sinhalese, have had to depend for their well being on employment secured through education, the government's language policy was bound to be an issue of great and wide concern. Hence it is no exaggeration to say that in the first two decades since independence the most important factor contributing to ethnic tension and violence in Sri Lanka had to deal with the bread-and-butter issue of "middle-class" and "white-collar" employment in the governmental and commercial sectors. This is why it is no distortion to say that although the educated "middle classes" among the Sinhalese and Tamils may not actually participate in the rioting—violence and thuggery is the play of the urban poor, the footloose, and the displaced—it is in their bosom that the ethnic conflict incubates. For "white-collar status," though achieved only by a minority, is nevertheless the aspiration of all those shut out from achieving it. The rice farmer, the harbor worker, the peon, the bus driver, all want their children to be pen-pushers. Such an aspiration can therefore serve as the clarion call for political mobilization and action on a mass scale, even though the prizes are few; indeed, precisely because they are few and reflect the scarcity of a zero-sum game.

Thus, when it came to implementation, Sinhalese gained the status of official language for purposes of central administration, while education at the primary and secondary levels was provided in two streams—Tamil and Sinhalese. This decision, once taken, dictated in due course that even at the university level the two languages would have to serve as the language of instruction, with English being used as a second language.

The debates on the language issue conducted in the 1950s showed a victorious slide in favor of the Sinhalese majority, to the growing chagrin of the Tamils. The discussions first proposed the thesis of the necessity for education in one's own tongue (*swabāsha*), then progressed to concede the parity of status of Sinhalese and Tamil as mother tongues and as national languages, and culminated in the victorious claim of "Sinhala only" as the official language of the country, championed by the SLFP, the Sinhala Mahā Sabhā, and a segment of the left led by Philip Gunawardene. This was the winning combination in the elections of 1956. The UNP's tardy espousal of Sinhala only on the eve of the elections was discounted by the public at large. The linguistic and educational policy subsequently implemented in the name of nation building and equitable democratization of the society served to deepen the Sinhalese-Tamil rift and increasingly to politicize and make collective adversaries out of the Sinhalese and Tamils. Previously Sinhalese and Tamil students studied together in those of the country's schools that taught in English—the urban schools in particular. In this environment it was considered improper by and large to invoke ethnic, caste, or religious affiliations, or let them interfere with interpersonal relationships, and with representation on the schools' teams and alumni associations. Indeed, those very schools founded by Buddhist and Hindu revivalists and reformers—such as Ānanda and Nālanda Colleges, and Viśākhā Vidyālaya—were also modeled on British public-school lines. The public-school ethos did produce an elite unified by certain traditions, aspirations, and norms, and this facilitated and maintained a social discourse between the Tamil and Sinhalese, between Christian, Buddhist, and Hindu, who in other matters, such as marriage or worship or party affiliation, went their separate ways.

But the provision of education in two separate streams isolated the two ethnic communities, and served to underscore the differences between students even when they attended the same school. Contact between Sinhalese and Tamil students was reduced to a minimum, and the social distance served in time to convert difference into enmity and confrontation, and to create distrust, dislike, and fear between the youth that had never before been experienced so vehemently in the island's cities and towns, including the capital city of Colombo itself.

In the long run, the implementation of the new language policy has worked to the detriment of Tamil interests, and Tamil fears regarding discrimination, especially in governmental employment, have materialized. For it has become the accepted thesis among numerous Sinhalese—including many segments of the educated middle classes—that the principle of majority politics entitles their government to insist on "affirmative action" on behalf of that majority. This affirmative action is defined as securing employment for the Sinhalese in proportion to their demographic strength. The same majority claim has stimulated populist politicians and monks to press for the granting of Sinhala "nationalism," with its potent mix of race, religion, and language, its "rightful place" in the island's political culture. Buddhism is today virtually the state religion of Sri Lanka. And most of the

Sinhalese majority, and the most important Sinhalese—
dominated political parties—the UNP, SLFP, and JVP—by
and large take for granted that discriminatory legislation and
the imposition of quotas in favor of the majority as justified
and justifiable action. There are no serious moral qualms or
conflicts of values experienced in this regard. Preferential
action on behalf of the Sinhalese is interpreted as an affirmative and positive corollary of the arithmetic of democratic
politics.

I may comment here that Sri Lanka presents us with the
moral ambiguity embedded in that kind of third-world rhetoric which waves the flag of "one-party government" and of
"popular consensus" as the legitimators of absolutist claims.
Insofar as it means the implementation of the rights of the
majority, this ideology puts in great peril minorities and
opposition groups—whether these be ethnic, religious, linguistic, or political minorities and dissenters, who can be
ground down by the juggernaut of majority consensus.

Be that as it may, as a result of what they perceived to be
increasing discrimination and their relegation to second-class
status, many of the Sri Lankan Tamils have become alienated
and have in increasing numbers united behind the TULF and
its cry for a separate state. This process of alienation has also
led many of the TULF politicians, and the insurrectionary
rebels, who seem for the most part to reject TULF reliance on
constitutional means for winning its goal, to seek support
from the political parties (DMK and AIADMK) and the
politicians of Tamil Nāṭu. Apart from the fact that Tamil
insurgents have sought asylum in South India, and are now
thought to have established their guerilla training camps and
hideouts there, some of the Tamil Nāṭu politicians, who have
their own dissensions and interests to promote within the
Indian state and federal arenas, have come to champion the
cause of their Tamil brethren in Sri Lanka. These attempts on
the part of the Sri Lankan Tamils to connect with South India
enrage the Sinhalese majority. Such attempts invoke in their
minds the specter of South Indian "invasions"—a specter that
has also been raised in the Sinhalese chronicles, and that was
advanced in earlier centuries as the reason why the Sinhalese
Buddhist nation and state must be vigilant and aggressive in

defense of its integrity. The last straw for the Sinhalese has been the leading Tamil rebel groups' adoption of the old Cōḷa tiger symbol, and their mounting attacks on the island's security forces and police—acts which they interpret as calculated to make the Sinhalese security forces and extremist politicians react with violence, thereby reducing the island to such disorder that foreign intervention (both by India and the western powers) might ensue and become the channel for a just settlement.

While one cannot condone the terrorist activities of the rebels, one must nevertheless realize that these are acts of desperation and hopelessness. And since the backbone of the rebels is made up of Sri Lankan Tamil youth, and their desperation stems from the certitude that there is no place of dignity or possibility of achievement in a Sinhalese-dominated country, I am compelled to advert to the puzzling nature of one kind of Sinhalese attitude.

I have previously referred to the Sri Lankan Tamil concentration on education in the British era, and the need for them to do so because of the meager economic resources of the Northern and Eastern Provinces of Sri Lanka. It is undeniable that the participation of Sri Lankan Tamils in higher education and the number of white-collar and professional positions they hold has always been proportionately higher than their demographic size. Yet it is also true that the Sinhalese chauvinists have always exaggerated the level of Tamil participation and their "privileged" position. In any case, as a result of the "affirmative" action on their own behalf, the Sinhalese have by now decidedly "corrected" the imbalance and tipped the scales in their favour (even in terms of demographic representation). Tables 5.1 and 5.2[7] based on government data, demonstrate how Sinhalese employment in the public sector and Sinhalese participation in higher education have now become greater than their population size would ordinarily warrant.

Part of the reason why much of the Sinhalese public persists in the belief that the Tamils have an unduly high share of the jobs in the public sector is that Tamils are visible in certain fields;[8] this reflects the traditional Sri Lankan Tamil concentration on these professional skills, which they have domi-

Table 5.1: Ethnic Representation in State-Sector
            Employment, 1980
            (excluding the corporate sector)

Percentages of:	Sinhalese	Tamil	Others
Professional and technical	82%	12%	6%
Administrative and Managerial	81%	16%	3%
All categories	84%	12%	4%

SOURCE: *Census of Public Corporation Sector Employment*, 1980.
Department of Census and Statistics and Ministry of Plan
Implementation.

Table 5.2: Ethnic Representation in the Public
            Sector, 1980
            (state and corporate sectors combined)

Percentage of:	Sinhalese	Tamil	Others
Professional and technical	82%	13%	5%
Administrative and Managerial	83%	14%	3%
All categories	85%	11%	4%

SOURCE: *Census of Public and Corporation Sector Employment, 1980*.
Department of Census and Statistics and Ministry of Plan Implementation.

nated under conditions of equal competition. But Sinhalese
perceptions go well beyond the objective facts, and since this
stereotypical exaggeration persists, is fostered and manipulated by politicians and state propagandists, we have to ask
the following questions: Does the popular Sinhalese charge
that Tamils enjoy an unfair advantage in the administrative
services and professions show signs of "overdetermination"?
Why are the Sinhalese so ready to credit "conspiratorial"
reasons for the talents the Tamils have carefully nursed? And
why do the Sinhalese disregard all the economic and commercial advantages, including those associated with the plantation
industry, and with peasant colonization, that have so pre-

dominantly accrued to them? It is undeniable that administrative and professional employment is the most vital competitive arena for all Sinhalese and Tamils. But this is not a complete explanation. For in order to discover the nature of the overdetermination of the Sinhalese response, and what in Tamil mores and conduct stimulates certain perceptions of Tamil exclusivity among the Sinhalese, we have to engage in some soul-searching and frank self-examination.Therefore I shall attempt in the next chapter to probe some aspects of the collective preoccupations, obsessions, and anxieties of the two communities, who are so similar in many respects and have yet drifted so far apart.

Let me conclude this chapter by referring to the changing and deteriorating fortunes of the Tamils, which they feel forces them to take a last stand. If language was the crucial issue for the Tamils in the 1960s, in the 1980s other issues have become preeminent because earlier battles to secure education and employment on equal terms have been lost. A regrouping of all Tamils is now felt to be the only efficacious strategy.

I have previously referred to the current "standardization policy" that regulates admission to the universities and how the weight given to population size in revenue districts (55% of the admissions) and to revenue districts deemed educationally underprivileged (15%) puts Tamil candidates at a grave disadvantage. The government's higher education policy is perceived by Tamils as having closed off that avenue for good.

Hence other issues have become salient because they are now felt to be the only guarantees of the security and integrity of the Tamil people in the future. One is the issue of peasant colonization and resettlement, which Tamils feel allows the infiltration of more and more Sinhalese into their own areas of dominance, thereby posing the danger that they may become a minority in their provinces. The slogan of "traditional homelands," whatever its objective truth, is first and foremost a political claim meant to ensure the security of the Tamils. This territorial issue is integrally connected to the present Tamil insistence on provincial or regional autonomy.

The second issue relates to the citizenship status of Indian

Tamils, whose "stateless" condition has been a matter of contention for several decades between the Sri Lankan and Indian governments. They, as we have seen, have been a primary target of ethnic violence and disparagement, and are increasingly joining hands with the Sri Lankan Tamils to protect themselves against blanket Sinhala discrimination. Thus in 1984 it was said that most Tamils would be willing to concede the dominance of the Sinhala language only at the center in exchange for autonomy for the Northern and Eastern Provinces and the granting of citizenship to Indian Tamils.

The Retrospective Overview

Standing back now and taking a long retrospective view, one can identify three major phases in the relation between Buddhism and politics. Phase 1 was the ideology promulgated in the *Mahāvaṃsa* concerning the integral symbiotic relation between the Buddhist orders of monks (*sangha*) and kingship and between the island of Lanka, the Sinhalese-speaking people, and their special stewardship of Buddhism. This formulation by and large served as a periodically invoked charter, especially during revivals and restorations of religion and state during the Anurādhapura period, and subsequently in the Polonnaruva epoch. This ideological package was crafted to accord with certain facts of political and economic existence of those early times. The political collectivities of the time— the multicentric principalities and kingdoms of Sri Lanka— were "galactic" in form, and the ideology was forged to preserve and maintain Sinhala-Buddhist kingdoms against the intrusion and invasions of similar "galactic" South Indian kingdoms, which increasingly, especially since Cōḷa imperial expansion from the eighth century onwards, fought under a banner of royal patronage of Hindu temple cults and devotional worship of the high gods Viṣṇu and Śiva.

But in all this, during phase 1, there was a fundamental contradiction and a charcteristic acculturation and assimilation process at work. The existence of Anurādhapura and Polonnaruva was predicated on a symbiotic relationship with South India, which was the source of their waves of immigrants, of craftsmen and soldiers and specialized castes, and also their chief partner in the exchange of Buddhist learning, lore, and monks. Until the Cōḷa period, South India had a strong Buddhist heritage concentrated in special areas. So at the same time that they revived and recovered lost territory, the Sinhalese kingdoms also assimilated and indigenized their South Indian infusions. These processes were also prominently at work in the Kōṭṭe phase in the fifteenth century in the southwest regions of Sri Lanka.

Phase 2 was the time of increasing Western colonial control, culminating with the British raj from, say, 1796 (or later) until 1948. This period saw the introduction and spread of the plantation economy, and of the transportation and export-import services. Together with them spread a certain amount of English and vernacular education under the auspices of the government and missionaries. Whatever the exploitative character of Ceylon's colonial economy during British times, the nineteenth and early twentieth centuries were a time of expanding horizons for the local populace, who entered into a more dynamic tenor of life and a greater social commingling than had been known before. An inevitable result of these colonial processes was the rise of "elites" among the local populace on the basis of local planting and commercial enterprise and educational attainments. In due course the British raj spawned its own antithesis in the form of a revival of Buddhism among the newly emerging elites, especially in the low country of the southwest, a pressure for a greater participation in governing the country, and a drive for a restoration and revival of traditional national culture. All these developments in a sense culminated and erupted like a volcano in 1956.

The developments exhibited two contradictions and tensions that continued into the 1960s. One was the collision between the old English-educated liberal elite, more or less committed to a "secular" politics uncontaminated by religious considerations and to the British conventions (the group to whom the British transferred power in 1948), and the newly arisen elite of largely Sinhala-educated rural leaders and purveyors of small commerce, committed to a Buddhist-Sinhala identity. It is the second group that won in 1956 under the leadership of Bandaranaike. But it in turn generated an unresolvable rift between, on the one side, the adherents of a revived Buddhism of a "puritanical" strand, emphasizing doctrinal aspirations of detachment, restraint, and morality and a "neutral" *sangha* dedicated to liberation, and, on the other side, the Buddhist monks themselves, banded in activist associations such as the Eksath Bhikkhu Peramuṇa, who, in reviving the *Mahāvaṃsa* ideology, also wanted the *sangha* to be a weighty political force in the shaping of a Buddhist state. And at this time the *sangha* did manage by and large to elevate its social status and its importance in the body politic. In the event this collision has not been resolved yet. The *sangha* has defied any attempt at state regulation of its affairs (a policy favored by the elite "orthodox" Buddhists), while at the same time it has burgeoned and harbored militant, chauvinist, and demogogic monks, who have added fuel to the radical political Buddhism of the 1980s. But it can no longer be said that the *sangha* is the chief torchbearer and formulator of a political Buddhism. For political Buddhism in its present flag-waving, content-less, plebiscitarian phase is the mirror image of the new political bosses. It taps atavistic emotions and pretends to no philosophical or ethical ambitions.

Thus in the 1970s and now in the 1980s, Sri Lanka has fully entered phase 3. Economically, the post-independence era was increasingly taking the shape of a "dependent economy," whose traditional pattern of export of cash crops such as tea, rubber, and coconut was reducing it to a peripheral status under conditions of worsening terms of trade, and whose internal population explosion was increasingly tending to produce a large segment of "rurban" underprivileged slum populations and déclassé peasants. A third world dependent economy can to some degree ease internal poverty by following subsidized welfare distributive policies, however much they stifle or slow down economic growth. But a liberal "market-oriented" free enterprise policy paradoxically generates unequal development internally, and pauperizes at least in the short run the poorer segments of the working and unemployed populations.

So this third phase of the country has generated its typical contradictions and paradoxes. A UNP government officially dedicated to free enterprise and development schemes and favoring the growth of a rich enterpreneurial class also spawns and harbors populist and chauvinist politicians who use the patronage system as a net in an ocean of an impoverished floating and thrashing urban and semiurban populace to catch shoals of clients and henchmen. They use this poor-quality catch to provide arsonists and thugs in their pursuit of power. By now, the pious adherents of doctrinal and puritanical Buddhism have retreated into private worship, while a non-unitary *sangha* continues, out of its diversity and fragmentation, to throw up maverick monks who preach Sinhala-racist-Buddhist-anti-Tamil cant. One of the results of this larger deterioration is the spate of riots against the Tamils, which have speeded up in recent years, and which seem to serve as valves for the temporary easing of a deep malaise through an easy formula of we and they. This formula is as spurious as it is ineffective.

The UNP regime from 1977 onwards has, as we have noted, sponsored an "open economy," puts its faith in competitive market processes, and, in tandem, initiated proportional representation and a presidential form of government allegedly in order to achieve political "stability" without eroding democracy. At the same time this regime has, by suppressing or banning opposition groups and placing restraints on the press and the judicial institutions, created for itself a seeming monopoly of power. It has full control of the patronage system, a crowning example of which is the "job banks." The pre-1977 years saw the growth of the "chit system," by which MPs sought to have their nominees appointed to government jobs. The MPs issued chits that informed the administrators screening candidates for jobs who they wanted appointed. The UNP regime went one step further and entitled each MP to distribute one thousand government jobs pertaining to the lower occupational ranges (such as peons, chauffeurs, hospital workers, etc.) to their favored clients.

This process of increasing monopolization of power and patronage has coincided with a social "homogenization" process that consists of large numbers of rural and urban people, many of whom are recent migrants, progressively losing their roots in traditional social forms, such as kin groups, village communities, and locality-based castes, and finding their compensation in an imagined collective Sinhala communal identity and in euphoric millenarian and ecstatic religious cults. At this point in the mid-1980s, this collective homogenizing "nationalism" energizes itself by actively and aggressively mobilizing against the Tamils as the ethnic enemy. The ethnic conflict has therefore reached a climax precisely because the present time is one when the social, economic, and political processes, which have been previously identified, have converged and fed on one another. But is this Sinhala ethnic nationalism such a compelling "inevitability" that it must be allowed to run its course, or must it be "stemmed" and "redirected" in the service of a more healthy national development? This is the question the politicians on all sides must face and tackle. Civil war is an easy destructive option that promises short-term power and populist euphoria. Political settlement is the harder constructive option, one that can only be gained through continual and statesmanlike deliberations.

This is the present overwhelmingly disconcerting news about the smiling island of Sri Lanka. In these circumstances, it would be difficult to deny the powerful logic of young "rationalists" and "secularists" on both sides, Sinhalese and Tamil, who argue that the old guard have neither the will, the commitment, nor the vision to work for a just society, that Sri Lanka can only be lifted out of its crippling parochial politics, and its inflammatory conflation of religion, race, and nationalism, by a new kind of egalitarian and universalistic politics that embraces a truly united citizenry of Sri Lanka.

There is a plausibility to the hypothesis—which, however, does not exhaust the whole truth, precisely because it relates to a short-term perspective—that in many third-world countries, of which Sri Lanka is one, multitudes are struggling to survive either in cities that are not industrialized enough to absorb them or in villages that are too overcrowded and poor to yield them a subsistence. Moreover, they are confronted with tantalizing imports of diverse commodities and consumer goods which they are unable to buy and thereby they experience an inescapable intensification of poverty and relative deprivation. This situation provides a fertile ground for uprisings of the urban and semiurban poor, who are ready to be

6
TWO SOCIAL PROFILES

The Ganges, though flowing from the foot of
Vishnu and through Siva's hair, is not an ancient
stream. Geology, looking further than religion,
knows of a time when neither the river nor the
Himalayas that nourished it existed, and an ocean
flowed over the holy places of Hindustan. But
India is really far older. In the days of the
prehistoric ocean the southern part of the
peninsula already existed, and the high places of
Dravidia have been land since land existed, and
have seen on the one side the sinking of a
continent that joined them to Africa, and on the
other the upheaval of the Himalayas from a sea.
They are older than anything in the world. No
water has ever covered them, and the sun who has
watched them for countless aeons may still discern
in their outlines forms that were his before our
globe was torn from his bosom. If flesh of the
sun's flesh is to be touched anywhere, it is here,
among the incredible antiquity of these hills.

E. M. Forster, *A Passage to India*

The Prior Truths of Prehistory

Most Sri Lankans, whether Sinhalese or Tamil,
are prone to think of their island as originally some kind of
empty space that was peopled by successive waves of migrants. While the Sinhalese story, propagated by the *Mahāvaṃsa*, asserts that the first colonizers were North Indians,

Tamil enthusiasts assert with equal justice that the South Indian seafaring peoples of yore were bound to have established settlements long before the coming of Vijaya and his band of followers. It is true that waves of migrations from India have come to Sri Lanka over the centuries, and their mode of incorporation is an essential part of our story, but there is a greater truth to establish first: that there were autochthonous people who have lived in Sri Lanka from pre-Buddhist and prehistoric times, and they included not merely the hunting-and-gathering stone-age Väddas, but also people who practiced pastoralism and settled agriculture.

Since independence, Sri Lanka has been more parochial than either India or Pakistan with regard to the pursuit of prehistoric archeology. Sri Lankan government-sponsored archeology virtually equates that field with the digging of Buddhist sites and the restoration of Buddhist monuments. Aside from the research of unusual scholars like P. E. P. Deraniyagala, S. Deraniyagala, S. P. F. Senaratne, and K. Indrapala, there has not been any significant interest in breaking the Buddhist time barrier: the historic period is defined as beginning with written documents or inscriptions, and since the Buddhist written records are the earliest, the beginning of Sri Lankan history is assumed to coincide with the coming of Buddhism, which, according to the Buddhist chronicles, was around the third century B.C., the time of Emperor Asoka.

Fortunately, within Sri Lanka itself, recent work by both Sinhalese and Tamil archeologists and historians is amply confirming earlier isolated discoveries that the earliest evidence of human life on the island goes back several thousands of years B.C., and, more important for us, that Sri Lanka is dotted with sites that span from the late Stone Age through Neolithic times, when pastoral and settled agricultural activities had begun, to the Iron Age, which in India and Sri Lanka probably began around 1000 B.C.

It is usual among prehistoric archeologists to divide the Indian subcontinent into three major regions: a western region centering upon the Indus system; a northern and eastern region centering upon the Ganges system; and a southern or peninsular system. It is now unequivocally clear that prehistoric Sri Lanka belonged to the southern or peninsular region, which had an internal unity of its own and a characteristic material culture.[1]

Initially, the economy of the Stone Age cultures was based on hunting and gathering, and nomadic life in the open has left behind both large "factory sites" that were used for making stone implements and rock shelters with paintings. The Bandarawela site in Sri Lanka, for example, has revealed large quantities of charcoal, which was used for heating pieces of quartz before they were shattered. Large factory sites of the late Stone Age are found in certain regions, notably in central India, north Mysore, and Sri Lanka, and they suggest a continuity of local tradition. The Väddas of Sri Lanka probably go back in time to this epoch.

In South India there are Neolithic sites that were established before the coming of iron, giving evidence of pastoral and agricultural activities. The settlements in Karnataka were established at least a millennium before iron became known. Moreover, there is a strong suggestion that the Indian humped cattle were first domesticated in the peninsula—they had achieved a dominant position in the earliest settlements of Deccan—and that food grains were cultivated in the region, some of them native to it.

But the richest archaeological evidence for South India and Sri Lanka pertains to Neolithic cultures of the Iron Age, in particular to those complexes of burials frequently known as megaliths. These burial sites have been reported in great numbers in Sri Lanka, the extreme south of India, and in most parts of the peninsula in which granites and gneisses are the predominant rocks. Perhaps some day in the future, when more systematic searches have been made, more impressive evidence will be found of complex settlement sites.

Outstanding burial sites have been excavated in South India—in Shorapur, Adichanallur (Tinnevelly district), Chingleput district, Trichur district, east Hyderabad and so on. In all the graves pottery, particularly black-and-red ware, has been found. Bridget and Raymond Allchin state that "other commonly found grave goods include etched carnelian and other beads, small gold ornaments, and occasional objects of copper, bronze or stone. But iron is almost universal, and the range of identical tool types repeated many times . . .

must testify to the diffusion of a fairly tight group of iron-workers."[2] Among the iron objects that have been found are flat iron axes, flanged spades, hoes, pick axes, sickles or bull hooks, a variety of knives, iron tripods or pot rests, many-armed lamp pendants, daggers and swords, iron tridents, etc. Another special group of objects includes house furniture. The Iron Age finds of South India show the consequences of both interregional contact within India and far-reaching external contacts as well, both overland and maritime.

It is both exciting and vastly important that in Sri Lanka, over a wide area that disregards present-day ethnic territorial claims, similar burial sites and settlement sites have increasingly been discovered, ever since Ievers found an ancient burial site in Gurugalhinna in the Anurādhapura district in 1896, and Hocart a megalithic cemetery in Pomparippu in 1924. In an informative essay, Susantha Goonatilaka,[3] summarizing findings and views of the best modern Sri Lankan archeologists, declares that a number of sites—such as Pomparippu, Gurugalhinna, Katiraveli, Podiyogampola, Walave Basin, all in the red-brown earth region of the country's dry zone, have an unmistakable affinity with the Iron Age megalithic culture of South India, and that before the advent of "Mauryan traditions" of the coming of Buddhism in the third century B.C., the local inhabitants cultivated rice through tank irrigation, and were culturally closest to the early Iron Age "megalithic" man of middle and South India.

James Rutnam,[4] in an essay that celebrates the theme that "a single matrix of culture and identity . . . bound South India and Sri Lanka in the past," reports more urn burial sites recently uncovered in the north in the Jaffna region, such as Kantarodai, where black-and-red pottery ware has been found, and Anaikoddai, where the discoveries include iron tools and the same kind of pottery.

Goonatilaka summarizes the significance of the findings for subsequent "Sinhala-Buddhist" times thus:

> The characteristics of this megalithic culture common to both Sri Lanka and South India are well known. "In one respect the settlements differed from each other; burial practices and funerary monuments varied. The variety includes dolmens, cists, stone squares and urn burials"

(Senaratna 1969 p. 30). Further, the culture was metal using, the pottery was of a black and red type and "a settlement had four distinct areas; a habitation area, a cemetery, a tank and fields. Irrigation was practised and the introduction of this technique to these regions is now thought to be the work of these people"(Ibid).

It is in these settlements associated with the South Indian megalithic culture, (which were from available physical evidence, practising an irrigated agriculture—before the so-called "coming of the Aryans") that we have to look for the first beginnings of our traditional culture, which, as is well recognised, is intimately tied with the growth and spread of irrigation in this country. The culture associated with this village tank based irrigation had also houses made of wattle and daub, (Deraniyagala 1972) used iron and pottery, (Senaratna 1969) had implements like grinding stones (the latter being found even in the late stone age of Sri Lanka) and very probably had wooden spoons, and artefacts associated with weaving. An important aspect of significance indicating the belief system of this culture were its funerary monuments. "Associated with these megaliths have been found urnfields in which the remains of the dead have been buried in large pots, together with the offerings made to them contained in smaller pots." (Paranavithana 1967 p. 8). Clearly the burial practices have a religious significance, as well as do the megaliths associated with it and here one finds a close identification of the irrigation tank and the religious/belief centre, a direct parallel between the dagoba and the tank of the later "Sinhala-Buddhist" times.[5]

The point of these archeological findings, as far as I am concerned, is not whether Tamils (or Dravidians) or Sinhalese (or North Indians) came first and colonized the island, but that there is an early historical context which, if properly understood, should establish from prehistoric times commonalities among the "dry-zone" settlements of Sri Lanka and of South India, which advanced in the direction of hydraulic technology, settled rice agriculture combined with shifting agriculture, and in time cumulatively provided the basis for those multicentric "kingdoms" that developed interesting legitimating ideologies and cultural practices uniting kingship, polity, and religious specialists.

Another significant implication is that these early settlement sites were already, by the early historic period, in indirect ways ultimately connected with far-flung civilizations through the flow of goods in an extensive maritime trade. As far as Sri Lanka was concerned, Tirukketisvaram and Mantai are cases in point.[6] Excavations so far have uncovered materials belonging to three successive epochs. The first was the middle medieval period (the eighth to the eleventh century A.D.), when Mantai was a crossroads in the Chinese ceramic trade and was thereby connected with ports on the Persian Gulf, on the Omani Coast, on the Sind coastline, and on the East African coast. The second is the early medieval period, dating from the late second or early third century A.D. to the mid-eighth century A.D., during which Mantai was tied to the far-flung networks of maritime trade that linked Sassanian Iran with India, Sri Lanka, and the Far East. The third layer of finds pertains to the early historic period (second century B.C. to the second century A.D.): finds of imported luxury rouetted ware, and reports of Roman coins from the site, as well as literary sources, suggest that Mantai may have been a major port in the development of Roman commerce in the Indian Ocean in the first centuries A.D.

So far no materials, ceramic or otherwise, have been found in Mantai related to an earlier megalithic period (ca. 800 to 400/200 B.C.). Only future excavations will show whether this site contains evidence of that final layer of prehistoric significance. If such material is found, then all Sri Lankans might come to marvel at the long continuity of the island's history, which has been as much local as cosmopolitan, and thereby declare as irrelevant the question of which ethnic group or religion or race or people first came to the island as colonizers.

The Sinhalese: A Majority with a Minority Complex

The Sinhalese manifest the features of a "majority with a minority complex" that is partly the product of Sri Lanka's minuscule size, both territorially and demographically, and the nature of the exchanges with India, especially South India, that have been interpreted in certain (tendentious) ways and inscribed in the traditional chronicles and transmitted as the true past.

There is in fact a deep paradox in the Sinhalese experience, which in part accounts for the "overdetermination" of their hostile attitudes to Tamils. For whatever reasons, the early centuries A.D. saw the composition by Buddhist monks, the only literati of that time, of the *Dīpavaṃsa* and *Mahāvaṃsa* chronicles, which, although they represented a breakthrough in historical writing, also formulated the founding myths and an ideological charter that conflated the unity of the Buddhist religion, the entirety of the island of Lanka, and the totality of the Sinhala people. Around the same period the Pali commentaries (*Aṭṭhakathās*), which hitherto had been orally transmitted, were committed to writing by famous authors such as Buddhaghosa and Dhammapāla. We also know that somewhat earlier, around the first century B.C., the Pali canon, the *Tipiṭaka*, which had been kept intact for centuries by remarkable techniques and traditions of oral transmission, were for the first time written down by monks who seemed to have been motivated by fears that the sacred knowledge might disappear owing to degenerating internal political circumstances that were worsened by invasions of South Indian warrior and raiding bands. In light of such suggestive evidence, I would propose that the politico-religious charter formulated in the *Mahāvaṃsa*, especially the story of Duṭṭhagāmaṇī, was born of earlier anxieties about the continuance of Buddhist monastic institutions, and of Buddhism itself, in the multicentric principalities that loosely formed the Sinhala polity in the early Anurādhapura period. A modern archeologist, Senake Bandaranayake, makes these supporting observations about the time immediately preceding and following the third century watershed:

> The myths, legends and the quasi-historical and historical materials relating to the transition from the Proto-historic to the Historic period reflect protracted and often violent conflicts between migrant settlers and indigenous peoples, between principalities and regional kingdoms, and competing religious and linguistic tendancies. . . . The Buddhist religion itself does not seem to have established undisputed

authority until the reigns of Duṭṭhagāmaṇī and Vaṭṭhagā-
maṇī (ca. mid-2nd century to mid-1st century B.C.), each of
whom had to re-establish the political supremacy of the
Sinhalese dynasty over Drāviḍa opponents.[7]

It would seem that once the politico-religious charter of
Buddhism and the Sinhala "nation" had crystallized, it was
periodically invoked and recapitulated many times, especially
during the tumultuous tenth to the thirteenth centuries, when
the Cōḷa Empire of South India made successful incursions,
and even ruled over the Polonnaruva kingdom for a while. In
any case, reviving "Sinhala-Buddhist" polities in the medieval
period—whether these political revivals were mounted by
"foreign" kings like Niśśaṅka Malla of Kāliṅga origins, or by
"indigenous" kings like Parākramabāhu I—are celebrated
not only for their "unification" of the island, but also for
having purified and restored the Buddhist religion. Here then
we have the transmission over time of an *ideology* that was
enshrined and objectified as a historical memory in the monkish chronicles, and which periodically, from the first centuries
A.D. right up to our own time, was available for invocation,
resurrection, and manipulation by zealots and political activists of different centuries, caught in differing circumstances,
and following objectives relevant to their times.

But this continuity of a Sinhala-Buddhist ideology stands in
dialectical discord vis-à-vis another aspect of Sinhalese historical experience, to which I alluded before. Throughout their
spasmodic and pulsating history, the "Sinhalese people" have
been enlarged and enriched by a number of discontinuous
infusions of South Indian migrants. Clearly in the medieval
Polonnaruva period and in the later Kōṭṭe periods there were
fairly extensive recruitments of militia and soldier mercenaries from South India. In the Polonnaruva epoch, aside
from the spectacular trauma of the Cōḷa emperor Rājarāja I's
virtual conquest and renaming of the capital as Jananāthapura, there were other more cordial and more symbiotic
interactions with and incorporations of South Indian people at
the level of military settlements (military corporations known
as *agampaḍi and vēlakkara* that were settled in villages),
religious worship (the dedication of temples [*dēvālēs*] to gods

of recognizably Hindu origin), guilds of craftsmen, and dynastic marriages, which at times allowed South Indian royal families to found for a while their own separate lines in Sri Lanka. It is because of these exchanges that G. C. Mendis, one of Sri Lanka's authoritative historians, concluded that "from that period [of Cōḷa influence] to the arrival of the Portuguese [in 1505], it is the South Indian influence that prevailed."[8] I would, however, underscore and celebrate the fact that the genius of the Anurādhapura and Polonnaruva civilizations consisted in the creative use of these infusions in the continuous development and maintenance of an indigenous Sinhala civilization that generated magnificent irrigation engineering,[9] great art and architecture, and a high literate Buddhism. These achievements have been amply described and commended by various scholars such as Paranavitana, Brohier, Nicholas, Geiger, Needham, Coomaraswamy, and Nell. I shall here only refer to Senake Bandaranayake's *Sinhalese Monastic Architecture, The Vihāras of Anuradhapura*,[10] which, while taking into account the "dialectical relationship" and "interaction between the local and imported forms," triumphantly acclaims "the continuing momentum of the indigenous tradition" which had "its own distinct character in the life of the country and people."

During the Kōṭṭe period, the Sinhalese principalities in the southwestern part of the island came into prominence as the center of gravity shifted in accord with the expansion of the international maritime trade, one of whose local nodes was the southwest coast of Sri Lanka. The southern and southwestern parts of the island were no doubt locations of very old Sinhala settlements, Buddhist temples, and monastic institutions that antedated the spate of new migrations from South India since the thirteenth century, and the arrival of the Portuguese in the east. Between the thirteenth and sixteenth centuries, there was implanted upon this older Sinhala substratum layer after layer, colony after colony of settlements of South Indian origin: "During the Kōṭṭe period, the Sinhalese royalty gets so mixed up with South Indian royalty, as to make it difficult, at times, to distinguish the one from the other."[11] At the highest levels of the society, princely generals like Alakēsvera (who fought for Kōṭṭe against the Tamil king

Āriya Chakaravarti of Jaffna), Champak Perumāl, and Tiruvē Bandaŕ became part of the polity. At a lower level there were "tribal clans" and other such collectivities imported and settled as militia in their own villages. Some of them certainly were the ancestor "clans" of the miscellaneous segments of the population that later came to be given collective caste names such s Karāva, Salāgama, and so on. What is important to note is that in the Sinhala and South Indian kingdoms and principalities of this time it was under the aegis of kingship that various honors (*mariyātai*), sumptuary privileges, and status emblems were distributed and land tenure rights allocated, such that a number of groups of agriculturalists-cum-soldiers, or artisans, or cinnamon peelers, or toddy tappers, or traders, or fishermen, arriving at different times and from different points of origin on the vast South Indian coastal areas on both sides, the Coromandel and Malabar, could be placed in the Sinhalese "galactic polity" by being awarded the above-mentioned privileges and residental locations, and at the same time assigned to different "departments" of state. (Since I have elaborated the concept of "galactic polity" elsewhere,[12] a condensed gloss is sufficient here. Many of the traditional kingdoms of South and Southeast Asia were arranged according to a galactic or *maṇḍala* scheme, wherein central domains were surrounded by satellite provinces, which were actually smaller replications of the former. A political arena was typically multicentric, composed of many such galactic polities, which episodically competed with one another. Because their domains of control expanded or shrank according to the fortunes of warfare, and satellites changed affiliation frequently, and the capitals themselves shifted or declined, they are best viewed as pulsating galactic polities. These very same features and processes enabled these polities to place and incorporate minorities, waves of migrants, and groups of war captives without trauma.)

The above-mentioned processes of incorporation also took place at all levels of the hierarchy in the Kandyan kingdom of central Sri Lanka, the last principality to come into its own, since it existed much as an enclave during the period of European maritime conquest and control of the spice trade.

To modern-day Sinhalese, the Kandyan kingdom represents their "traditional past." It is true that the Kandyan kingdom, because it was the last polity and territory to be conquered by the British in 1815, and because it was far less affected by changes introduced by the Portuguese and Dutch in the maritime areas, has come to represent for the Sinhalese people the embodiment of their traditions. But one does not subtract anything from its coherence as a civilization to admit that Kandy, like Kōṭṭe and Polonnaruva before it, profited both culturally and demographically from symbiotic exchanges with South India. The most spectacular feature of the South Indian connection—which is well known to any Sri Lankan historian—is the actual enthronement in Kandy of the Nāyakkar kings. I refer my readers to one informative work, L. S. Dewaraja's *The Kandyan Kingdom 1707–1760*,[13] which documents in rich detail the traffic between South India and the Kandyan kingdom. An extraordinary feature of the South Indian connection was the pattern of alliances, both military and dynastic/marital, actively sought and solicited by the Kandyan royalty with the Nāyakkar rulers and warrior elements of South India, particularly those established in Madurai, in order to keep at bay the threats posed by the Dutch colonialists. Although there are several recorded instances of previous intermarriages between Sinhala ruling families and South Indian royalty or nobility, it was "in the late seventeenth century that it became a matter of policy for the chief queen or queens to be obtained from Madura."[14] There is no doubt that the legitimacy of the Kandyan ruling house depended on the prestigious marriage connections it could establish with the Madurai court (Dewaraja documents that the Kandyan court did not always receive princesses of rank). Moreover, as Seneviratne reminds us, the Tamil language and other allegedly "imported" cultural forms enjoyed prestige, and were copied by the socially "mobile" sections and courtiers of Kandyan society. Thus it comes as no surprise when finally, there being no heir of blood born of the union of both the Sinhala and Nāyakkar royal houses, a brother of an imported Nāyakkar queen ascended the throne in 1739 as Śrī Vijaya Rājasiṃha and founded the Nāyakkar dynasty in Sri Lanka.[15]

The most illustrious of the Nāyakkar kings in Kandy was Kīrti Śrī Rājasiṃha (1747–82), who, if not unconscious of his foreign origins, and allegedly prone to daubing holy ash on his forehead in Śaivite fashion, had also unmistakably absorbed the Kandyan ethos, and conscientiously sponsored a Buddhist religious, cultural, literary, and artistic renaissance, and a reestablishment of a vigorous *sangha* (order of monks), which unarguably constituted the last great creative gasp of the Kandyan civilization. Kīrti Śrī's reign was no bed of roses: having survived an assassination attempt by some disaffected nobility and monks, he consolidated his position and consummated his reign's achievements. Like many other local dynasties, the Nāyakkar dynasty, which as Professor Seneviratne reminds us should not be considered "alien,"[16] was also short lived. The last king of Kandy, Śrī Vikrama Rājasiṃha, also of Nāyakkar origin, whose loss of legitimacy and misrule hastened the British takeover through local rebellion and defection, signifies the terminal loss of vitality and integrity of this last Sinhala stronghold. In these days of uninformed slogan-mongering, it may be salutary to remind the zealots on *both* sides that the treaty of 1815 signed by the Kandyan chiefs with their British victors contains some signatures in Sinhala script, some in Tamil script, and others in a mixture of the two.[17]

Dewaraja also documents other kinds of influxes of South Indian immigrants into the Sinhala kingdoms of Kōṭṭe, Dambadeniya, and Kandy, especially between the thirteenth and sixteenth centuries. Most of these immigrants were in due course incorporated into the Sinhala "farmer aristocracy," the *govikula*.[18] The Muslim conquests in South India accelerated the influx of Brahmins, who had lost the patronage of their Cōḷa masters, into Sri Lanka. Perhaps the most interesting of the immigrants were those whom Dewaraja identifies as *panṭāram*s, or non-Brahmin priests usually of the Veḷḷāla caste, who came from various parts of South India. In the reign of Bhuvaneka Bāhu I (1272–84) of Daṁbadeniya, a group of *panṭāram*s came from the Cōḷa country

> together with all the paraphernalia, attendants, craftsmen and mendicants connected with their Siva temples. When they were ushered into the presence of the king they were given *radala* and *mudali* titles, such as were always given to

the higher subcastes of the *govikula*. Villages were also given for their maintenance. A considerable group of immigrants headed by the *paṇṭārams* came from Malayāla or modern Kerala in the reign of Bhuvaneka Bāha VI (1470–78) of Kōṭṭe and received lands and titles from the king.[19]

Similar facts can be adduced for the time of Rājasiṃha I (1581–93). It is significant that the Sinhala title *baṇḍāra* taken by princes and nobles was most likely borrowed from these immigrant *paṇṭāram*s, and in turn by the seventeenth and eighteenth centuries *"paṇṭāram*s had become part and parcel of the Kandyan nobility, and their title too became popular among the high nobles of high rank."[20] Dewaraja also refers to the influx of Śaivite mendicants called Āṅḍi at the time of Rājasiṃha I, who had embraced Śaivism, and their infiltration into various parts of the Kandyan region. It is no surprise then that "the strong influence of South Indian religious beliefs and practices Kandyan society was undoubtedly due to the absorption of [all] these immigrant groups."[21]

Let me now advert to some implications of the origins and distributions of the Sinhalese people for their social, religious, and political conduct in the time of the Western colonial powers, especially during British times, and in the postcolonial decades. Many Sinhalese of the coastal areas north of Colombo all the way to Puttalam were relatively recent migrants, and they were distinctive for two reasons. Large numbers of them converted to Roman Catholicism in the time of Portuguese control, and have remained more or less true to their faith right up to the present. Second, in these areas, the Karāva people bore the marks of their Tamil origins in their clan/*varige* names, in some of their religious cults,[22] and while they have become, or are progressively becoming, speakers of Sinhalese as their major language, they have not entirely lost their knowledge of Tamil. Stirrat, who recently has done field work among the Karāva of the northwest coast, affirms their long-standing bilingualism, and reports that "Tamil tends to be the language of the home and the sea; Sinhalese the language of the marketplace and of dealings in general with outsiders." However, "since the early sixties, Sinhalese has become more and more important . . . , a process encouraged by the Catholic Church."[23]

Another classic region whose peripheral location made it oblivious to nationalist revivalist exclusivist slogans of race and religion is the deep interior of the Eastern Province, where Sinhalese and Tamil peasants lived side by side on the frontier zone, sometimes in the same villages, intermarried, and shared certain parallel religious cults such as the worship of Pattini and cultural performances such as folk opera. Whereas the Puttalam area north of Colombo, when left to itself, would have quite naturally and organically become more and more Sinhala, the Pānama and Akkaraipattu areas of the east coast would have continued with their easygoing symbiotic duality and exchange.[24] But such traditional patterns of peaceful interaction between Sinhalese and Tamils, and the organic transformation of Tamil people into Sinhalese, suffered a drastic re-sorting and dichotomization in the pressure chamber of post-1956 politics. The coastal peoples north of Colombo have had to renounce and suppress whatever remained of their South Indian traditions, and in the Eastern Province the creation of the Gal Oya multipurpose hydroelectric and peasant resettlement scheme saw the introduction at the source of the works of a politically self-conscious Sinhala peasantry and of construction workers from the south and highlands who, as far back as 1958, began the ethnic riots against the Tamil colonists and peasants living down-river at the periphery. By now the Sinhala-Tamil split in that region between those who live at the head of the scheme and those who live at its tail end has become decisive. In these two cases, of coastal peoples north of Colombo and interior peoples of the Eastern Province who have shifted from a relaxed symbiosis to an imposed Sinhala identity, we see one reason for the "overdetermination" in the anti-Tamil attitudes of certain segments of the Sinhalese population.

But there is a much more potent and explosive breeding ground of "overdetermined" hostility south of Colombo, in Sri Lanka's coastal southwest all the way to Mātara and Hambantota. I have previously referred to two important circumstances. The southwest region, as, for example, identified in later times with the Kōṭṭe kingdom, was an area of old Sinhala Buddhist settlement and culture, which came fully into its own in the fourteenth and fifteenth centuries. The same period saw

the numerous migrations and infusions of South Indian peoples, who were variously settled as militia, or were engaged in
sailing and fishing, or were employed as artisans, and who
were later aggregated as the Karāva caste, the Salāgama
caste,[25] and so on. These people faced two problems of incorporation. The first was the easier, and involved being placed
in the Sinhalese polity under the aegis of kingship as settlers
accorded "feudal" or "caste" privileges, honors, and tasks.
The second was more difficult: not merely to learn the
Sinhalese language and make it their own, but also to become
Buddhist in a region of historic Buddhism. Not only did they
make both conversions, but throughout the nineteenth century, when British rule initiated economic expansion and
opportunities, the inhabitants of the southwest littoral of Sri
Lanka were to become the most vociferous and dedicated
revivalists and upholders of Buddhist Sinhala religion and
culture.[26] I would surmise that this effervescence had a twofold aspect: its positive side was that social mobility and
economic success and expanding educational horizons produced an efflorescence, both religious and cultural; its negative side was that the recent emigrants faced anxieties and
problems of identity, of becoming true Sinhalese and true
Buddhists, of invidious comparison with the older inland
people, which in its first manifestation broke as the so-called
caste rivalries and contests between Karāva, Salāgama, and
Goyigama. In its second manifestation, this was transformed
into the larger and more enduring claims of Sinhala Buddhist
nationalism, whose byproduct is the rejection of the Tamils as
the alien "other." In sum, the continuing transmission of the
Mahāvaṃsa ideology in the context of a melting pot of diverse
peoples of South Indian origin becoming Sinhalese has in
good measure motivated the "overdetermined" attitude of
hostility toward and rejection of the Tamils. The claim of
dark-skinned Sinhalese to be Aryans is the last absurdity
of this posture. In a curious and interesting sense, the contemporary consciousness of ethnicity is a politicized product of
post-independence "democratic" politics, chauvinist rhetoric, and state-building. Its present transformed and explosive
manifestation has risen on a base that has contained older
ingredients, and experienced prior bakings. Deeply ignorant

of their past, the young adults and youth of today, on both the Tamil and Sinhalese sides, educated in two different linguistic streams and exposed for over two decades to notions that Sinhala-Buddhist and Tamil-Hindu identities are mutually exclusive, have come to think and feel as two separate peoples, two ethnic species, locked in a man-made battle for survival.

The Sri Lankan Tamils:
A Minority with a Parity Claim

If vast numbers of the Sinhalese people have been historically the cumulative result of streams of South Indian migrant groups arriving at different times and slotted into different positions and roles, who became Sinhalized by incorporation into the extant indigenous Sinhala galactic polities, the Sri Lankan Tamils, whose heartlands today are in the Northern and Eastern Provinces, evidence the same patterns of migration and incorporation.

The diversity of the Tamil peoples is signaled by certain distinctive labels. "Vanniyārs" was the label for the people who lived in the intermediate zone south of the Jaffna peninsula and north of Anurādhapura; they had martial traditions as well as their traditional chieftains and made their accommodations with the Sinhalese polities of the south and the kingdom of Jaffna in the north.[27] Similarly, the name "Mukkuvārs" referred to peoples with matrilineal customs who occupied the sparsely populated areas extending from the eastern end of Vavuniya into the Eastern Province. The codified customary laws of the Jaffna Tamils, called *Tēcavaḷamai*, differ from the customary laws of the Mukkuvārs.[28]

The political and social heart of the Sri Lankan Tamils has been and continues to be the Jaffna peninsula, because there alone a Tamil polity was established: the kingdom of Jaffna, which thrived in the centuries before the arrival of the Portuguese; its history is more accurately known from the third quarter of the fifteenth century until the time of its Portuguese subjugation in the 1620s. It is doubtful whether the Tamils of the Eastern Province were subjects of this kingdom: traditionally, that region lay at the outer perimeter of the Kandyan

kingdom, enjoying much autonomy as did many of the Vanniyārs from the centers of political influence like Kandy and
Jaffna. Thus traditionally, and especially after the kingdom of
Jaffna was overtaken by the Portuguese and thereafter by the
Dutch, the Tamils of the north and east had neither strong
social interconnections nor acted as political collectivities—
though no doubt their speaking a common language, worship
of the same or similar "Hindu" deities, and practice of similar
cults and customs gave them a recognizable affinity. (But
then, perhaps in only a slightly weaker sense, the same could
have been said at the dawn of modern times of the Sinhalese
and Tamils living side by side in the Northwestern and the
interior Eastern Provinces.)

Now, if we focus on those members of the Tamil population
who are referred to today as the Jaffna Tamils, and who are in
this century, and especially today, the principal challengers of
Sinhalese domination and discrimination, we can discern the
interesting ways in which they parallel the Sinhalese profile
and also differ from it.

At a formal level the kingdom of Jaffna must have been
structured on the same lines as the Kōṭṭe and Kandyan kingdoms, particularly as regards its economic basis and the distribution of powers and constellation of castes. These traditional features have left their mark on present times. There
was a formal similarity between the Kandyan kingdom, whose
kingship and political integrity was closely tied to the cult
focused on the Temple of the Buddha's Tooth relic, and the
Jaffna kingdom's close association with the temple cult
focused on Śiva and his son Subramaniam or Kantacāmi
(Skanda). In fact, this blueprint was most in evidence in the
Vijayanagara and Cōḷa kingdoms of South India.[29] The castes
of Jaffna most definitely paralleled the distributions and con-
figurations prevalent in the Sinhalese Kōṭṭe kingdom at the
same time, the dominant and majority caste being the Veḷḷāla,
which paralleled the Goyigama. Around them were deployed
various subordinate service castes, some in servile status and
some in dependent artisan status. There was no indigenous
Brahmin caste of any size or influence. Brahmin priests were
imported from India to serve as ritual functionaries. The
Karaiyār, who parallel the Sinhalese Karāva (who were de-

rived from multiple origins), were Jaffna's second major caste traditionally associated with coastal trading and fishing, and around them were also deployed a (lesser) array of subordinate service castes. As in the case of the Sinhalese, it is better to view the traditional caste constellation in terms of parallel structures cohering around two dominant local castes: it is only in the era of the British raj that problems of status competition between the castes, previously dominant in their regional locations, emerged when an attempt was made to place them in a unitary society-wide hierarchical caste system. Jaffna too boasted its version of the Sinhalese Karā-Goi contest. The Karaiyār-Veḷḷāla rivalries, which were much less acrimonious in the past because they did not directly compete in British times, today have ironically surfaced at the time of the political mobilization of all Tamils. These rivalries are alleged to have some salience among the Tamil "freedom-fighting rebels," who are said to be split into rival factions, a major split (but not the only one) being between the Karaiyār-dominated rebels drawn from and based in the coastal settlement of Valvettithurai (famous in recent times for its successful smuggling operations linking Jaffna and the Coromandel coast) and those with Veḷḷāla affiliations. In any case, the dual structure of the dominant castes of Jaffna reflects its traditional economic basis: agriculture—a mixture of rice cultivation and of cash crops like tobacco, and market gardening of vegetables—was and is the major concern of Veḷḷāla landlords and farmers and their allied castes; while traditionally, and right through the times of Portuguese and Dutch control of Jaffna, extensive trade in tobacco, spices, salt, cloth, and fish products linked the coastal trading communities of Jaffna and the Coromandel and Malabar coasts. Thus, like Kōṭṭe, Jaffna's political economy rested on a dual dependence on agriculture and trade.

There is still another resemblance—little appreciated, especially by the Sinhalese chauvinists—that makes the Sri Lankan Tamil predicament similar to that of the Sinhalese. In the case of the Sinhalese peoples of today the process of Sinhalization and of "passing" as Sinhalese is accomplished by conforming to the strong diacritical markers of speaking the Sinhalese language and practicing the "Buddhist" religion (which is minimally achieved by "taking the precepts" recited by the Buddhist monks, and in return giving gifts (*dāna*) to them). In the case of the Sri Lankan Tamils, their social separation from South India, and their "parochialization" and "indigenization" as a dialectal variant of South Indian Tamil Nāṭu society and culture, while important to recognize, is more difficult to describe, because most of the ingredients of Sri Lankan Tamil culture, religion, and social practices bear a distinct family resemblance to those prevailing now in Tamil Nāṭu. And yet the physical separation from India has also become over time a social separation, and by the same token, the engagement in intensified local relations and endogamous marriages has invested them over the same time with a distinct Sri Lankan Tamil identity. A recent study comments of the majority of Jaffna Tamils that they "have no tangible connections to South India, nor are there any collective recollections of such connections."[30]

Indeed, it is this very parochialization and indigenization of the Tamils of the north that paradoxically gives the Sinhalese people of the island the strong impression that the Tamils are "clannish," "communal-minded," and motivated to form strong networks to protect and promote their interests. There are both cultural and sociological reasons for this Sinhalese perception of Tamil exclusiveness. Although the traditional pattern of caste relations in Jaffna was similar to those in the south, the Tamil variant was more rigidly bound by stricter notions of purity and pollution, of food taboos and avoidances. Vegetarianism was practiced by certain segments, and the eating of beef was prohibited and the prohibition strictly observed by all the "clean" castes. Moreover, the north contained larger segments of degraded low castes (outcastes) of servile status such as the Parayar, Paḷḷar, and Naḷavar (the Roḍiyās and Kinnaras of the Kandyan region are very small in number), and women of upper-caste status were more hedged in by severe rules of premarital chastity, were more confined to the home, and had less freedom of physical movement and social intercourse than their Sinhalese counterparts. And precisely because the north was an isolated part of the island that did not participate in the commercial and plantation developments of the nineteenth century but exported to the rest of the island educated young men who were married according to tightly controlled and arranged marriage preferences, the severity of the Veḷḷāla Tamil caste domination in the north has prevailed to this day in a form that is unknown in contemporary Sinhalese society. Furthermore, like the interior Sinhalese regions, but unlike the western or southwestern coastal areas, the numerical strength of the Veḷḷālas in Jaffna makes them the majority group in every electorate and this has ensured their political dominance and encouraged their social solidarity. By comparison, the low-caste groups of the Sinhala coastal regions are large enough to mobilize and win parliamentary seats—and over time even the more degraded communities have found their political voice. Cyril Mathew, a product of such low-caste mobilization is a dubious example of "social emancipation" and overdone Sinhala Buddhist identity.

If all these features I have listed made the northern Tamils a privileged and strong-knit "protectionist" minority in Sinhalese eyes, they also made the Jaffna Tamils a proud community whose experience of social dominance in their own region and whose sense of greater "orthodoxy" and "orthopraxy" in matters of caste and religious observances made it impossible for them to accept a position of subordination in a polity composed of a Sinhalese majority, who by their standards were inferior in their purity of customs, inferior in talent, and had no historical claim to rule or encompass them.

Like many ethnic minorities living in the towns and cities, the Jaffna Tamils have congregated in recent times in their own enclaves or "ghettos" in Colombo—for example in Wellawatte, Ratmalana, and parts of Dehiwela wards. And many young Tamil youth of poor circumstances in the north, but committed to education as their only salvation, have, when they have secured their white-collar jobs, lived frugally in Sinhalese areas, because they were constrained to send home money to educate their younger siblings, or to help parents amass dowries for their marriageable sisters. This pattern of frugality and white-collar ghetto residence has shaped the Sinhalese stereotype of Tamils as ambitious, exclusive accumulators of money. And this is a matter for invidious comparison, since there are no Sri Lankan Tamil slums in Colombo

paralleling those of the Sinhalese. That there have been numbers of Sri Lankan Tamils of elite and affluent origins, who
live the same kind of life as the elite Sinhalese and, barring
intermarriage, move in the same social circles and clubs of
Colombo, has scarcely affected the basic Sinhalese negative
stereotype of Tamils as described above.

As a countervailing feature to those differences, one can
cite a norther Tamil cultural and religious process which paralleled—even slightly preceded—that which occurred among
the Sinhalese at roughly the same time. Late nineteenth- and
twentieth-century Sinhalese religious revivalism, with its literary propagandist output, its "puritanical" overtones in the
name of "religious orthodoxy," its borrowing of proselytizing
and educational techniques from the Christian missions, and
its founding of schools to disseminate Buddhist and Sinhala
values, had its counterpart in Jaffna. If for the Sinhalese this
movement was personified by Anagārika Dharmapāla (1864–
1933) the corresponding figures for the Tamils were Ārumu-
gam Nāvalar (1822–79), a Śaivite of Veḷḷāla family origins,
and his disciples and followers. His reaction to the threatening
success of Christian missionaries in making converts, and his
resistance to the spread of deracinating westernization, are
embodied in his writing. Perimbanayagam describes his reformist posture thus:

> In Ārumuga Nāvalar's case, he declared war on all de-
> partures from written orthodoxy and excoriated various
> practices of the folk religion. His aim was to return the
> people to a strictly textual religion bereft of both the devia-
> tions that carelessness had wrought in the practice of
> Śaivite religion and the vulgarizations of the folk cults—the
> cults of goat sacrifices, nautch dancing, and wordless pūjas
> performed by the "unclean" and the uninitiated.[31]

Nāvalar's reformist Śaiva Śiddhānta movement, while
demonstrating that the Buddhist and Hindu reactions—especially among the educated "traditionalist" elites—were similar and even homologous, also shows a self-consciousness on
the part of the northern Tamils as a cultural, linguistic, and
religious collectivity with its own local religious and cultural
center and identity. Indeed, in a remarkable essay, Kailasap-

athy has documented that Arumuga Nāvalar, who spent
several years in Madras as a publisher, writer, and polemicist,
along with his many talented desciples who held positions in
government service in South India, such as C. W. Tamotaram
Pillai (1832–1901), contributed richly to South Indian Tamil
literature and philosophy. Kailasapathy claims that "during
the time of Nāvalar and about three decades after his death it
was the 'Jaffna School' that dominated the literary scene in
Madras."[32] At the same time it should be noted that these
educated Jaffna Tamils were champions of "high culture,"
which included classical Tamil (*Sen Tamil*), Bharāta Nātyam,
and Carnatic music, and were thus the flower of an elitist
revivalism that was a reaction to the stimulus and irritant of
colonial attitudes, Western knowledge, and missionary education. Ārumuga Nāvalar himself acquired his knowledge and
literary skills while helping a Methodist missionary, the Reverend Peter Percival, in the Tamil translation of the Bible.

What is important for our story is that the championing by a
Jaffna Tamil local elite of Tamil literature and art forms, and
their propagation of Śaiva doctrines, represented a heightened cultural and linguistic consciousness that naturally
emphasized the distinctiveness of the vocal Tamil revivalists
from the Buddhist activist movements in the south, and this
sense of difference also affected the political question of
majority-minority relations.

Indeed, the political postures of the Sinhalese and Sri
Lankan Tamil leaders at the time of the Donoughmore Commission hearings and during the period when the Donoughmore Constitution was implemented give us an insight into the
counterproductive misunderstandings that directly fed into
the cesspit of future ethnic conflict. As K. M. de Silva explains
in an illuminating discussion, in the eyes of the commissioners—in tune with the liberal political theory of the time—the
introduction of territorial representation and of expanded
suffrage, and the elimination of provisions for the special
protection of minorities, were in line with "progress" in
politics.[33] The Sinhalese politicians concurred, and, except for
their incriminating blind spot regarding the rights of Indian
Tamil plantation labor, they sincerely preached and believed
in these constitutional principles. In their eyes, therefore, the

Tamil (and Muslim) special pleading for minority "communal" privileges was a case of self-interested obstruction of progress and of a march toward self-government. And when the Tamils boycotted the elections of 1931, their action confirmed in Sinhalese eyes their willingness to impede the political advance of Ceylon by placing their minority privileges before the national interest (though in fact some of the Tamil liberal politicians who joined in the boycot did so because they held that the reforms had not gone far enough in granting self-rule). There was a repetition of minority pleading before the Soulbury Commission some fifteen years later, led by certain Tamil politicians, which similarly irritated the Sinhalese and did not convince the commissioners. (At the time Lord Soulbury believed that the Tamil fears were exaggerated, and that to write special provisions into the constitution for the protection of minorities would be retrogressive. After the riots of 1956, Lord Soulbury publicly deplored his midjudgment and regretted his omission.)

Be that as it may, from the Tamil point of view it is a piece of tendentious and insensitive pleading for President Jayawardene, and many other Sinhalese politicians and officials, to make this exonerating comment: "After all, the Sinhalese have nowhere else to go, while the Tamils have a homeland in South India." For that matter, the original homeland of most Sinhalese and Tamils is the same, and the Tamils, like the Sinhalese—whatever the historical past—feel that their home is Sri Lanka, and that South India is not their motherland.

But recent ethnic politics and the deepening polarization of Tamils and Sinhalese have in fact begun those social and political interconnections between South India and the Tamils of the north, in the same way that common discrimination and a blanket violence against all Tamils have begun to bring together all the island's Tamils as the victims of a common enemy.

There is no doubt that in the last few years the rebels have found refuge and established training camps and bases in South India. TULF politicians similarly have found refuge, support, and sympathy for their cause among South Indian politicians and well-wishers. Moreover, thousands of Tamil civilians, especially those living on the northern coastline, which is subject to army and navy surveillance and punitive action, are fleeing to South India and creating a refugee problem there. Protest processions, sympathetic strikes, the temporary closing of schools, and urgent telegrams to New Delhi are the order of the day in Madras. If the Tamils of Sri Lanka, both "indigenous" and "immigrant," make common cause with Tamil Nāṭu, that would be the final chapter, indeed a final consequence, of a train of events, rather than its antecedent and initiating cause. Then indeed the Sinhalese will surely witness the birth of their self-fulfilling phophecy that South India threatens to engulf them. An in desperate fear they may attempt to perpetrate their final solution—the genocide or expulsion of all Tamils from Sri Lanka. These are the "black holes" that await us, and before they can suck us all in, a negotiated political settlement *must* take place.

There is no denying now that the cause of the Sri Lankan Tamils and of the Indian Tamils in Sri Lanka is increasingly becoming interlocked with the political sentiments and political issues prevalent in Tamil Nāṭu in South India. There is no need for me here to repeat the trajectory and the dialectics of Tamil Nāṭu's politics in the twentieth century, for it has been amply documented.[34] One of its major features was the anti-Brahman movement of the non-Brahman castes with its many-faceted programme which rejected alien Sanskrit elements in language and literature, alien brahmanic elements in religious ritual and practice, contested the social and political dominance of the Brahman minority, and mobilized the DMK (Draviḍa Munnētra Kazhagam) as a politcal majority and the ruling power in Madras. It too generated a new sense of social and cultural identity, a revivalism in literature, and a reformism in religion, and while seeking pristine roots and releasing creative impulses also spawned tendentious mythohistory, and preached and paraded a chauvinist militant Tamil nationalism. The hoary and fabled North-South, Aryan-Dravidian divides were resurrected and made politically alive in terms of a twentieth-century democratic politics in which majorities sought to wipe out historic wrongs and to engage in corrective affirmative action in a theater of populist rhetoric and ethnic nationalism. In many ways Tamil Nāṭu politics parallels that of Sri Lanka, though there are also distinct differences between them.

At the present time, in the 1980s, the DMK movement itself has lost its monolithic unity and fragmented into two parties, the DMK and the AIADMK (All India Anna Dravida Munnētra Kazhagam), with the latter in power now, and both have again fragmented into their several factions. Not only are the Tamil Nāṭu politicians embroiled in their internal rivalries, they also bargain, sometimes all together and sometimes in smaller pressure groups, on behalf of "collective" Tamil interests with New Delhi, the federal center and capital. Internal rivalries and individual political ambitions therefore make the present predicament of the Tamils of Sri Lanka a rewarding issue for Tamil Nāṭu politicians to champion and exploit, irrespective of the larger fact of South India's genuine feelings of concern for and amity with their "brethren" in Sri Lanka. There are good reasons why New Delhi, in the face of pressure from Tamil Nāṭu and Sri Lanka, strives to be guarded, evasive and noncommital. The lesson to be drawn by the Sinhalese politicians of Sri Lanka is that it is infinitely safer and saner for them to arrive at an amicable settlement with their own "brethren," the Tamils of Sri Lanka, rather than pump up an Indian invasion hysteria. Thereby they will not only extricate the island from a messy international tangle, but also resist the temptation to seek the armed embrace of Western powers, who have their strategic eyes set on the incomparable port of Trincomalee.

A final word on behalf of all Sri Lankans abroad who are the deposits, in other countries and foreign parts, of a continuing diaspora. It is said that in our present epoch of "nation states" it is a grave and universally recognized insult to say that a person has no country. It is an even graver charge to say that he or she has no birthplace, for that involves canons of parentage as well. Recently each race riot, punctuating a campaign of increasingly hostile and emotionally draining discrimination, has sent wave upon wave of Tamil refugees and emigrants to seek safety and new fortunes elsewhere. In the past many Tamil (and Sinhalese) professionals chose to live abroad because of the better prospects found there. But in recent years the refugees pushed out of the island far outnumber the voluntary emigrants. It is well known that colonies of Sri Lankan Tamil professionals—doctors, engineers, teachers, accountants, etc.—are establishing themselves in the United States, Britain, Australia, and in many third-world countries. They are prone to combine an understandable nostalgia for their birthplace with a deep resentment of Sinhalese governmental policies. In this estranged frame of mind many of them have felt driven by the logic of their situation to support extremist policies at home, including the giving of financial and moral support to the violent guerilla activities of the rebels. (Similar behavior has characterized other overseas migrant communities, such as the Irish in the United States and the Sikhs in Britain, Canada, and the United States.) This expression of vicarious revenge is self-defeating, and it might in the long run be suicidal. For it too in time might realize its self-fulfilling phophecy of genocide: it is likely to result in the massive annihilation of the Tamil civilians and the razing to the ground of their villages and towns of birth. Thus the fate that was anticipated will have been made to happen by the victims themselves.

For their part, the Sinhalese people should realize that the very causing of a diaspora of fellow Sri Lankans has boomerang effects. Those forced abroad do not forget their homeland. They form their associations abroad, collect and distribute information through their newspapers and through all the modern media of communication, and are in a position to effectively air their grievances to their host governments, and to appeal to the highest international courts of justice in terms of universalistic standards of human rights and civic freedoms. And such erosion of the credibility of Sri Lanka as a democratic polity will not abate, because the very experience of diaspora among expatriates, their collective memory of wandering and exile, is indissolubly and indivisibly linked to an indelible imprint of a native place of birth and origin that serves as a focus of constant recollection, and a point of reference for all those traditions and customs that give them an identity. In short, a cultural identity fundamentally implies a place of origin.

Unfortunately for Sri Lanka, the degenerating spiral of factional politics and a constricting economy is causing the diaspora of the most educated and talented members of the Sinhalese intelligentia as well. These are the very folk committed to universalistic norms, and capable of a distanced rational understanding of the mainsprings and futilities of the current turmoil. And those among them who are still committed to remaining in Sri Lanka feel unable to act or, seeing the growing polarization of the country, will be forced to be passive observers of the scene, or to avert their faces from its unsavory appearance, or even to give tacit approval to injustice and genocide, as long as the dirty work is done by others.

7
REFLECTIONS ON POLITICAL VIOLENCE IN OUR TIME

There is in the world today a widespread resort to violence by radical groups on both the left and the right, and by the armed cadres of authoritarian governments as well as by private armies and resistance groups functioning outside the umbrella of governments. They range from West Germany's Bader Meinholf gang, through the rival Protestant and Catholic fanatics in Northern Ireland, to politically displaced minorities like the PLO and the army-backed right-wing groups of Brazil. At the most amoral end of the continuum we have professional assassins and mercenaries of one kind or another. Around October 1983, when I was first putting down my thoughts on this issue, there occurred another incredible staging of political assassination: a visiting South Korean delegation to Burma was the target of an explosion in which eighteen, including four cabinet ministers and two advisers, were killed. It is believed that this act was perpetrated by the North Korean government.

Planned episodes of violence on an international scale have become possible and deadly in their accuracy for two reasons: first, because of the easy access to modern weaponry, which is eminently marketable and therefore profitable. This has led not only to gunrunning by private profiteers but also to the sale of arms and aircraft by profit-hungry and equally amoral governments, be they "democratic" or "communist" in posturing. Second, because "resistance groups" and "security agencies" of diverse origins, and following diverse and unrelated programs are inclined to provide each other with services, protection, and training. It is not unrealistic that a Japanese left-wing resistance group could have links with a PLO group, and the P.L.O. with a West German revolutionary group. Nor is it unrealistic for the

CIA to finance and arm a "tribal" resistance group against a left-wing government in Nicaragua, and at the same time shore up a military clique in the country next door. It is rumored in Sri Lanka that the Tamil rebels have established links with the PLO, while it is an established fact that the UNP government has imported Israeli government agents from the Mossad, and British ex-SAS commandos considered experts on fighting "terrorism," to help eradicate the rebels. Thus we are confronted with the reproducing of Middle Eastern Lebanese and Palestinian politics in the Indian Ocean, and with the unusual conjunctions between a theater of the absurd and professionalized violence, between anarchical tendencies by underground resistance groups and subversive ploys in other people's back yard by well-heeled generals. The net result is a contemptuous disregard of institutional safeguards of the basic liberties and rights of persons.

While the Sri Lankan turbulence is affected by and linked with this wider international setting and cannot be divorced from it, my essay is primarily devoted to a focused analysis of the Sri Lankan situation per se, and to suggesting indirectly how it may be capable, as a case study, of illuminating a world larger than itself, and revealing more general truths regarding political processes in many other parts of our globe.

The Sri Lankan situation has two interwoven implications concerning the phenomenon of violence. One is the tragic circumstances by which two closely interrelated peoples, calling themselves Sinhalese and Tamils, have progressively resorted to violent action as a way of resolving their differences. This violence, which is ethnic fratricide, cannot settle their differences, and can only polarize their imagined differences and real grievances. The other implication is the progressive steps taken by successive Sri Lankan governments—and the present one in particular—to dismantle democratic institutions and procedures in order to eliminate or incapacitate their political opponents, whether these be Sinhalese opponents, the Tamils, left-wing groups, or elements of the press. Moreover, the ethnic conflict itself has become justification and an umbrella, through the imposition of martial law and curfews and through enactment of legislation such as the Prevention of Terrorism Act, for the erosion and elimination of various civil liberties and freedoms that guarantee a democratic system of government for all Sri Lankans. This is why it is in the interest of *all* citizens of Sri Lanka, whether they be Sinhalese, Tamil, Muslim, or Eurasian, to contemplate the consequences of the violence and coercion that are endemic in the society as a whole, in their various forms, and to take urgent action to prevent the country from sliding into a state where the mobilization and use of force become the sole and unstable arbiters of political life. Thus ethnic fratricide and the demise of democracy in Sri Lanka are two sides of the same coin.

We have in Sri Lanka today several kinds of political violence and terrorism. There is the violence *in potentia* widespread among certain segments of the Sinhalese population, which is tapped, triggered, and intensified by political patrons, bosses, politicians, and business *mudalālis*, who use it to further their populist causes. The government in power, the UNP, is not a stranger to this use of organized force, just as its predecessor, the SLFP, was not. Then there is the desperate, armed resistance and guerilla action of increasing numbers of Tamil youth in the north, whose "righteous cause" as freedom fighters, as they see it, does not erase the fact that they are engaged in terrorism. Third, there is the deadly terrorism and intimidation practiced by the armed forces. Thus we have violence committed by a majority, which includes, beside that perpetrated by private gangs, the repressive use of the country's armed forces and the police force, who, let us not forget, are armed with modern weaponry and strategies of destruction.

I have in previous chapters documented the cumulative unleashing and use of these forms of violence, the accompanying dismantling of several democratic institutions, and the whittling away of judical safeguards and civil liberties, as Sri Lanka slides simultaneously toward authoritarianism, undisciplined security forces, factional politics, thuggery, and mob violence. The holding of elections in an atmosphere of intimidation and impersonation has now reached a point when the presiding governing officials themselves, carelessly throwing to the winds their canons of fair play and neutrality, function as election agents of the government in power. Thus orderly elections are becoming a thing of the past, and the peaceful turnover of governments an unlikely occurrence. The ultimate hell of political life is reached when threats of protests and processions by "right-wing" or "extremist" elements in one's own party or in another party become the overriding considerations by which the game of politics is played. Thus today shapeless, hungry ghosts and monsters called "militant Sinhala Buddhist nationalists" freeze President Jayawardene and his lieutenants into a fear of inaction, and any ennobling ideas of the role of a statesman in forming public opinion, or in leading a country out of a crisis, are abandoned because they seem too utopian to contemplate.

In the meantime, as violence escalates in the ethnic conflict between Sinhalese and Tamils, a distant observer ruefully and despairingly delineates how the Sri Lankan case, like many others of a similar nature, displays certain patterns and tendencies. There occurs an increasing "theatricalization," and an accompanying ritualization and polarization, in the escalating contests of violence between ethnic, religious, linguistic, or political minorities on the one side and the majority collectivities and established governments on the other. In the increasing theatricalization of the political process, there occurs a twofold magnification. On the one hand the majority community in power is impelled to locate, define, and sharply demarcate its enemy within the body politic, an enemy which is not only a minority but is also usually located at the territorial margins of the country. It tries to do so by organizing periodic military exploits and forays against its alienated "enemy," by incarcerating the leaders of the "rebellious" or "deviant" groups, by organizing rigged trials of alleged "traitors" and insurgents, and by indiscriminately arresting youth and transporting them to concentration camps.

On the other hand, the embattled minority community dialectically produces mirror images of the same phenomena. There is no doubt that in Sri Lanka the punctuated Sinhalese riots against the Tamils, and the increasing severity of the exclusions, discriminations, and quotas imposed on the Tamils, have reaped their reward in Tamil guerillas, and the progressive pushing of larger and larger numbers of Tamils into demanding a separate Eelam state. For their part, certain segments of the resisting minority are also interested in radicalizing their stance, and to this end mouth their own populist dogmas, invent a new history of their past, and engage in spectacular and spasmodic feats of guerilla warfare against the bulwarks of the establishment, and against those among their own people who have been branded as collaborators, spies, or quislings and thus deserving of extinction.

So in the country at large, marauding armies of government forces and pockets of assassinating rebels fire at each other across a landscape of perplexed and confused ordinary people who are the victims of the excesses of both sides. But as the violence mounts, the histrionics progressively produce whirl-pools that engulf the bulk of the ordinary people caught in the middle, who, whatever their private misgivings and equivoca-tions, would rather be left alone, and who in any case do not wish to be plunged into the violence. But many of these ordinary folk are finally forced into one camp or the other as a result of protracted and mounting exchanges of verbal rhet-oric and violent acts. The mass media ensure that the public is bombarded as much as possible with inflammatory news. Politicians, bazaar merchants, and brokers order their private gangs of thugs to stage mob violence, which in turn attracts the hoodlums and vagrants who loot and destroy property and kill terrified humans. The people are in effect pressured and blackmailed and massaged into taking sides, and once this polarization takes place, the confronting majority and minor-ity communities may reach a point of no return, a point beyond any future mediation of their differences or any rap-prochement. Sri Lanka is dangerously close to this rupture now.

Let us recapitulate the diabolical byproducts that have been spawned on the road to the total estrangement between Sinhalese and Tamils, which is itself a result of the dramatiz-ing and stereotyping of violence.

1. The Sinhala-Tamil conflict is, from a world perspective, still another example of the *internationalization* of violence— violence as an exportable technology from one resistance group to another, or from one government to another.

2. There is a *routinization* of violent action as the ordinary mode of settling differences rather than as a measure of last resort.

3. Violent encounters progressively *impersonalize* the adversaries, the adversary is first declred to be an enemy, and

the enemy in turn becomes an abstract, dehumanized entity, an object. Modern weaponry also encourages long-distance exchanges of fire and destruction without personal combat, and thus contributes further to the *depersonalization* of human beings.

4. The stepping up of the violent exchanges in turn tends to encourage among all segments of the population a *condoning of the erosion* of the society's norms and institutional safeguards.

5. Together with this increase of general tolerance of intolerance in the public at large goes the tendency of the government in power further to *politicize* and to *impair the neutrality* of the agencies of law and order, the law courts, the civil service, the police, the postal service, the welfare agencies, and, unbelievably, the state hospitals as well. (During the riots of 1983 some hospital staff in Colombo refused to give medical aid to injured Tamil victims who had been attacked on the roads or in their homes. There were also reports that some Tamil patients were killed, and one woman doctor was raped by hospital staff.)

6. The adversaries on both sides who are the day-to-day combatants progressively refine and perfect their organizational techniques for the recruitment and maintenance of highly disciplined and professionalized militant "cells," "regiments," "societies," and so on. Other features of the *professionalization* of these groups is their development of secret codes and communication patterns, and of special checks and balances, for linking these bodies with a larger movement that is simultaneously hierarchical and dispersed to ensure maximum security and efficacy.

7. Both sides develop their own *heroes*. The "populist activist" in the majority community is fantasized as a reincarnation of one of the mythic royal heroes and founding ancestors, such as the Sinhalese hero Duṭṭhagāmaṇī or the utopian monarch to come, Diyasena. Correspondingly, the resistance heroes on the Tamil side, willing to die for their people's cause, unequally pitted against an unrighteous enemy and bent on a suicidal mission, are in turn romanticized and assimilated to equally heroic figures on the Tamil side. We might well see the invocation of some great Cōḷa and

Pāṇḍyan names, as well as those of local Tamil "resistance heroes" of the past.

8. In the end, as I have said before, this course of events results in the *polarization* of the body polity into two camps, clinging to distorted and stereotyped perceptions of each other, unwilling to communicate, negotiate, or compromise, and convinced that they are totally *separate* peoples in terms of culture and origin. The truths concerning the common historical origins of both Sinhalese and Tamils become impossible to contemplate, and those scholars who speak the truth are likely to be branded as traitors.

The awful existential fact in a society that has become totally polarized is that its minority of activists, populists, and terrorists on both sides holds the entire society as its hostage. And the sad fact is that the main body of the people caught in between—ranging from those few who find violence of any-kind repugnant to those many who are ambivalent and confused about the rights and wrongs of the rival "ethnic" claims—are inexorably seduced and forced into taking sides as the spilling of blood on both sides heightens the emotions and sentiments cohering around such primordial themes as kinship, people, religion, language, and "race."

In the case of the Sinhalese people, their periodic staging of riots since 1956 has occurred in an educational context that has separated their youth from Tamil youth, and in a political atmosphere that has tolerated the preaching of the allegedly justifiable dominance of the Sinhalese people as their historical destiny. One result of this collective populist emphasis has been the muting, if not the total eradication, of hoary rifts: of invidious internal caste differences and comparisons (such as the Goyigama versus the Karāva), of regional differences between allegedly exploitative and intrusive low-country people and the exploited and backward Kandyans,[1] and of religious differences between Buddhists and Christians (especially Roman Catholics). Now there is a conspicuously visible collective scapegoat against which all Sinhalese can unite and vent their frustrated passions.

A parallel process has been encouraged among the Tamils, although their homogenization has not reached the level found among the Sinhalese. As I have said before, the Tamils are not a unitary group either. The east coast Tamils are not the kinsmen of the Jaffna Tamils, and both have traditionally felt separate from and superior to the recently arrived Indian Tamils of the tea plantations in the central provinces. And the Veḷḷāla-Karayār caste differences, as well as others, persist in the north, in an atmosphere of Veḷḷāla "dominance" of a kind unknown today in any Sinhalese region.

But when shops and houses are burnt in Trincomalee, when soldiers rape Tamil girls, burn down shops and libraries, and mow down innocent civilians in the bazaars of northern towns; when schoolgirls taking examinations are forcibly taken to police stations in Batticaloa; when in the "upcountry" Indian coolies are mercilessly beaten and driven from their miserable coolie lines into pitiful refugee camps; when all these events happen simultaneously as actions taken against "the Tamils," then it is inevitable that Tamils of all varieties will see themselves as sharing a common condition, and as victims of a blanket violence on the part of the majority community. The Tamils too are on their way to becoming a single political collectivity, proclaiming themselves to be a distinct nationality with rights of self-determination and entitled to their homelands, and, perhaps more than any other factor in recent history, the repeated discrimination and aggressive acts of the Sinhalese will have produced this result. As things are now, this may be a fortunate circumstance for the Tamils, a serendipitous and unanticipated aid to their future negotiations.

8
WHAT IS TO BE DONE?
A Prescription for the Future

A black hole threatens to engulf both the Sinhalese and Tamil communities. On their part, large segments of the Sinhalese population have engaged in a shameful violation of the basic tenets of a religion founded on nonviolence, noninjury, compassion, and detachment. The new face of political Buddhism is ugly. The ethnic riots have shown a fairly high propensity to violence in Sinhalese society at many levels, and the government in power has grossly violated basic human rights. The danger in Sinhalese belligerence is that the Sinhalese may be tempted to resort to violence in a situation of increasing entropy in order to settle all contentious political issues. Moreover, if today it is Sinhalese Buddhist versus Tamil, tomorrow the victim may be the Muslims, and the day after the Christians. The same danger exists in the relations between political parties within the Sinhalese body politic: the UNP, SLFP, JVP, and the leftist groups.

The Tamils for the immediate future are in even more desperate straits. Unless they have the courage, imagination, and realism to negotiate a settlement that a government representing and accountable to the Sinhalese can, on its side, realistically accept, they may themselves become increasingly involved in violence with the ensuing risk of a diaspora. People on both sides will have to work toward a sane solution compounded of restraint, empathy, and generosity. It is inevitable that any agreement that is reached will in the short run completely satisfy no one, and be repugnant to the extremists on both sides on the grounds that too much has been given away and too little gained.

These are the contours of a possible solution:

1. The polity must restore the rule of law, repeal its disproportionate and counterproductive Prevention of Terrorism Act (and other excessive legislation), and law enforcement agencies must be neutral and even-handed in the administration of justice, the provision of protection to persons and property, and in restraining violence. In other words, the country as a whole must consciously come to see the necessity to "secularize" and "liberalize" its politics, and to accept a definition of citizenship in which religious and ethnic affiliation play no part.

2. Together with the foregoing, a nation constituted of all Sri Lankans can be formed only if the nation is recognized to be a *plural society*. Such a society, in its role as a collective political actor, while recognizing pluralism to be a fact of life, must not seek to legislate for all time decisive quotas as divisions of spoils on behalf of any component group, for such allocations of benefits will freeze social differences and prevent the unfolding of an open-ended future in which religion and ethnicity are irrelevant.

3. The disaffected segments of the Tamil population must renounce not only "terrorist" activities—for they are plainly suicidal in consequence—but also "separatism," that is, the concept of an independent state of Eelam. Aside from the question of its economic and territorial viability as a separate state, there are other roadblocks. The Tamil language cannot be the basis of a linguistic state for two reasons: on the one hand, the Muslims of the Eastern Province, who are predominantly Tamil speakers, have not so far cared to belong to Eelam; and on the other hand, the Tamils themselves have their internal divisions—the Indian Tamils vis-à-vis the Sri Lankan, the Jaffna Tamils vis-à-vis the Batticaloa Tamils, and so on. In the past, large segments of the Sri Lankan Tamils did not vote for the TULF or a separate state, and the Indian Tamils showed little enthusiasm about belonging to a state of Eelam. The Sri Lankan government in its propaganda document *Sri Lanka—Who Wants a Separate State?* has advanced arguments for the rejection of Eelam whose force the Tamils cannot dismiss or fail to address. I reproduce this document as appendix 5.

If they are to comprise a single political community, the

Tamils of the various regions must strive for at least a political homogeneity by eliminating the discriminatory implications of caste, as well as regional and other divisive affiliations. Here the Tamils should learn the lesson taught by the Sinhalese: if in the nineteenth and early twentieth centuries Kandyan Sinhalese thought themselves to be different from and exploited by the low-country Sinhalese and therefore wanted their separate quotas and guarantees, today that dual identity and antagonism do not hold; if during that same period, the Goyigama "establishment" and majority caste was the object of invidious comparison and equal-status claims by the socially mobile and economically affluent Karā-va-caste (and Salāgama-caste) elites, the so-called Karā-Goi contest is no more a salient or overriding feature of Sinhalese party politics. Low-country and Kandyan Sinhalese are inextricably mixed up today.

What the Sri Lankan government is achieving by its persistent military action and terrorizing of all Tamils is to drive the latter, both Indian and Sri Lankan Tamils, toward the imagined haven of Eelam and toward a blanket ethnic solidarity. After several punitive actions, many Indian Tamil plantation workers have found themselves as refugees or are voluntarily migrating to the north and east. And the armed forces, by another ironic twist, are forcibly repatriating them to their plantations and estates in the hill country. When history plays such tricks on the Indian Tamil laborer, he may well begin to lose all hope of "emancipation," and may well imagine that the Sinhalese conspire to keep the Indian Tamils as hostages not only for reasons of national politics but as a bargaining chip with India as well. Thus, in the end, the case against a separate state of Eelam may be not that all Tamils do not want it, but that it is impossible to wrench it from the Sinhalese, or to demarcate its borders, let alone defend them.

4. A major viable solution, as matters stand now, is a genuine devolution of powers as envisaged in a provincial or regional-councils plan. The provinces or regions should be able to enjoy autonomy in matters of local government, local revenue collection, primary and secondary education, peasant colonization, and so on. In the areas where the Tamils are in a majority, they should be able to feel that they control

some significant part of their destiny. And given the present poisoned ethnic relations, it makes sense to grant Tamils provincial or regional "autonomy," which would imply the larger grouping of Tamil districts for the purpose of following certain larger collective goals. This would also give them a sense of greater security within the larger polity of Sri Lanka. The Tamils should be assured a major role in the constitution and use of security forces and police in the areas in which they predominate. The government should guanantee a system of fair allocation of central government funds to the local units. It should devise and implement a fair plan that will integrate higher education (university, training colleges, and professional schools) at the national level. There should be open recruitment on the basis of merit alone to those national institutions of higher education that teach medicine, engineering, and so on, and are the avenues to professional employment. These places of higher learning, like the professions they lead to, cannot be subject to quotas on the basis of race, religion, or any other attribute irrelevant to applicants' level of knowledge. Finally, there should be a determined effort to establish national "nonpolitical" organizations, such as a university grants committee, an advisory economic council, and so on, which will deal with the entire country in an even-handed way, and yet seek to give additional help and provide better facilities to those segments of the population that are most disadvantaged.

The Tamils on their side must realistically accept Sinhalese as the only viable and economical language for much of the country's administration. Tamils must acquire competence in Sinhalese if they wish to serve as administrative officers in districts where the Sinhalese are in the majority.

The formation of provincial or regional councils and the granting of regional or provincial autonomy should not result in restricted mobility. Any Sinhalese or Tamil, as a citizen, should be able to reside in any part of the country, and be eligible for all facilities, privileges, positions on universalistic criteria of fitness, merit, and performance.

5. A majority government of the Sinhalese people in Sri Lanka is a fact of life. Such a government, and the Sinhalese people as a whole, are rightly proud of their historical and

cultural achievements, which are integrally and indivisibly linked to Buddhism, not merely as a religion in the narrow sense but as a civilization in a total sense. A Sri Lankan goverment must therefore feel free to sponsor the restoration of Buddhist monuments, celebrate past literary achievements, and initiate new endeavors that will recover as much as is possible of the past. It would also behoove a Sri Lankan government to recognize at the same time that there are monuments, archeological remains, and literary and cultural treasures that are neither Sinhalese nor Buddhist as these labels are understood today. There is a prehistory in Sri Lanka that antedates the coming of Buddhism. And in historic times many different peoples have lived on the island and left legacies that the labels "Sinhala Buddhism," "Buddhist Sinhalese," and so on do not include and cannot ignore. Moreover, the labels themselves pertain to entities that were vastly enriched by external borrowings that argue against a fictitious ethnicization.

It would not be a wise or fully representative government that, while celebrating Sinhala and Buddhist pasts, moved in the 1980s and thereafter to enshrine Buddhism as a state religion. Just as it must hereafter renounce discriminatory legislation on the basis of fictional concepts of race, so must it also cease discrimination on the basis of religion. And it is a manifestly dangerous and an explosive promise to rely on millenarian Buddhism or the charisma of parochial monks to generate a genuine nation in a plural society. Sri Lanka, especially in the three decades after independence, has had ample time to recover and relish its Buddhist past, and for its majority to define their identity after a period of colonial rule. Sri Lanka as a nation and polity at the threshold of the twenty-first century must think of its future and not live in its past, must forge new programs of action to create a more prosperous and richer society, for there are new frontiers of knowledge to master, new technologies to exploit, and new values to define that will build on the best in our heritage. History is an open-ended process, not a futile opening of doors that have closed behind us.

I can do no better than quote the sage words of Raymond Aron, the French sociologist and political analyst, who uttered them a few days before his death: "Intellectual and spiritual pluralism does not pretend to offer a truth comparable to the truths of mathematics or physics. But nor does it offer merely opinion. Pluralism justifies itself by the falseness of the beliefs that oppose it." If the West cannot live—cannot survive—except by pluralism, neither can the East. This is an enduring truth. It was well known to India's greatest "universal king" (*cakravartin*), Asoka, who fostered all religions and diversity in custom, and ruled according to the tenets of *dharma* (righteousness) and not by violence. And according to Sinhalese traditions it was this sage king who sent the gift of Buddhism to Sri Lanka.

The 1950s and 1960s were optimistic and hopeful decades when it was imagined by foreign-aid experts and local politicians alike that the road to utopia consisted in hitching the newly founded post-colonial countries to "economic development" and "nation building," as two horses running in tandem. Both horses have often enough run off course. A word about nation building is relevant here. Nation building was frequently conflated with "national integration," and that in turn came often to be interpreted, as in Sri Lanka, as the right of a majority in power in a plural society to enforce a homogeneity on the population, whether linguistic, or religious, or political. The result has been the breeding of a militant nationalism on the part of the majority that sometimes borders on racism and on internal colonialism. This in turn has bred the opposition of minorities, who too have dialectically emphasized their linguistic or political or religious or historical distinctiveness, to preserve, combat, or promote their own interests. It is difficult to define ethnicity, but in our time ethnic conflicts are some version of this general problem. Having witnessed a few decades of internal turmoil in many newly founded states, both political scientists and politicians are now seeing more clearly the advantages of devolution, decentralization, and regional and local autonomy as ways of maintaining and stimulating the growth of plural societies. They agree that national integration can and must accept pluralism as not inimical to its objective, but indeed as essential to its achievement. Recently Loki Madan argued a similar thesis for India: that "national integration," which has created resistance to national unity, should be replaced by a policy of "national accommodation."[1] As our analysis shows, "ethnicity" is a man-made identity. But once it has crystallized it cannot be dismissed (as was done by an earlier group of theorists of "modernization") as a "primordial" loyalty that will automatically dissolve in the crucible of economic development, social class formation, and the generation of special interest associations and secular political parties. Ethnicity exists, and at best it cross-cuts and intersects with these newer associations in diverse ways. It may be the refuge and resort of the poor at the bottom of the heap here, the defensive weapon of an oppressed minority there, or the engine of political mobilization and of destruction by a ruling group elsewhere.

9
EPILOGUE:
Biographical Interweavings

I cannot deny my past to which my self is wed
The woven figure cannot undo its thread.
     Louis MacNeice

I see two perspectives and attitudes of mind reflected in the push and pull of Sri Lanka's politics since independence which were reiterated at another level in the careers of Sri Lanka's two most illustrious prime ministers, Don Stephen Senanayake and Solomon West Ridgeway Bandaranaike, who arguably might be garlanded as the two founding fathers of the new nation state. These perspectives, both intenally ridden with contradictions and ambivalences, also compete as rival interpretations and justifications of the current crisis. At a humbler level the same dualities affected my own intellect and emotions as I grew from adolescence into manhood in the years when these two men presided over the affairs of the new nation.

The first perspective and attitude of mind was quintessentially represented by Senanayake, who, as the island's first prime minister from 1947 to 1952, proudly received the transfer of power from the British raj and hoisted the lion flag on Independence Day. A giant of a man with a walrus moustache luxuriating on an immense, benign, elephantine face, he was descended from a line of "low-country" district chiefs (*mudaliyār*s) who came into prominence as agents and collaborators of the British rulers in the nineteenth century. The family's wealth derived from land, and, following British entrepreneurial activity, the Senanayakes established coconut estates and engaged in graphite mining.

Don Stephen Senanayake began his political career as a
leader of a Buddhist-inspired temperance movement directed
against the British-encouraged "arrack renting" that, while
providing revenue to the rulers through an expanding liquor
trade, also corrupted and ruined the ordinary people. And
since this agitation coincided with the 1918 Sinhalese riots
against the Muslims, the British temporarily incarcerated
Senanayake together with other Sinhalese agitators. But
although this beginning catapulted him into politics, throughout the 1930s and thereafter Senanayake wore the garb of a
"constitutionalist," who peacefully pressured the British into
the granting of dominion status, and of a "secularist" in that
the sponsorship of Buddhism (or any other religion) was not a
significant part of his political platform. In fact, D. S. Senanayake (unlike his able brother, F. R. Senanayake, who died
early in his political career) was not a dedicated "religionist"
at all, and would have felt distinctly uncomfortable if he had
been called upon to wave the Buddhist flag for political purposes. Moreover, Senanayake by and large, while proud of
the Sinhala heritage, and while believing in the Sinhala destiny to rule the island, was not a "communalist," that is, was
not an ethnic chauvinist, and although right through the years
of the Donoughmore Constitution he participated in a Sinhala
domination of the Executive Councils, he did not care to
exploit the ethnic issue for his own political aggrandizement.

Senanayake's noncommunalist attitude toward the island's
minority groups—Tamils, Muslims, and Eurasians—was
partly influenced by the pragmatic realization that the British
would not countenance progress toward independence unless
he and other Sinhalese leaders came to a reasonable understanding with the minorities. But his noncommunalist, nonre-
ligionist, and pro-constitutionalist attitude was also fostered
by the kind of education he received and the kind of elite
members of all ethnic groups he consorted with at St. Thomas'
College, one of Sri Lanka's famous "public schools" run by
the Anglicans. Though a Christian institution, St. Thomas'
(like many other missionary-run public schools in the island)
fostered a liberal ethos that considered the promotion of
religious and ethnic affiliations and ethnic identities for socially or politically divisive purposes to be in extremely bad

taste. This liberal, pluralistic attitude was encouraged by the fact that all the boys and girls who went to such elite schools spoke to one another in English rather than in their mother tongues. Indeed, since English was the primary language of instruction, tongues such as Sinhalese and Tamil were downgraded, and the students were at best indifferently taught them. It is these circumstances that gave birth to the Sri Lankan expression "the English-educated elite," a segment of the population on whose heads many sins have been heaped.

Don Stephen Senanayake, who founded the United Nationalist Party, on the whole recognized that Sri Lanka was a plural society with a Sinhalese majority, and that politics had better be a "secular" affair. He was, in the years before and after independence when he was in power, even chary of approaching the question of replacing English with Sinhalese (and Tamil) as the national languages.

Finally, Senanayake was by preference and bent a "gentleman farmer" who was deeply interested in agriculture, and showed a benign paternalist sympathy for the peasant farmers and rural folk. He imagined the ideal Sri Lankan society as constituted of numerous free, independent, peasant smallholders, and, more than all the politicians of his time, he was committed to reclaiming the dry-zone jungles of the island through hydraulic engineering and the eradication of malaria for peasant resettlement. Though not the originator of these settlements he was the accredited father of the peasant colonization schemes (which ironically, are the volatile political arenas of today).

But despite such deep concerns, the tenets of the UNP and the Senanayake-type paternalist, elitist, traditional political leadership were challenged and overthrown by 1956 by a more dynamic, revivalist, demagogic political movement led by S. W. R. D. Bandaranaike, which claimed to initiate a "social revolution." Don Stephen had died in 1952, and by 1956 his successors, including his son, Dudley, were painted as old-fashioned liberals, collaborators with the British, committed to a capitalist, colonialist economy that the British rulers had bequeathed them. But above all, the UNP was rejected in 1956 because its politics was seen as tired and without luster, because it lacked a revivalist and populist message and ideology that could speak to the pride, identity, and collective consciousness of the people at large, particularly the Sinhalese, in terms of a religious, linguistic, and ethnic revivalism and nationalism, of the sort proclaimed so long ago in the *Mahāvaṃsa*. Senanayake did not care to appeal to a bygone national identity and national pride that would redeem the people from their degraded colonial bondage; his sense of historical legacy appealed more to the glories of ancient agriculture and irrigation works than to those of Duṭṭhagāmaṇī and his holy wars.

A second perspective and attitude of mind burst like a dam in the 1956 elections, when Solomon West Ridgeway Dias Bandaranaike and his coalition (whose major component was his own Sri Lanka Freedom Party) won a landslide victory. Bandaranaike also came from a line of "low-country" chiefly *mudaliyār* aristocrats. Indeed, his family and extended kindred claimed a superiority of rank over the Senanayakes, who were newcomers compared with the longer history of patronage enjoyed by the Bandaranaikes under the British, and before them, under Dutch rule. Moeover—and this is one of the complex undercurrents in the makeup of low-country Sinhalese and Jaffna Tamil elites—the Bandaranaike clan was ostentatiously and proudly Anglican (they even had their own church in Mutwal, and had spawned an Anglican canon). S. W. R. D. Bandaranaike's father was by government appointment made the chief of the native chiefs (*mahā mudaliyār*). His wealth, too, was in land, especially coconut estates, and he had his country seat in Horagolla. He rode horses, and dressed and lived like an English country gentleman. He was a loyal conservative, indifferent and hostile to the political aspirations of the leaders of the Ceylon National Congress, who peacefully agitated for representative government. And in the tradition of many another local patriot and admirer, invested his son with two middle names borrowed from a British governor (Sir J. West Ridgeway was governor from 1896 to 1903). (Incidentally, some decades later my father, following the same tradition, invested me with a name borrowed from Sir Herbert Stanley, the governor at the time of my birth.)

S. W. R. D. Bandaranaike also had his early education at St. Thomas's College, but he did not leave a mark there, nor has the school ever claimed him as its own, while it has fulsomely feted D. S. Senanayake as its most illustrious old boy. Bandaranaike was duly sent to Christ Church at Oxford, where he is alleged to have been the contemporary of Anthony Eden. But, soon after returning from Oxford, the son of the foremost titled chief and foremost Anglophile supporter, entered local politics (his initial entry benefited from his aristocratic connections), discarded Western clothes, put on the "native costume," and in due course also renounced Christianity and espoused Buddhism. And although he was earlier an active member of the Ceylon Ntional Congress and later, with the granting of independence, belonged to that sprawling group of politicians to whom power was transferred and who banded together as the UNP, Bandaranaike was not a conformist, and was considered not *pakkā* enough in his political style to be considered fit for succession as a UNP prime minister.

Bandaranaike was slight in physique, and wore spectacles on a pinched and thin-lipped face that was prematurely aged. But while the physically imposing and benign Senanayake was slow of speech, Bandaranaike was an orator in both English and Sinhalese, and was cut out to be a campaigner. And unlike most of his political contemporaries in power, he had, along with his change of religion and dress, participated in organizations such as the Sinhala Mahā Sabhā, whose membership tended to come from village and local elements somewhat cut off from the preoccupations of the "English-educated elite," and who were genuinely interested in the revival of "traditional" Buddhism and the promotion of Sinhala language and literature. They were also, as a matter of self-interest, impatiently demanding a more "egalitarian" and "democratic" form of government that would open up educational and employment opportunities to the socially mobile within their ranks. These activist elements, with their grass-roots support and knocking at the doors of privilege, were composed of vocal Buddhist monks (whose religion had been disestablished by the British and whose status had declined), pious Buddhist members of temperance societies, village elites of vernacular teachers (who suffered in comparison with their English-educated counterparts), ayurvedic physicians (whose "science" was rated inferior to that of Western medicine), and the newly rich merchants and *mudalālis*, who were the objects of the snobbery and disdain of the traditional rural headmen and chiefly families and the English-educated professionals and estate owners.

The so-called social revolution of 1956 reflected the interests of these segments of the population, who were the touchstone for the masses at large. Though these segments were not destined to effect a fundamental or radical reordering of society, they did inject leavening influences, unleash creative energies, and support the attainment of a greater degree of social justice and opportunity in the society at large. Most importantly, they exposed the unwieldiness and injustice of conducting administrative affairs and legal proceedings in English, which about 85 to 90% of the population did not speak or write, and they assiduously addressed the question of education at all levels in the native languages.

Nevertheless, a disturbing and sobering fact about the Bandaranaike era was that this charismatic politician, who voiced many of the political sentiments and aspirations of the Sinhalese masses, proved unable to direct or control them, and was extinguished by the very forces he had helped attain to dignity and power. Bandaranaike was assassinated in 1959 by a Buddhist monk who was the tool of a larger monkish plot. His career as prime minister lasted a mere three years. Perhaps the greatest tragedy suffered by Sri Lanka since independence is that such a gifted politician, who might have presided over a radical reordering of a "colonial society," had not the statesman's stamina, guts, and greatness to implement solutions to the country's ailments, including the spiraling Sinhalese-Tamil ethnic conflict, whose outlines he saw quite clearly.

Let me now describe how the perspectives and actions of these two prime ministers in the 1940s and 1950s affected me as a Sri Lankan and as an academic, and to suggest how my own location within Sri Lankan society might have influenced the ideas that I have set out in this book.

At independence, when Senanayake became Sri Lanka's

first prime minister, I was a high-school student at St. Thomas'
College, that same school to which he had gone, and of which
he was the most illustrious old boy. I inevitably shared in the
Senanayake heritage in many ways. My public school
friendships transcended ethnic barriers (to this day I have
Sinhalese, Tamil, Muslim, and Eurasian friends), and we
were warned that invoking religious caste, or communal
affiliations and loyalties would lead to unhealthy divisiveness.
Moreover, my father's political connections linked us with the
Senanayake tradition and the UNP in an unusual way that,
while unorthodox and peculiar from a Tamil point of view,
had a positive feature from a "national" point of view because
it sought to transcend ethnic separatism in politics. In a rough
way, my parental social origins could be thought of as a
northern Tamil provincial version of the landed segments of
the low-country Sinhalese with traditional chiefly connections, and ownership of coconut plantations. For reasons
similar to those of their low-country counterparts, my parents'
forebears had become Anglican Christians, while large numbers of their kin remained Hindu. My father was for the most
part educated in Colombo's Christian public schools (St. Thomas' and Wesley), became a lawyer, and returned to Jaffna to
practice his profession and indulge his hobby as a "planter."
He was a close friend of Arunachalam Mahadeva, the son and
nephew respectively of two famous Tamil politicians, Sir Ponnambalam Arunachalam and Sir Ponnambalam Rama-
nathan, who together with Sinhalese politicians led the
Ceylon National Congress in the early decades of the twentieth century. Mahadeva was the only Tamil minister in the
Donoughmore era, and was in turn a close friend of Senanayake and a founding member of the UNP. My father,
though not politically inclined, consented, as an ally of
Mahadeva, to contest the first parliamentary elections in 1947
under the UNP ticket, at a time when the Tamils of Jaffna
were closing ranks behind a purely Tamil party, the Tamil
Congress, led by a fiery orator, G. G. Ponnambalam, who had
vainly argued before the Soulbury Commission for more
minority safeguards in the proposed constitution. As expected, my father and Mahadeva were heavily defeated. Subsequently Mahadeva was honored with a knighthood and my

father was awarded the Order of the British Empire. My family (together with a few others in Jaffna) have remained for a long time loosely and sentimentally attached to the secularist, noncommunalist, nationalist postures and goals of the Senanayakes, though none of them has actively engaged in politics again. A brother of mine, a surgeon, has served as the head of the Army Medical Corps; another is presently a judge of the Supreme Court; and a brother-in-law has been the warden (principal) of St. Thomas' College.

To return to myself. When I returned to Sri Lanka in 1955 from my studies abroad to teach at the University, one side of me was well aware that my own professional career and social existence would be meaningful only in an "integrated" society, whose pluralism could not, and must not, be undermined by legal definitions and quota allocations in favor of any segment, whether the majority or a minority. I feared that the freezing of communal and ethnic boundaries, and the perpetuation of certain kinds of sectional loyalties, would make their future dissolution in favor of a pluralistic society impossible. By temperament I am not a political being—if I had any political sympathies at all in the 1950s it was for the radical Marxist groups led by impressive intellectuals who stood at that time for an entirely secular conception of socialist politics and an even-handed policy toward all ethnic groups.

But another important side of me—influenced and informed by my anthropological and sociological concerns—was powerfully touched by the events of 1956 and thereafter, when Bandaranaike drenched the country with the aspirations of revivalist Buddhism, a national identity rooted in the traditions and achievements of the precolonial past, and a more just and egalitarian social order. The euphoria of 1956, in which many of my Sinhalese friends, including the most creative, imaginative, and sensitive of them, participated and rejoiced, created in me an ache to achieve an empathetic understanding. Although by virtue of my minority status and my school and university upbringing I could not emotionally fully identify with it, I was intellectually moved to positively understand the phenomenon of Buddhist-Sinhala (religio-linguistic) nationalism. It was imperative that I grasp its historical underpinnings as well as its powerful movement into the future.

In 1958, while I was leading a research team composed of University undergraduates, all of whom were Sinhalese, that was engaged in a sociological study of peasant colonization in Gal Oya, ethnic riots unexpectedly broke out in our midst, and at Amparai Sinhalese public works laborers went on the rampage in hijacked trucks, attacking Tamil shopkeepers and Tamil peasant colonists. My students, very solicitous for my safety, insisted that I stay behind closed doors while they stood guard. And I was later hidden in a truck, and spirited out of the valley to Batticaloa, a safe Tamil area. That experience was traumatic: it was the first time the ethnic divide was so forcibly thrust into my existence. And intuitively reading the signs, I wished to get away from the island, for I experienced a mounting alienation and a sense of being homeless in one's own home.

And then a remarkable opportunity came my way, which enabled me to positively sympathize with and creatively study the phenomena in another country that I could not do in my own. I went to Thailand to do research and teach on behalf of UNESCO. I was able to study with the double posture of rapport and distance in someone else's country many things that I could not aspire to do, or do well, in Sri Lanka. How Buddhism as a classical heritage and a popular religion was integrated with all aspects of life in a Thai village was the subject of my first book.[1] In the following years, having returned to academia in Britain and then in the United States, I studied the roots and manifestations over time of the complementary relation between Buddhism as a vocation of renunciation and its larger linkage with the polity under the aegis of Buddhist kingship, a kingship whose ideal role was that of a righteous regulator of society and the foremost lay merit-maker toward, and protector of, the *sangha* (monastic orders). My second book, *World Conqueror and World Renouncer*,[2] is a statement of the overarching ideological nexus between Buddhism and the polity, which in my view, has relevance not only for Thailand but also for Sri Lanka, Burma, and Laos.

In a complex way, I sense that this book was an attempt at an intellectual and emotional confrontation with and resolution of my own personal situation with regard to Sri Lanka, and the conflicts and urges it gave rise to. My third book, *Buddhist Saints of the Forest*,[3] destined to be seen as part of a trilogy, tells the story of the esoteric forest monk saintly Buddhist tradition in Thailand, its classical precedents and its present political and social ramifications. As an anthropologist of Sri Lankan Tamil origins, I like to think that I have contributed as much as any indigenous Southeast Asian scholar to the positive understanding of the interrelation between Buddhism and politics. And if there has been a certain "overdetermination" in my views, I hope I have erred more on the side of generosity than on the side of deprecation.

While all these intellectual and emotional strivings and resolutions are still a part of me, I have now reached a point when I must sound warnings. Today the continuing ethnic animosities and violence in Sri Lanka are paralleled in Burma by the persisting opposition and rebellions of ethnic minorities, such as the Shans and Karens, against the domination by the majority Buddhist Burmese, and in Thailand by vocal opposition on the part of the minority Muslims in the southern provinces (and in Bangkok) to the restrictive and homogenizing administrative and educational policies of the central Thai Buddhist-dominated government. These resistances, rebellions, and oppositions should warn us of the encompassing and dominating urges of majority peoples and of majority politics in pluralistic societies and countries. In the case of Thailand, the Thai governmental and civilian attitudes and policies toward the "hill tribes" (*chao khao*)—exemplified by administrative penetration by Thai officials, border police, and army; by the "missionary" activity of Buddhist monks; and by the compulsory spread of education in the Thai language—are menacing in their discriminatory and hierarchical implications. Keyes reports that a local district officer in Mae Sariang in north Thailand asserted in the course of an argument with an American Baptist Missionary working among the Karens: "To be a Thai is to speak only Thai, to be a Buddhist."[4] Parallel expessions regarded as self-evident truths are on the lips of their counterparts in Burma and Sri Lanka.

These convergent attitudes, which are commonplace in these three Theravāda Buddhist countries of Southeast Asia, should warn us about the militant and chauvinistic resonances that have constituted the dark underside and the other terrifying face of Buddhism as a religio-political complex, which in its positive aspects has attained to great humanistic conceptions and civilizational triumphs. This other face presents itself in the twentieth century as a distorted "political Buddhism" emptied of its ethical content and inflated with the poison gas of communal identity. Under its banner populist leaders mobilize masses who are losing their traditional roots and their traditional Buddhist moral restraints, and whip them into a heady collective identity and a fury of displaced and misplaced anger against the alien others, the minorities, who are seen as a challenge to their chauvinistic manhood.

Traditionally, the overarching cosmological and ideological frameworks of the (Buddhist) peoples of Sri Lanka, Burma, Thailand, and so on were predicated on a shared formula: that there is a special relationship between the *sangha* (the community of monks) and the polity, between the Buddhist quest for salvation of the renouncer and the Buddhist lay ethic of the wider society of householders capped by kingship, the role of which was to institutionally support, materially nurture, and physically protect the *sangha* as the exemplar that guarantees the dignity and authenticity of the whole. In this larger formulation, the ideology linked the religion (*śāsana*) with the polity, and acclaimed it as the special heritage and destiny of a people—the Sinhalese, the Burmese, the Mons, the Thai, the Laos, and so on—who were shaped to think of themselves as a "race" cum "nation," with a special historical mission indissolubly linked with Buddhism. This framework, this mold, was constructed and set in place at the critical phases when, at various times, these Buddhist polities attained their political consolidation, and claimed their religious and moral legitimacy from Buddhist monastic communities which, in addition to their work at the center, also acted as civilizing agents at the expanding periphery. The monks in turn required the patronage of rulers to secure their material needs, and to guarantee their safety from invaders and the vagaries of political uncertainty and instability. Thus when, at critical historical watersheds, the political and clerical elites defined their societies, contours, and ideological charters, these contours and charters in due course hardened into constraints and immanent styles that locked their societies within certain parameters that encouraged certain developments and were hostile to others. Once in place, these frameworks became the bases for a long-term trajectory in precolonial times, with its continuities as well as its tensions, its pulsations as well as its oscillations.

In the long run, such crystalized frameworks, with their inflexibilities, may incapacitate these societies with their distinctive political cultures in making adaptive transformations in changed contexts that pose new tasks and challenges. Is it possible for majorities like the Sinhalese, Burmese, and Thai peoples with "Buddhist," "linguistic," and "racial" identity claims to contemplate living in plural societies in which diversity rather than homogeneity of religion, language, and ethnicity is accepted as a necessary and normal fact of life?

As I have previously argued, the traditional precolonial "galactic polities" of South and Southeast Asia not only could, but also did, tolerate, positively place, and mutually benefit from satellite principalities, specialized minorities, and heterdox communities all incorporated in cosmological and politico-economic frameworks deployed on a maṇḍala pattern of devolution and replication. Indeed, it was this galactic blueprint that positively enabled in Sri Lanka over time the continuous peaceful and *uncoerced* Sinhalization and Buddhicization of diverse South Indian peoples and gods. But during British colonial times there occurred the introduction of new populations as well as the bringing together of previously separated regions and loosely connected peoples within the same politico-economic space, under the aegis of an imperial power that combined a tolerance of diversity of social customs within an administrative structure orchestrated in the English language by British officers and their native agents and interpreters. In a sense the British experience left a confused message to Sri Lankans: on the one hand, an authoritarian regime of white sahibs exercised in theory a total power backed by the technology of centralized power developed in the West; on the other hand, these same autocrats distributed in driblets in their own time more and more powers of elective representation and self-government to the natives, who were being progressively educated to the procedures and norms of democracy, rational administration, and civil justice. When the British left the island they hoped they were leaving behind a viable nation state (constituted of groups of multiple linguistic, religious, and ethnic affiliations) unified by a single administrative structure and by a defined territorial boundary. These were major new circumstances that comprised the British legacy to Sri Lanka at the time of independence. However much the revival and reassertion of their traditional religio-political-linguistic ideology by the Sinhalese majority has served in the short run to liberate collective energies, to politicize the ordinary folk, and to enable them to participate in a democratic form of politics, yet that same ideology in some of its exclusive, restrictive, and intolerant aspects has functioned as a suffocating straitjacket, and by the norms of the twentieth century it is an unjustifiable engine of domination and an ineffective system of knowledge and technique for coping with the problems of a third-world country in our time.

APPENDIX 1:
FROM *THE TIMES* (OF LONDON), 18 JANUARY 1984

Fears of mob law in Sri Lanka

Judges come under attack

From Michael Hamlyn Colombo

A number of Sri Lankan lawyers are unhappy about what they see as a deliberate attack by the Government on the independence of the judiciary here. Although the constitution introduced by President J. R. Jayewardene in 1978 enshrined the concept of a separate and free judicial system, a series of actions by his ministers and officials have gone a long way to eroding it.

The moves against the judges include the promotion of police officers condemned by the courts for human rights violations, the terrorizing of judges by organised mobs of "demonstrators," and the establishment of a select committee of governing party MPs to investigate actions of the Supereme Court.

Although the United National party of Mr. Jayewardene praised the activities of the civil rights supporters in condemning actions of Mrs. Bandaranaike's Government, and although the constitution promulgated by him was on the whole an improvement over Mrs. Bandaranaike's 1972 constitution, the legal profession was startled by what happened to all the judges of the High Court and Supreme Court when his new constitution came in.

Their duties were reshuffled and a number of them were sacked, while others received promotions. One judge, Mr. K. C. E. De Alwis, received a double promotion, from the district court up to the Court of Appeal, without ever having been a high Court judge.

Mr. de Alwis had been a member of the special tribunal which had been set up to hear charges against Mrs. Bandaranaike and her nephew and Minister of Justice, Mr. Felix Diaz Bandaranaike, and which sentenced both to loss of civic rights. Mr. Bandaranaike sued in the Supreme Court, accusing Mr. de Alwis of misconduct and the court found in his favour, causing deep embarrassment to the Government.

The Government promptly set up the select committee with the Minister of Justice in the chair to investigate the court.

Under the constitutional amendment the MPs and all Government servants including the judges had to take an oath forswearing separatism. The Government took the view that the Supreme Court judges should have taken the oath in front of the President, and since they had not done so they announced that they could no longer sit, and put armed guards on their offices to keep them out.

During the referendum campaign in 1982 under which the Government won approval to extend the life of the Parliament for a further six years, police seized leaflets produced by a Buddhist organization called Voice of the Clergy. The leaflets urged a vote against the government proposal, and afterwards a Buddhist priest sued the police superintendent, claiming that his fundamental rights of freedom of expression had been infringed. The judges agreed and ordered the policeman to pay 10,000 rupees (£300) damages and 2,100 rupees costs.

The police officer was promoted instantly, and the Cabinet decided that the damages and costs should be paid from public funds.

An exactly similar thing happened when a veteran left-winger, Mrs. Vivienne Goonewardene, was arrested and ill-treated by police when demonstrating last year against the President's relection.

The court awarded her compensation, saying that demonstrations were not illegal, but the Ministry of Defence instantly promoted the police officer. Three days later a series of squads and hooligans paraded up and down outside the homes of the three judges concerned, shouting obscenities and causing damage.

APPENDIX 2:
THE SINHALESE-TAMIL RIOTS OF 1958

(From W. Howard Wriggins: "Ceylon: Dilemmas of a New Nation," pp. 268–70. Copyright © 1960 by Princeton University Press. Reprinted by permission of Princeton University Press.

The *crisis of June* 1958, therefore, drew near with the government's law-enforcement agencies weakened. As yet no end to communal tension was in sight. The one effort to reach a compromise solution that would reassure the minority had miscarried.

The Federal Party's annual public meeting was called for late May. The conclave was to decide whether or not to undertake a *Satyagraha* campaign now that the prime minister had withdrawn his support from the agreement he had endorsed a year before. The outbreak of violence began when a train, presumed to be carrying Tamil delegates to the meetings, was derailed and its passengers beaten up by ruffians. The next day Sinhalese laborers set fire to Tamil shops and homes in nearby villages where they lived intermingled with Sinhalese. Police stations were surrounded by large crowds and their communications cut so that effective protection to scattered Tamil residents could not be assured despite many instances of police heroism. Arson and beatings spread rapidly to Colombo. Gangs roamed the districts where Tamils lived, ransacking and setting fire to homes and cars, and looting shops. Individual Tamils were attacked, humiliated, and beaten. Many were subjected to torture and some killed outright. The outbreaks threatened to become religious riots when a Hindu priest and temple were burned and a Buddhist temple demolished. Some ten thousand Tamils were reported to have fled their homes to seek safety in improvised refugee camps established in requisitioned schools and protected by police and army units. Many fled to the north by sea. About two thousand Sinhalese in the north similarly sought camp protection.

The troubles had begun on May 23. After three days of terrifying disorders, the prime minister broadcast a message to the people, urging them to remain calm. But his reference to a prominent Sinhalese who had been killed in Batticaloa only incensed the Sinhalese masses the more and the riots grew in intensity. On May 27, the prime minister finally made his decision and asked the governor general to declare a state of emergency. The toll during the days of disorders included an estimated 300–400 killed, over 2,000 incidents of arson, looting, and assault, and 12,000 Ceylonese transformed into homeless refugees.

The governor general then became the effective center of government. The armed forces received orders to shoot if commands were not obeyed. Groups in the streets were to be disbanded. Houses could be entered without a warrant. A strict curfew was imposed and the most stringent censorship of the press introduced. The Tamil Federal Party and the most extreme Sinhalese group (the small, but incendiary, Jatika Vimukti Peramuna) were both proscribed and their members placed under house arrest. The troops methodically set about clearing out the trouble spots of the capital.

The Federalist leaders and a few Sinhalese leaders were held under house arrest from June until September. During that period, legislation was finally passed concerning the "reasonable use of Tamil." Tamils were assured that they could continue educating their children in Tamil and that they could use their language in corresponding with the government and in local government affairs. Tamils could compete for government service examinations, although they would have to develop proficiency in Sinhalese if they were to continue in the service and be promoted. However, since the Tamil spokesmen were not in parliament when legislation concerning them was brought forward, all but two members of the Opposition walked out. The bill that passed, therefore, lacked the sanction of a fully representative house. From the Tamil point of view, it also fell short of the Federalist requirements—and the Bandaranaike-Chelvanayagam Pact—for it made no reference to the proposed developments of regional councils and promised no assurance of greater regional autonomy in cultural and administrative matters.

The tragedy of these events is heightened by the realization that if these safeguards of Tamil interests—all of them included in the preliminary draft legislation proposed by the M.E.P. parliamentary party in 1956—had been passed two years before, both the 1956 and 1958 riots might have been avoided.

APPENDIX 3:
SRI LANKA'S
ETHNIC PROBLEMS:
MYTHS AND REALITIES

*(Report of the Committee for Rational Development,
November 1983)*

The Committee for Rational Development *was formed during
the aftermath of the July 1983 violence. Its members include Sinhalese,
Tamils, Muslims, and Burghers of different political pursuasions. The
objective of the Committee is to assist in the finding of solutions to
contemporary social problems of Sri Lanka on the basis of strengthening democratic institutions and the rational processes in society.*

Semi-truths tear at the fragile fabric of a united Sri Lanka. In this pamphlet we shall try to examine some key areas that have become a focus of
ethnic resentments and hostilities. We shall take up certain widely prevalent
myths and contrast them with the realities, which we have endeavoured to
discern without prejudice or partiality.

There are two possible ways of looking at how the various ethnic communities have fared in various fields of national life. One is by taking the
population figures of each community and measuring them against their share
of jobs, university places and their other indexes of social attainment. This
method is the one that has most often been used in recent discussion of the
subject—sometimes selectively or inaccurately. There is another method that
is relevant in certain contexts. This is to take the geographical areas where
particular ethnic communities are concentrated and to compare the levels of
social attainment in these areas with others. We shall use both these methods
of analysis in this pamphlet.

Population:

According to the Census of Population completed in 1981, the total
population of Sri Lanka was estimated to be 14.85 million. The percentage of
each ethnic community was as follows:

Table I

Sinhalese	74.0%
Tamils	18.2%
(Sri Lankan Tamil	*12.6%*
Indian Tamil	*5.6%)*
Muslims	7.4%
Others	0.4%

(Source: Census of Population and Housing, 1981)

While the Tamils—Sri Lankan and Indian—are around 18% of the national population, they are 92% of the population in the Northern Province and 68% in the Eastern Province. (See the ethnic breakdown, North and East, in Appendix A.) For a correct undertanding of our ethnic problems, both these sets of figures must be borne in mind. Ethnic groups diffused uniformly throughout the island do not develop the same consciousness, and do not face the same problems, as those which are highly concentrated in certain areas. Governmental policies must also cope with this reality.

We have used classifications as stated in the relevant government statistics. In most cases the government has classified both Indian Tamils and Sri Lankan Tamils as Tamils in general. Similarly, low country Sinhalese and Kandyan Sinhalese have been categorized as Sinhalese in general. It must also be understood that during times of communal disturbance these distinctions are usually not relevant with regard to victims of violence. Misperceptions about an ethnic community attach to that community as a whole whether they be Ceylon Tamil or Indian Tamil, Kandyan Sinhalese or Low Country Sinhalese, rich or poor.

The Committee for Rational Development recognizes that gross disparities exist **within** each ethnic group—disparities which are far greater than those which exist **between** ethnic communities. Income distribution figures clearly reveal this aspect—the highest ten percent get 32 times what the lowest ten percent get. (Report on Consumer Finances and Socio-Economic Survey p. 96).

Discussion on ethnic quotas and the like often serve to conceal the real inequalities and the nature of poverty which exists in our society.

Geographical zones:

We adopt in this pamphlet the division of the country into five regional zones used by the Central Bank:

Zone I: Colombo District (excluding the Colombo Municipality) Gampaha, Kalutara, Galle and Matara Districts. Wet zone, predominantly Sinhala areas.

Zone II: Hambantota, Moneragala, Amparai, Polonnaruwa, Anuradhapura and Puttalam Districts. Dry zone, predominantly Sinhala areas.

Zone III: Jaffna, Mannar, Vavuniya, Trincomalee and Batticaloa Districts. Dry zone, predominantly Sri Lankan Tamil areas.

Zone IV: Kandy, Matale, Nuwara-Eliya, Badulla Ratnapura, Kegalle and Kurunegala Districts. Predominantly Sinhala, with a concentration of Indian Tamils in the hill country.

Zone V: The Colombo Municipality. Predominantly Sinhala.

Employment in the State Sector

Q: *Do Tamils have a disproportionate share of jobs in the public sector?*
A: No, the latest published figures—for 1980—give the following picture:

Table II

State Sector (excluding Corporation Sector)			
Category Percentages of:	*Sinhalese*	*Tamils*	*Others*
Professional and technical	82%	12%	6%
Administrative and Managerial	81%	16%	3%
All categories	84%	12%	4%

Table III

Public Sector (State and Corporation Sectors Combined)			
Category Percentage of:	*Sinhalese*	*Tamils*	*Others*
Professional and technical	82%	13%	5%
Administrative and Managerial	83%	14%	3%
All categories	85%	11%	4%

Source: Census of Public and Corporation Sector Employment, 1980 (Department of Census and Statistics and Ministry of Plan Implementation)

Q: *How do these percentages compare with the ethnic breakdown of population?*
A: Compare them with the figures in Table I. With 74% of the population, the Sinhalese have 85% of all the jobs in the public sector, 82% in the

professional and technical catgories, and 83% in the administrative and managerial categories. On the other hand, the Tamils, with 18% of the population, have only 11% of all public sector jobs, 13% of professional and technical posts, and 14% of administrative and managerial positions. Confirmation of this position is to be found in the UNP election manifesto of 1977. That manifesto said:

> 'The United National Party accepts the position that there are numerous problems confronting the Tamil-speaking people. The lack of solution to their problems has made the Tamil-speaking people support even a movement for the creation of a separate state'.

The manifesto went on to say:

> 'The Party, when it comes to power, will take all possible steps to remedy their fields of such grievances as . . .' and it then listed four such fields, in which the fourth was: 'Employment in the Public and semi-public Corporations.'

So, in 1977 the present governing party felt that those who had a genuine grievance regarding public sector employment were the Tamils.

Q: *Why then is there a popular impression that Tamils have an unduly high share of public sector jobs?*

A: The impression has been created by taking figures in selected Government departments, or in selected fields like accountancy and engineering. For instance, it has been claimed that in these fields the figures are around 22% and 42% respectively. (This is the Truth p. 19)

Q: *Would this position be changed by an ethnic quota for public sector employment, as some people have suggested?*

A: It could, but since an ethnic quota would have to be applied throughout the public sector, it would mean that the Sinhalese presence in certain sectors would be reduced from its present levels. A few Sinhalese professionals would gain jobs as doctors, professionals or engineers, but a large number of poorer Sinhalese in Government departments, corporations or the armed forces would have to lose their jobs to Tamils.

General Employment

Q: *How do the ethnic communities stand in relation to employment in general?*

A: Table IV gives the relevant statistics.

Q: *What do these figures show?*

A: Though Tamils have a higher proportion of their labour force employed than the Sinhalese in general, the Kandyan Sinhalese, the Low country Sinhalese and the Indian Tamils have a larger proportion of the total population in their communities in employment than Sri Lankan Tamils.

Q: *What do these last-mentioned facts mean?*

A: The figures for Indian Tamils are explained by the fact that whole families are employed on the estates, and at the wage levels at which they are employed, the entire family earnings go into their subsistence. On the other

Table IV: Employment by Community—All Island

	Percent of Labour Force in the Community					As a Percent of the Total Population in the Community				
	Self Employed	Employer	Employee	Unpaid Family Worker	Total Employed	Self Employed	Employer	Employee	Unpaid Family Worker	Total Employed
Kandyan Sinhalese	24.62	1.07	40.12	20.33	86.14	9.79	0.43	15.96	8.09	34.27
Low Country Sinhalese	18.80	1.57	52.17	8.97	81.51	7.03	0.59	19.52	3.35	30.49
Ceylon Tamils	27.52	0.95	51.78	8.96	89.21	8.63	0.30	16.23	2.81	27.97
Indian Tamils	1.80	0.17	91.54	0.87	94.38	0.93	0.08	47.50	0.45	48.96
Moors	25.16	2.58	50.58	7.87	86.19	6.79	0.70	13.64	2.12	23.25
Malays	9.72	1.39	63.89	4.17	79.17	3.14	0.45	20.63	1.35	25.57
Burghers	3.23	0.0	67.74	0.0	70.97	1.22	0.0	25.61	0.0	26.83
Others	33.33	0.0	66.67	0.0	100.00	10.00	10.00	20.00	0.0	30.00
Total	19.59	1.24	52.95	11.49	85.27	7.45	0.47	20.13	4.37	32.42

Source: Report on Consumer Finance & Socio-Economic Survey 1978/1979 p. 72 Table 56

hand, in the case of Sri Lankan Tamils, it is evident that the few who do earn
have a greater number of individuals to support.
  Q: *What is the unemployment rate for each community?*
  A: Table V gives the figures:

Table V: Unemployment (1979)

Community	Unemployment rate (% of labour force)
Kandyan Sinhalese	13.9
Low country Sinhalese	18.5
Sri Lankan Tamil	10.9
Indian Tamil	5.6
All-island	14.8

Report on Consumer Finance and Socio-Economic Survey 1978/1979
page 82, Table 66).

  Q: *If the Tamils have a low rate of unemployment why are the youth so dissatisfied?*
  A: Though the Tamils have a low unemployment rate on average, The Labour force and Socio Economic survey published by the Ministry of Plan Implementation and the Department of Census and Statistics 1983, show that the unemployment rate among young Tamil males who have passed the G. C. E. A/L Examination is 41 percent while their Sinhalese counterparts suffer an unemployment rate of 29 percent (Page 44). This may help us to understand the phenomenon of the militant youth movement in the North.
  Q: *If Tamils are under-represented in public sector employment, why is their unemployment rate lower?*
  A: This would indicate that Tamils have moved away from employment in the public sector and have had more success in finding employment in the private sector. However, a good deal of this is self-employment, as Table IV shows (27.52 of the labour force in the case of Sri Lankan Tamils is self-employed). Both Jaffna Tamils and Kandyan Sinhalese traditionally engaged in agriculture have a relatively lower rate of unemployment.
  Q: *Can a system of ethnic quotas work in relation to employment outside the public sector?*
  A: Apart from the fact that it would mean again that large numbers of Sinhalese would lose their jobs to Tamils in those sectors where they are overwhelmingly dominant at present (e.g. the Free Trade Zone projects), an ethnic quota would be extremely difficult to enforce in a free economy such as that created under the present government. Further, it has been pointed out that many Tamils, because of the language and other barriers to employment in the public sector, are finding self-employment or setting up their own enterprises. Government interference in these sectors would not only be very difficult but would also be immoral. It would also create further bottlenecks in a nation-wide situation of frustrated aspirations.

Income Levels

Q: *What is the position of the different ethnic communities in respect of income levels?*

A: It is possible to arrive at an approximate answer by taking the income figures in respect of the different geographical zones listed in the Introduction. Table VI gives the figures.

Q: *What do these figures show?*

Table VI

Zone	Without Univ. degrees (OL)	Average income	Without Univ. degrees (AL)
	Rs.	Rs.	Rs.
I	974.62	631	926
II	909.25	713	768
III	888.11	746	903
IV	770.71	512	987
V	1743.20	1137	4986

(Report on Consumer Finance and Socio-Economic Survey, 1978/1979 p. 115 Table 99)

A: The Colombo Municipality has the highest average income level and the predominantly Tamil areas (Zone III) comes next. But averages can be misleading.

Q: *Why?*

A: The high incomes earned by a small percentage of Tamils who have university degrees skew the figures. This is evident if one looks at the average incomes for people with OL and AL qualifications. Here Zone III ranks fourth, in both cases. Again, this may help us understand the militant youth phenomenon in the North.

Education

Q: *That last answer leads one to the subject of education, which has been one of the storm-centres of inter-ethnic controversy. Is it true that Tamils gain admission to the universities in numbers far in excess of their proportions population—wise?*

A: This is not really true. If we look at the total number of admissions, to University, Sinhalese have averaged around 74%. Let us look at the table on admission figures for the last three years—

Q: *What do they show?*

A: Tamil admissions to University have not been over ten percentage points of their ethnic proportion in the population. However these statistics which group Sri Lankan and Indian Tamils together obscure the fact that

Admission Figures 1981–1983

	1981			1982			1983		
	S	T %	O	S	T %	O	S	T %	O
Arts	82.8	13.3	3.9	79.4	16.3	4.3	77.1	16.4	6.6
Physical Science	63.5	31.8	4.7	61.1	33.5	5.5	73.4	23.1	3.6
Biological Science	72.5	24.3	3.2	71.7	26.1	2.2	70.3	23.1	3.6
Engineering	67.2	28.1	4.7	66.9	28.5	4.5	66.4	28.1	5.1
Medicine	72.7	23.1	4.3	72.4	25.3	2.3	72.8	22.1	5.1
Law	73.0	16.2	10.9	68.8	24.0	7.3	78.5	11.5	10.0
Total	76.4	19.2	4.4	74.0	22.0	3.9	75.0	19.3	5.7

Source: (Division of Planning and Research University Grant Commissions 1983)

Indian Tamils are under represented in University education. Nevertheless, the figures run counter to popular perception about Tamil students in the coveted faculties of Medicine, Law and Engineering usually place their participation at 50%. Secondly, what is also intersting is that except for Engineering, the representation of Sinhalese is near their ethic proportion in the population.

Q: *'This is the Truth' and other publications show different figures with a greater concentration of Tamils in Medicine and Law?*

A: Those figures are based on the present composition of the student body. In the years 1978 and 1979 before the District quota was imposed, there was a larger Tamils intake to these faculties. However, these two years have not been representative since the year 1975. (See Appendix B)

Q: *Why then is there a popular impression among Sinhalese that Tamils are privileged in respect of university admissions?*

A: Because in the past, before 1974, in certain coveted university faculties such as medicine, engineering and the physical sciences, there were more Tamils, percentage-wise, in relation to their proportions in the population.

Q: *Weren't these the faculties which matter most?*

A: Yes, in the sense that they are the faculties which matter most to elite groups competing in the fields which are most privileged in respect of status and material rewards. But while this is certainly an important part of the social reality, we must also remember what a small part of the nation is engaged in this race. For a complete picture of opportunities and attainments in education in respect of different ethnic communities, we must look not only at the whole range of university education but also at the totality of education, since university students are themselves only the narrow apex of a broad pyramid. For many people, what happens lower down makes a greater impact on their lives than what happens at the top.

Appendix B: Admission Figures 1975–1980

	1975			1976			1977		
	S	T	O	S	T	O	S	T	O
		%			%			%	
Arts	85.5	10.1	4.4	87.6	8.4	4.0	86.8	9.0	4.3
Physical Science	76.4	20.3	3.3	64.7	31.4	3.9	69.6	26.8	3.0
Biological Science	78.3	18.3	3.7	79.1	18.5	2.4	81.0	16.7	2.3
Engineering	83.4	14.2	2.4	75.0	23.3	1.7	79.5	19.1	1.4
Medicine	78.9	17.5	3.6	65.9	30.4	3.7	68.0	27.8	4.1
Law	75.0	15.4	9.6	63.6	25.5	10.9	86.0	8.0	6.0
Total	82.4	13.7	3.9	80.6	15.7	3.79	81.9	14.4	3.7

	1978			1979			1980		
	S	T	O	S	T	O	S	T	O
		%			%			%	
Arts	83.0	11.3	5.7	80.4	13.8	5.9	82.0	13.7	4.3
Physical Science	73.8	24.1	2.1	65.3	28.9	5.8	71.3	25.2	3.5
Biological Science	54.4	42.8	2.8	67.9	29.3	2.9	78.4	17.5	4.1
Engineering	58.8	36.6	4.7	65.4	30.0	4.6	70.1	29.7	0.2
Medicine	56.6	39.7	3.7	57.8	39.9	2.3	75.3	22.1	2.6
Law	77.8	16.7	5.6	68.9	24.4	6.7	76.1	22.5	1.4
Total	75.9	19.7	4.3	73.6	21.3	5.1	79.2	17.3	3.5

Source: (Division of Planning and Research University Grant Commission 1983)

Q: *But why should Tamil students have fared better in the competition to get into certain faculties?*

A: The limitations on agricultural development placed by the natural conditions of the Jaffna peninsula and the meagre growth of a modern commercial economy led to the fact that for Tamils the main avenue of social mobility was entry into the professions. This led to a high value being placed on education and an intense concentration on the development of educational faculties. This process was helped by the fact that some of the Christian missionary educational bodies took Jaffna as their main area of activity, thus giving Tamils in the north a head-start in this respect. Jaffna was also probably more receptive to missionary education, not only because it was welcome as a means of social advancement but also because there was in Jaffna no strong priestly caste to offer resistance to missionary education, whereas in the South the Buddhist Sangha who had in pre-colonial times been the sole transmitters of education and knowledge, were naturally opposed to the spread of missionary schools.

All these historical and sociological factors combined to give Tamil students certain advantages in competition for entry into those University faculties which were the point of entry to the professions. At present, however, this gap is closing due to concentrated efforts to increase educational facilities in Sinhala areas.

Q: *What about ethnic quotas in this field?*

A: Any such solution would have to be approached very warily in the light of the fact that media-wise standardization between 1970 and 1977 was one of the principal causes of frustration among educated Tamil youth which fueled anti-State violence and the separatist movement.

Q: *What about the allegation that Tamil examiners have cheated?*

A: When the allegations were first made, a Commission of university dons looked into them, in 1970, and resolved that wide-scale cheating was not a possibility and that these allegations were therefore misconceived. In 1979, when the Minister for Industrial and Scientific affairs put forward further allegations, dons at the University of Colombo (both Sinhala and Tamil) demanded a public commission of inquiry into the matter so as to establish the facts in an objective manner. This demand was not acceded to. In the absence of such an inquiry, it is impossible to say whether there have in fact been any cases of false marking in either medium. On the other hand, the slur cast on Tamil examiners as a body, accusing them of cheating on the basis of unproved allegations has done great damage to relations between the two ethnic groups. The 1975 Report of the Sectoral Committee chaired by Pieter Keuneman, a minister in the government which first introduced the policy of media-wise standardisation said that:

> 'Organised manipulation of marks in one whole medium in a deceptive manner is neither possible nor probable, and while the possibilities of correcting examiner variability through standardisation was slight, its contribution both to deepening and indeed institutionalizing suspicion between communities and promoting distrust in the fairness or impartiality of public examinations was considerable.'

Q: *The point was made earlier that the educational opportunities available to and the levels of educational attainment of each ethnic community cannot be judged purely on the basis of figures of university students. What is the total picture?*

A: First, it must be realized that less than 1% of all students get into the universities. To judge a community's educational levels by this minority alone is to ignore the needs and aspirations of the other 99%. In fact, the majority of Jaffna Tamils, like their Sinhala counterparts, have only secondary schooling, and 21.60% have no schooling at all. Table VII gives the figures.

There is a further important fact that emerges from this table—that aggregating educational statistics for Tamils is grossly unfair, to the Indian Tamil community, who are the most underprivileged in respect of education. This in spite of the fact that the labour of Indian Tamil estate workers produce a great part of the wealth on which we all live. Consider in Table VII the illiteracy figures for estate populations (43.58%) and the zero figures of AL qualified undergraduates, and degreed persons. All the agitation against an 'excess' of Tamil students in particular faculties never refers to this fact. Nobody who asks for ethnic quotas in education thinks this principle should apply to Indian Tamils.

Table VII: Percentage of Population Classified According to Educational Status and by Sectors and Zones 1978/79

Educational Status	Urban	Rural	Estate	Zone I	Zone II	Zone III	Zone IV	Zone V	All island
No Schooling (Illiterate)	18.57	22.47	43.58	19.47	25.38	21.60	27.10	19.08	23.40
No Schooling (Literate)	1.09	0.92	1.08	0.67	0.70	2.92	0.83	1.25	0.97
Primary	33.89	39.55	47.39	36.70	42.36	37.22	40.94	32.41	38.92
Secondary	31.80	27.12	6.67	31.04	23.72	25.81	22.81	31.76	26.43
Passed SSC/GCE (OL)	12.38	8.60	1.28	10.23	6.58	11.53	7.24	13.11	8.84
Passed HSC/GCE (AL)	1.35	0.84	0.0	1.19	0.64	0.79	0.66	1.36	0.88
Under- graduate	0.18	0.14	0.0	0.21	0.12	0.05	0.10	0.16	0.14
Passed Degree	0.60	0.29	0.0	0.36	0.42	0.18	0.30	0.65	0.34
Other	0.14	0.07	0.0	0.13	0.08	0.10	0.02	0.22	0.08
Total	100	100	100	100	100	100	100	100	100

(Report on Consumer Finance and Socio-Economic Survey 1978/79
p. 28 Table 15)
(Note Zone I and Zone V have better literacy figures)

Q: *Is it possible to measure in some way the general level of educational attainment among each ethnic community?*
A: This is done through the Index of Education attainment. The figures for 1978/79 show that it is the low country Sinhalese who have a better educational level than the Sri Lanka Tamils, and that the Indian Tamils rank lowest in the scale.

Table VIII: Index of Education Attainment

Kandyan Sinhalese	4.40
Low country Sinhalese	5.26
Sri Lankan Tamils	4.94
Indian Tamils	2.10
Moors	3.91
Malays	5.48
Burghers	6.44
Others	6.50

(Source: Report on Consumer Finance and Socio-Economic Survey, 1978/79)

Agriculture

Q: *Since for most people in this country, farming is still the major source of livelihood, it would be good to take a look at agriculture. How do the different ethnic communities fare in this respect?*

A: Let's start with this fact. Most of the farming in Sri Lanka is carried out in the Dry Zone, and the critical resource needed for farming in the Dry Zone is water. To ensure an adequate water supply, irrigation is of paramount importance. Recognizing this fact, successive governments have invested heavily on irrigation in the Dry Zone. The Mahaveli project is the most important of the commitments made to farming and irrigation. However, the Dry Zone Tamil areas lag behind, and appear to have been neglected. This is brought out able IX, which shows the extent of land irrigate in key Sinhala and Tamil farming areas in the Dry Zone.

Table IX: Land Size and Percentages of Sown Land Irrigated in the Dry Zone (Maha 1979/80)

Sinhala districts	Percentage irrigated	Average size of holding
Puttalam	79.7	3.4
Moneragala	63.2	3.9
Anuradhapura	92.7	4.1
Polonnaruwa	95.3	4.0
Hambantota	92.5	3.0

Tamil districts	Percentage irrigated	Average size of holding
Jaffna	31.6	1.3
Vavuniya	83.4	5.7
Mannar	94.7	3.7
Trincomalee	56.6	3.1
Batticaloa	30.4	2.7

(Department of Census & Statistics. Ministry of Plan, Implementations, Socio-Economic, Indicators of Sri Lanka, February 1983, p. 232/p. 102)

Q: *What does this table show?*

A: That except for the Mannar District the other Tamil areas have had much scantier irrigation facilities than the Sinhala areas.

Q: *What is the relevance of the figures indicating average size of land-holding?*

A: Their significance comes out when you set them side by side with the figures in Table X, which shows the percentage of fallow (unutilised) agricultural land in each zone. When considering the lack of irrigation, it is not surprising that the proportion of land left uncultivated is highest in zone III, that is, the Tamil areas of the North, despite the fact that the average size of landholding is smallest in the Jaffna district.

Table X: Unutilised Agricultural Land (1978/79)

Zone	Percentage of fallow land
I	10.3
II	11.8
III	20.6
IV	14.5
V	13.8
All island	13.7

(Report on Consumer Finance and Socio-Economic Survey, 1978/79 p. 49 Table 33)

Q: *Is true that Sinhalese cannot buy land in Jaffna?*
A: That is completely false. Muslims, Burghers and Sinhalese have in fact bought land in Jaffna.

Q: *Then why is there a popular perception that Sinhalese cannot buy land in Jaffna?*
A: Under the Thesawalamai, there is a concept of pre-emption under which co-owners, co-heirs and adjacent landowners—who had a mortgage over property located in the Northern province—have the first option of purchase. It is not racial exclusion but an exclusion peculiar to the nature of an agricultural community. Today in fact the owner only need give notice before selling in the open market. It must be remembered that the Roman-Dutch law also entertains a similar concept.

Q: *What is the Thesawalamai?*
A: The Thesawalamai like the traditional laws of the Kandyan Sinhalese is a system of customary law which existed before the colonial era and is applicable to all persons who are "Malabar Inhabitants of the Province of Jaffna."

Q: *Why are there so few Sinhalese settled in the Northern Province in recent years?*
A: Migratory patterns in Sri Lanka have pushed members of all communities who wish to better their prospects to the cities such as Colombo and its vicinity. Besides, land in Jaffna is relatively unfertile and would not have attracted migrants interested in an agricultural livelihood. It could be argued that the paucity of Sinhalese settlers in the Northern province exists for the same reason why there is a paucity of Tamils settlers in Hambantota. (See Appendix C)

Central Government Capital Expenditure

Q: *There is an impression that the Jaffna District is specially favoured with regard to Government capital expenditure. Is this correct?*
A: No. In the District Budget for the year 1982, the amount allocated to the Jaffna District for new works is only Rs. 27 million. This shows up the

smallness of the District Budget and its very limited capacity to spear-head decentralised development.

In the case of the Central Budget, an analysis of the figures in the Ministry of Plan Implementation Performance, 1981, shows that capital expenditure in the Jaffna District was only Rs. 260 million—that is, only 2.6% of the national capital expenditure of nine billion rupees.

Q: *How does this work out in terms of per capita expenditure?*

A: The per capita capital expenditure in the Jaffna District is Rs. 313, while the national per capita expenditure is Rs. 656. In addition, foreign aid utilisation in the Jaffna District for the period 1977–82 was 0.

(Sources: Analysis from Ministry of Plan Implementation Performance, 1981; Central Bank Review of the Economy, 1981; Government Budget Estimates, 1981).

Q: *Aren't these figures of per capita expenditure affected by the fact that national expenditure on special projects such as the Mahaveli, Housing and the Free Trade Zone are targeted for certain areas and none of them are located in the North?*

A: That is so, and for the same reason, other areas unaffected by such projects—such as Galle or Kalutara—show figures similar to those of Jaffna. Also Jaffna District has been unrepresented in successive governments, and therefore has benefited little from Government development policy. However, what the figures do show is that the Jaffna District is clearly not a most favoured district, as some people have tried to make out.

The Private Sector

Q: *There is an impression that the private sector of the economy is dominated by Tamil interests? Is this correct?*

A: In the large public quoted companies there is a diversity of shareholders, interlocking directorates, bank indentures etc. The large industrial houses are not and cannot be run like corner boutiques with a single proprietor making lone profits. The interconnections between different interests are still more difficult to ascertain today because of increasing foreign investment. However, as far as predominantly Sinhala-owned or Tamil-owned enterprises are concerned, the Gnanams and Maharajahs are surely matched by the Upali Group, Dasa Group, B. P. de Silva Group, Maliban Group, Nawaloka enterprises, Ebert Silva, De Soysa's Associated Industries, Wijewardene's Group etc.

Q: *Are the sources of credit for business controlled by Tamil interests?*

A: No. The main sources of credit are the banks. The Bank of Ceylon, the People's Bank, the State Mortgage and Investment Bank, the Development Finance Corporation, etc. are state enterprises. The primary shareholders of the Hatton National Bank are Browns Ltd., a company with a majority of Sinhala shareholders. All other banks are controlled by foreign shareholders with foreign managing directors who assess projects on viability alone.

Q: *What explains the fact that trade and business have been one of the main avenues of social advancement for Tamils?*

A: The Tamils were never large landowners or estate owners like the Sinhala upper classes. Only a handful were affected by land reform. The most lucrative export sector of tea, coconut, and rubber even before nationalisation, was never dominated by Tamils. It has been observed in many societies that those who do not hold land tend to go into professions and business. The Tamils as an ethnic group have followed this path, like many ethnic groups before them in Europe, Asia and Africa. There is nothing sinister, deceptive or exploitative about this: it is an understandable social phenomenon.

Q: *Are there any published statistics of the Ethnic Composition of directors and proprietors in private sector companies?*

A: No, but an analysis the Commercial Company list in Ferguson's Directory 1981–1983 (pages 1201–1249) shows that 20.45% of Directors, 21.16% of Chairmen, 17.65% of Partners/Proprietors in these companies are Tamil. This proportion does not significantly exceed their proportion of the national population.

Q: *Why should Sinhalese not overreact to statistics?*

A: The recent agitation over statistics on Tamil dominance avoids one inescapable fact. At present the Sinhalese are in **absolute** control of the national legislature and therefore in absolute control of national economic policy. Very few Tamils can receive jobs through state patronage, they can only succeed in private self-employment or in the professions. With control over national economic policy the Sinhalese have the absolute power to direct the course of our economic future. Statistics and social figures can be managed and changed over time, to maximize opportunities for all communities. The inability to do so is not the diabolical plot of an ethnic minority but the failure of our political leaders to direct and manage a modern, equitable economy.

Political Violence

Q: *Everybody knows that all this violence is really the natural result of the Separatist cry and the Terrorist movement in the North?*

A: That is to some extent an oversimplification. Though these movements have accentuated the crisis, our problems are much deeper. In 1958, the Tamils did not ask for a separate state and only used non-violent tactics but violence was directed against them. At that time, they were asking for language rights and federalism and even with that cry the Sinhalese felt their national identity was threatened. If we are to truly understand our predicament, the national state must also bear its share of responsibility for the accelerating crisis in the North. We must also try to understand the social and historical reasons which gave rise to the above movements if we are to find an effective political solution. We must learn not to give into a blind sense of loyalty without a rational and historical appreciation of the facts.

Q: *The violence of the State organs has always been a response to the violence of the Northern Terrorist.*

A: This is not entirely correct. As far back as 1961, forces were sent to Jaffna. In 1972 Amnesty International reported the arrest and detention without trial of 42 young members of the Tamil community who were staging peaceful protests, such as the display of black flags against the policy of standardisation and the Republican Constitution. Annual reports from Amnesty International and the ICJ from 1976 detail torture inflicted on Tamil youths held in detention. In January 1974, police used force against the crowd at the scene of a Tamil cultural show held at the closing sessions of the prestigious conference of the International Association of Tamil Research. Eight persons died. Though the magisterial inquiry exonerated the police, an unofficial commision of inquiry came to a different conclusion. In any event a full fair and independent inquiry was not held. The use of force by the police at a prestigious international conference of Tamil scholars only accentuated Tamil perceptions of injustice. It was after 1977 that Tamil youths began their systematic campaign of violence. At present of course the situation is far more complex and it is difficult to assess cause and effect, in the increasing cycle of violence and destruction.

Q: *Are your trying to justify the violence of the Northern militants?*

A: No. As a Committee which wishes to strengthen rational and democratic processes we are opposed to violence. At the same time we must look at the accelerating crisis with fairness and impartiality, especially since our media continues to give us only one side of the question. The present situation is a result of many complex factors. It is often difficult to separate cause and effect. Unless we look at the issues with clearsightedness, we will not be able to provide the social and political solutions necessary for the resolution of the present conflict.

Q: *But they, the Tamils are trying to destory us, how can you be so calm and detached? We Sinhalese have no-where else to go, this is our only home.*

A: If we feel we are an united nation, there can be no question of "we" or "they." Justice is not only supposed to be rational but **race** blind. If we continue to think in terms of "we" and "they" we will turn the present conflict into a savage tribal war. Those who over-react to problems and thereby destablize the country and the region, will create the very nightmares they so desperately fear.

Decentralisation

Q: *Why are the Sinhalese so afraid of conceding regional autonomy to Tamil dominated areas?*

A: Because they are afraid that this will be a first step toward Eelam.

Q. *Is their fear justified?*

A: No, in other countries this has not always occured. In fact most often the issue subsides. With greater regional autonomy, the Quebec nationalists, the Basque nationalists and even Tamil Nadu nationalists have begun to work within the framework of a united state.

Q: *Will the northern extremists be satisfied?*

A: Even if they are not, a solution agreed to by a moderate majority in Jaffna and supported by the Indian government will alienate the users of violence from their own people. This occurred in Quebec and is now happening in the Basque region of Spain. After a period of amnesty, with the help of the Indian government through extradition agreements and the like, it will be easier to control their violent activities.

Q: *Why do you envision a role for the Indian Government in solving our problem? What business is it of India's to interfere in Sri Lankan Affairs?*

A: Let us look at India's possible role in a different and more constructive light. The Indian government is the only factor which can influence the TULF and other Tamil political parties to give up their demand for a separate state. Mrs. Gandhi has categorically stated that she stands for an united Sri Lanka. If the problem of extremist violence persists even after a political solution is implemented it will be necessary to get the assistance of the Indian government to overcome the problems. Elements within the Indian government have already expressed fears about a revival of Tamil Nadu nationalism as a result of recent events. It is in India's self-interest to help Sri Lanka resolve the current crisis not only for political stability but for strategic reasons as well. Instead of being paralysed by a historical sense of fear we should attempt to maximize the opportunities afforded by our government's acceptance of India's offer of good offices.

Q: *Aren't these "decentralisation" ideas new to Sri Lanka?*

A: Actually these ideas have been circulated since the beginning of the twentieth century. In 1925, SWRD Bandaranaike himself, put forward a federal structure of government for Sri Lanka with nine separate regional units. Before him the Kandyan leaders in the Ceylon Congress also put forward ideas for a federal structure consisting of three units. In 1940, the colonial government introduced Provincial Councils but though approved in Parliament they were not implemented.

Q: *Have any of the major Sinhalese parties after independence ever entertained such a scheme?*

A: Both the UNP and the SLFP had before 1977 negotiated decentralised arrangements but failed to implement them. The Bandaranaike-Chelvanayagam Pact for example agreed to the creation of two or more decentralised regions and allowed room for parliament to delegate powers in certain areas. It was a very comprehensive Federal solution. The UNP in 1965 also concluded a fairly similar Pact but it too was not implemented.

Q: *Why aren't the Tamils satisfied with the DDC scheme?*

A: The DDC scheme, in some ways, falls short of the other Pacts for the following reasons:

a) The District Minister, an appointment of the President—is chairman of the Executive Committee and can block all decisions of the DDC, if he chooses to.

b) The Line Ministries must approve all projects of the DDC, in their area. As we all know, ministers jealously guard their preserves and do not often like to share power and control.

c) The District Budget so far has been very small, 40 million for both old and new works for each District. Considering the wide range of projects that the DDC's may wish to engage in, the budget so far has completely limited their scope.

d) Any decision agreed to by the DDC can be overridden by a simple majority in Parliament, in addition the President also has the power to remove and appoint members of the Executive Committee.

e) The DDC is only statutory legislation and has no constitutional validity. It can easily be swept away by a simple majority vote in Parliament. The DDC's then are mere administrative arrangements vulnerable to the contradictory personalities of ministers and the sudden shifts of presidential and Parliamentary power.

Q: *What kind of schemes do other countries have?*

A: In most democratic countries with an ethnic minority which is territorially placed, decentralisation has been the political answer. In addition, for administrative reasons, countries prefer to have a decentralized political structure for effective planning and diverse development. In India, US, Australia, Canada etc . . . the federal system gives much power to the decentralised units. These units have their own courts, own executive, own legislature, and the federal government can only interfere in situations of national concern such as foreign policy, interstate commerce, defense, currency, taxation, immigration, protection of fundamental rights, the national development plan etc. Except in these specified instances, the decentralised units may govern themselves though they may look to the Central Government for additional financial resources and projects. In other countries of Europe, France, Spain, Federal Republic of Germany—similar arrangements exist.

Q: *Aren't those large countries? Isn't Sri Lanka far too small for this type of arrangement?*

A: No, we have before us the example of Switzerland. In tourist literature we are often called the Switzerland of the East.

Q: *What is the Swiss solution like?*

A: The Swiss system has some of the following features:

a) A federal system composed of 22 cantons—each with its own elected Legislature and Executive.

b) The cantons, commune have extensive spending & taxing powers. In addition the cantons have legislative powers within their area of jurisdiction.

c) Each canton has its own Constitution and its own system of courts but with a superceding Federal Court to determine issues of national importance—or inter-cantonal disputes.

d) Though there are certain national standards, each canton has its own system of schools and Universities.

e) The Federal Legislature itself contains two houses—the first is like our Parliament and called the National Council, the second contains two representatives from each canton and is called the Council of States.

f) The Federal Assembly only has certain specified legislative powers in the Constitution, all residual powers vest with the cantons. The Federal powers are related to defense, posts, army, national economic policy, foreign policy, currency etc . . .

g) The Swiss Constitution recognizes three official languages—German, French & Italian. All cantons also have an enlightened policy of extending official recognition to all the spoken languages.

h) Religion—the people of each canton are free to determine the nature of state-religions relations. This is due to the fact that there is a large non-Catholic minority in Switzerland.

i) Each canton is also responsible for public order within it's boundaries—own police force and public service.

Q: *Isn't that too much for Sri Lanka?*

A: We don't have to adopt their model completely but just learn from their example. Switzerland is a country where modern leaders from traditionally warring communities have managed to negotiate an enlightened settlement.

Q: *Isn't all this too risky and uncertain, why should we even begin to think in this manner?*

A: We stand at the cross-roads of history. We can either become the Switzerland of the East by following the middle path of negotiation, conciliation and goodwill or the Lebanon of South Asia where intransigence, violence and hate have made it a playground for destruction in which all the powers of the world have a stake.

Appendix A: Ethnic Breakdown—North & East

NORTH	Total	Sinhalese	Tamils	Moors	Indians	Others
Jaffna	831,112	4,615	792,246	13,757	20,001	493
Mannar	106,940	8,710	54,106	28,464	14,072	1,588
Vavuniya	95,904	15,876	54,541	6,640	18,592	255
Mullaitivu	77,512	3,948	58,904	3,777	10,766	117
	1,111,468	33,149	959,797	52,638	63,431	2,453
		2.98%	86.35%	4.73%	5.71%	.23%
EAST						
Batticaloa	330,899	10,646	234,348	79,317	3,868	2,720
Amparai	388,786	146,371	78,315	161,481	1,410	1,209
Trincomalee	256,790	86,341	86,743	74,304	6,767	2,536
	976,475	243,358	399,406	315,201	12,045	6,465
		24.92%	40.90%	32.28%	1.24%	.66%
OVERALL TOTAL						
	2,087,943	276,507	1,359,203	367,839	75,476	8,918
		13.24%	65.10%	17.62%	3.61%	.43%

(From Census of Population and Housing 1981)

Appendix C: The Percentage Ethnic Breakdown in the Jaffna District and Hambantota District over Time

	1921	1946	1971	1981
JAFFNA				
Sinhalese	.32%	1.1%	2.9%	.6%
Tamils	98.24%	97.3%	95.5%	97.7%
HAMBANTOTA				
Sinhalese	96.17%	96.6%	97.1%	97.4%
Tamils	.86%	1%	.6%	.5%

Source: Census of Bureau of Statistics Population Surveys 1921, 1946, 1971, 1981.

The Colombo district must of course be dealt with separately since it is the capital of the country and capitals throughout the world are cosmopolitan in character and composition. The Nuwara-Eliya District must also be regarded differently because of the plantation sector, and the presence of Tamil estate workers.

APPENDIX 4:
REPORT MADE TO THE UNITED RELIGIOUS ORGANIZATION, 25 JULY 1984

The following is the main text (minus the affidavits of certain witnesses) of the report written by a group of leaders, both clerical and lay, who visited Jaffna and Trincomalee and other parts of the Tamil north and east. On their way from Colombo to Jaffna, the team stopped over at Kegalle, Kurunegala, and Anurādhapura. They visited many sites and interviewed many persons, both lay and religious, and presented their report to the United Religious Organization, which represents all four religions: Buddhism, Christianity, Hinduism, and Islam.

The leader of the URO team on the "Journey for Harmony" was Father Tissa Balasuriya of Colombo. The other members were Venerable Rakupola Ananda Nayake Thero of Kuliyapitiya, Venerable Weerambuwe Vinala Bharathi Thero of Jaffna, Venerable Gnanaratne Thero of Kurunegala, Bishop Andrew Kumarage of Kurunegala, Reverend Udeni de Silva of Kurunegala, Father Paul Caspers of Kandy, Mrs. Millicent Loyola of Colombo, and Mrs. Sriyani Perera of Colombo. All members of this team (except one) were Sinhalese, and they subscribed to the Buddhist and Christian faiths. Three of them were Buddhist monks.

The Itinerary of the URO Team

The team arrived in Jaffna by the inter-city train on 16 July, and were put up at the bishop's house. The women were lodged at the Holy Family Convent and with relatives.

7/16, afternoon:	Meeting with an inter-religious group.
7/17, morning:	Continued meeting with inter-religious group, and afterwards meeting with Tamil Refugee Rehabilitation Organisation.
Afternoon:	Visit to a fishing village.
4:00 P.M.:	Visit to a Muslim center.

167

7/18, morning:	Visits to Nāga Vihare, Sinhala Mahā Vidyālaya, Our Lady of Refugee Church, and other sites in the town; and to the Home of Human Rights.
9:00 A.M.:	University of Jaffna.
11:00 A.M.:	Divine Life Society Centre for a Hindu service and lunch.
3:00 P.M.:	Public Meeting at Divine Life Society Centre.
5:00 P.M.:	Meeting with Citizens' at the bishop's house.
7/19, morning:	Left by private van for Anurādhapura; visit en route to Kilinochchi and Murugandi refugee settlement; arrived by noon at Anurādhapura.
3:00 P.M.:	Public meeting at International Buddhist Library; URO section set up for Anurādhapura.
7/20, morning:	Left for Trincomalee by van; visit to Welgamvehera Rājamahā Viharaya.
10:00 A.M.:	Arrival in Trincomalee; reception at Jayasumanarama Temple Bodhi Pooja and prayers of all religions. Afternoon from 2:30 P.M.: Meeting of small groups.
2:30–3:30 P.M.:	Hindu Delegation.
3:30–4:00 P.M.:	Muslim Delegation.
4:00–4:30 P.M.:	Christian Delegation.
4:30–5:00 P.M.:	Buddhist Delegation.
5:00–7:30 P.M.:	Public meeting in the Town Hall.
7:30–8:30 P.M.:	Session with small Muslim group and with Hindu group.
7/21, morning:	Return by train to Colombo.

The Report

The atmosphere in Kegalle, Kurunegala and Anurādhapura was calm and quite different from those in the Northern Province and Trincomalee where there was much tension, insecurity and fear.

In Jaffna and Trincomalee

We met with persons of different social strata and of all the four religions during the short time of our stay. We did not meet the youth militants or the military. The former cannot be met as they are underground and a proscribed group. The Brigadier in Charge of the security forces was away in Colombo and so we could not meet him. Our views are therefore those obtained from ordinary citizens who are non-combatants in this situation of undeclared war.

Fear

Fear and lack of confidence were the two sentiments most consistently and strongly expressed by the groups we met in Jaffna Peninsula, Kilinochchi and Trincomalee. They fear the presence of the armed services whom they see going about fully armed and with their fingers at the trigger. These service men, though themselves so armed, lived in constant fear of instant annihilation by some ambush as in July 1983. People in general fear that the armed services, provoked by an attack on them by the militant youth, will again run amok and indiscriminately attack them and their houses.

They fear that their male children between the ages of 15–30 may be taken into custody on suspicion or in retaliation against attacks by militants whom they cannot apprehend. Sometimes when a youth sought is not at home, his brother or close relative is taken in as ransom. It is alleged that youth taken into custody have been made to undergo torture or threatened with torture to obtain denunciations of other youth. Sometimes the youths are asked for the names and addresses of their friends and their friends are then apprehended. Recently a blindfolded youth had to identify "terrorists" at a mass parade of people rounded up in a public place. The people in the North and East feel that their young people are harassed for no other reason than that they are Tamil and young and are therefore suspected of being linked in some way to the underground militants. Even elderly persons complained of undue humiliation during such large-scale public investigations which the media term mopping-up operations to flush out "terrorists."

The poor fisherman of the North are rife with resentment, less at the Surveillance Zone, which has destroyed the fishing economy, than at the unrestrained abuse of power that takes place even within that zone. Their situation makes them ask how long can their boats be rammed, their nets costing thousands of rupees cut, the best of their catch confiscated, their fuel tanks emptied in high seas, their identity cards tossed into the sea, their persons assaulted without alienating them totally from the State?

Fear is the most debilitating emotion. People live in constant fear of death, and loss of all their property and savings. The armed services are the main agents of such attacks on the people at large. The youth militants on the other hand attack specific military targets and persons considered informants or social miscreants. They generally warn such persons and leave a charge sheet near the bodies of the persons slain by them. The attacks by youth militants receive large scale media coverage, without much censorship. But the main attacks on the Tamil population by the armed services do not get such publicity. Hence there is much public resentment in the South against the Northern militants, but ignorance of the suffering of the people at the hands of the armed services.

In either case there is no just legal process that can satisfy fair-minded people. The militants are under no law, the military have been given powers under the law to dispose of bodies of persons shot dead by them in their efforts to combat "terrorism." The fear of the militants and the military of attack by the other increases their tension and that of the citizen body in these areas.

The delegation of the URO sought to ascertain the number of youths and other persons thus taken in during the course of 1984. No one was ready even to hazard a definite estimate, but several said the number must be counted in hundreds. This lack of information adds to the people's fear and sense of hurt. The number detained maybe less than is imagined. Sometimes those who have left their homes to join the militants may also be presumed to be under detention. The parents and relatives thus live under great tension and apprehension. Only the State can allay anxieties and give the correct answer. The delegation therefore appeals to the State to provide lists of persons taken in, the date, cause and place of their arrest and subsequent detention.

Tamil Refugee and Rehabilitation Problems— Jaffna and Trincomalee

A. The Jaffna team was met by the Chairman of the Tamil Refugee and Rehabilitation Organisation (TRRO) Mr. K. Visvalingam. He outlined the problems of the Tamils displaced by ethnic disturbances both in 1977 and in 1983.

The TRRO had established small industries for the rehabilitation of families in their care. These families could not be settled permanently as no land was available. All available land was Crown land.

Displaced persons in Welfare Centres had the option of taking an inducement allowance and leaving the Centre. Such persons could not be readmitted to a Welfare Centre, nor could they qualify for land settlement in the Northern and Eastern provinces. When they arrived in Jaffna, for instance, and found that they had no means of sustenance the TRRO was being taxed for relief. It was essential that the URO represent refugee needs and request the government to alienate some land for the relocation of refugees.

B. The Government issued 24 permits to the *Trinco Development Association* to build huts. The permits were issued on a basis of annual revalidation. 15 more huts were built on private land. Some of these permits were not renewed, through oversight or ignorance. On 5th July, the Army and Navy levelled 39 huts irrespective of whether the landholders were entitled to be there or not. Now these refugees were squatting on unauthorised land causing new problems.

C. *The Kilinochchi Welfare Centres* were administered by the Social Services Department along with the good offices of the Parish Priest of Kilinochchi. The team's visit to one of these Centres was met with tales of looting, arson and physical violence in their home areas. The Parish also overlooked a settlement of refugee families of 1977. This settlement had a grave need of water. The required funds could be obtained but the permits to dig wells, although repeatedly requested, were not forthcoming.

The refugees from the 1983 violence live in huts in very precarious conditions without any income or employment.

March–April 1984

In April of this year, Jaffna was filled with greater dread than usual. Men, young and old, who left for market or to their work-places did not return home. Shooting was heard, curfew was declared and yet the shooting did not stop. When the curfew was lifted charred bodies were found on the roadside. Over 50 persons never returned home. In the South it was reported that these same events reflected a success of the armed forces over "terrorists." It is in a situation like this that those who take up arms against the State win the sympathy of the people and grow in numbers. An oppressed people tends to support them. A mentality of resistance to the state that includes all the people is likely to grow. After an ambush attack on a service vehicle, the Church of Our Lady of the Refuge in Jaffna, and the Cooperative Society were particular targets of the military. Others in retaliation attacked the Naga Vihare and the Sinhala Mahā Vidyālaya. The services attacked people at random in the city centre.

Along with this fear, a *lack of confidence* in the rulers and in the majority Sinhala people is growing in the minds of the Tamil people. They are becoming increasingly conscious of being an unprotected minority that has been subjected to blind and merciless murder, arson and loot during two generations. 1956 and 1958 are recalled as sad and tragic memories. Since 1977 it is an almost regular litany of woes: August 1977, 1979, 1981, May–August 1983 and March–April 1984.

When and where will the next outburst be is the ominous question. They feel that others who are not Tamil do not understand their feeling of vulnerability, helplessness, powerlessness, and defencelessness. They are being reduced to a state of desperate hopelessness. In this situation their resourceful youth militants appear to them as their only safeguard against the violence of the armed services. To them these are their "boys" who are sacrificing their life for their future as a people.

The collapse of the forms and norms of democratic rule has rendered the people of the North utterly voiceless in the Councils of the State. Their representatives have been excluded from Parliament for over a year. District Councils and the Municipal Council of Jaffna have ceased to function. Village Councils are non-existent. This is worsened by their understanding of recent history as a series of breakdowns in political negotiations due to promises broken by successive Sinhala dominated Governments.

They have no one to whom to turn in their distress. Hence they turn to India where the roots of the culture of all our peoples lie. They are being pushed towards South India by the failure to respond to their desires for political rights and to their pleas for security of life itself. Over 30,000 of them have fled to India so that their lives may be safe. The 35,000–40,000 refugees from the Estates now in the Kilinochchi area feel utterly neglected by the State which should care for them.

Resignation to Resistance?

In this helpless and sad situation without hope most people in the North still express a desire for a united, peaceful and just Sri Lanka in which they can live with dignity and security. However day by day the number of such people seems to be decreasing.

Many are resigned to a fate they cannot control. They seek safety of life and possessions and leave home only on essential tasks. Usually they are home from dusk to dawn. When a child does not come home after school, when the police do not know his whereabouts, and not even the G. A. can help, to whom are parents to appeal to? To go to the armed forces is a risky and difficult task. The Courts of Law have hardly any jurisdiction over security activities in this area of virtual martial law or undeclared war. Resignation is sometimes coupled with indignation at this sorry state of affairs. They are unable to wean away either the State military or their militant youth from the widening armed struggle.

Resistance is the response of the youth militants. Both boys and girls tend to share this mood. The hopelessness of their people leads them to the violence of the underground resistance. We were told by the university students they have the impression that the gun is the only power to which the rulers give heed. They seem deaf to all other pleas. It must also be understood that many of the older people also feel that resistance seems to be the only way—given the absence of any meaningful response from the powers that be.

The basic situation in these areas is that there is:

—no peace, no security of life
—no inquiry into death and destruction caused by the military
—no compensation for such damage to innocent persons by agents of the State
—the militants cannot be controlled or convinced to be peaceful
—no representatives of the people
—no one to complain to in case of loss of life, a person kidnapped, abducted or detained.

The people are like orphans with no representatives of the people. As a 64 year old retired Government servant from Atchuvely lamented after being injured by a gun shot. "I do not understand why the armed forces should be allowed to shoot around at innocent people so wantonly and with such impunity."

Growing Divisions

Man-made barricades and the massive presence of the armed forces in some parts cannot detract from the geographical unity of the whole that nature conferred upon this island. But for more than the 200-odd miles that separate the north from the south it is *the conflicting perceptions* that exist in the minds of Sinhalese and Tamils, and the destructive actions these lead to, that are dividing Sri Lanka as surely as they have divided other countries.

Divisive thoughts and actions, however, do not arise because people are intrinsically divisive or bent on destruction. They arise because people lack the ability to put themselves into the other's position when they are ignorant of facts. Thus, though neighbours and kinsmen, the Sinhalese and Tamils are strangers to each others' problems and sorrows. The gap that separates the Sinhalese and Tamil brethren of this country can be seen most clearly in their conflicting ways of looking, for instance at the practice of democracy, violence and the role of the clergy in particular of the Buddhist Sangha, to mention the most pertinent factors in the present crisis.

Democracy, the rule of the people, has been precious to Sri Lankans who turn out in numbers unparalleled in the world to cast their vote with free will and elect a government of their choice. Thus, it is a national tragedy that the Tamil people of the North and East believe that they are ruled, with no reference to their wishes, by a Sinhalese majority who can change or keep governments while they cannot change their MPs. This is what the referendum showed to them.

Instead of civilian rule by their elected representatives the people of the North and East are under *military rule*. The chief representative of the State in the North is the army Brigadier; in the East it is the Navy Commodore. In 1971 the revolting Sinhala heartland was under military rule for a relatively short period. Yet many thousands died among whom were an unknown number of innocents. In the North and East military rule and the violence directed against it is protracted and bitter. It has been escalating in a sad spiral of violence during a decade since 1974.

Few men are capable of wielding power justly and with restraints. These few are men of rare calibre. Few of those who join the military are such men. The virtual all-Sinhalese nature of the military contributes a communal flavour to the power that corrupts. Power may well flow from the barrel of the gun, but the gun alone can never bring about peace with justice which is the cornerstone of democracy for all.

A Way to National Harmony: A Just Political Solution

Among the Tamils of the North and East there is a sense of togetherness of people in opposition to the State. What is taking place today in the North and East is essentially not a conflict between Sinhalese and Tamils, but an unorganized movement of resistance against the State in which all Tamils virtually are involved. The idea of resistance to the State and its armed forces takes precedence over such communal slogans as Eelam at the present time.

When the killing of policemen and politicians, incidentally all of whom were Tamil first took place the great majority of the Tamils opposed the actions of the militants. But today, in a situation in which they are politically voiceless and militarily defenceless confronted by the armed power of the state, for better or for worse, they look upon those whom we in the South call "terrorists" as their protectors, their "boys." What we in the South are informed is the murder of Harijans, the people of the North say is the elimination of known criminals who use the unsettled conditions to prey on the people.

Acts of violence against the State must stop. But it is only a *just political solution* acceptable to the people of the North and East that will possess the power to isolate, and rid society of, the true terrorist who kills for a cause that is rejected by the people themselves. A just solution in the context of a united country would be welcomed, even at this late stage, by the people. At present the use of the armed power of the State to enforce a solution on a hostile populace has only served to bring about an unhappy union of "terrorists" and those who struggle for a cause that is supported by the great majority of the Tamil people of the North and East.

Where in a communally divided society the resistance of one section to the State has grown to the extent it has in this country, *a limited political autonomy* under a central government has proved, in other parts of the world to be the major part of the solution. This was the case in Canada, Spain, Sudan and Belgium to name but a few countries that were threatened with similar conflict. A limited political autonomy is important because it ensures in a communally divided society that citizens belonging to minority communities enjoy equal rights, in theory as well as practice, to share in the political power that is necessary to obtain employment, education and land. Here it must be noted and emphasised that such a limited political autonomy is not the precursor to separation. *Never been so.* If it did then countries such as the above mentioned four, and many others such as Finland, Yugoslavia and Malaysia would be on the way to division which is not the reality.

Such a political autonomy means greater scope for democracy. It means that if a village wants tube wells instead of a conference hall it can say so to government officials whose offices are 10 miles away instead of 200. It means that if there is an abuse of power those with the capacity to remedy the situation are close at hand. It means that the elected representatives of the people have power to assist their constituents and are readily accessible to them. It means that people look after the affairs of their own areas while the central government looks after those affairs that the concern the entire country.

Thus while sectoral authorities have control over education, law courts, law and order economic development and cultural affairs in their own areas, the central government will have full control over foreign affairs (aid, trade and embassies), immigration and emigration, the Central Bank, the issue of currency notes and postage stamps, the Supreme Court and the defence of the country.

The areas that are to have autonomy would best be decided by the people of the districts themselves in a democratic manner such as by means of district-wise referendums.

It is because so little is known about what limited political autonomy means that fanciful fears are easily aroused. In countries threatened by separatist movements and violence (Canada, Sudan and Spain for example) methods of political autonomy have helped to diffuse the crises and restored communal harmony. In no country in the world has the granting of such limited political autonomy led to separation against the wishes of the state. However, countries that denied such autonomy to dissatisfied territorial groups have ended up being partitioned (e.g. Ireland in 1920, Pakistan in 1971 and Cyprus in 1983).

The leaders of the religious and citizens groups that we met in Jaffna stressed the urgent need of a political solution. For it is not possible they said even with the goodwill of the rulers and the military commanders, to prevent such outrageous excesses of the army against innocent persons of all ages—both men and women—as occurred in May–July 1983 and March–April 1984.

The message of history is a compelling one to be ignored at great risk by those whose resolute desire is a united country. The equally compelling message of the great religious stresses the ceaseless operation of the law of cause and effect. The way we set about resolving our national problem, whether with minds and compassion or with guns and hatred, as much as the content of that solution, will determine not only the future of Sinhalese-Tamil relations but also the character of our people as human beings and of our civilization.

The Task of the Religions

In the North and in Trincomalee there was great interest in the work of the URO. Some, however were sceptical about the goodwill of religious leaders or of their ability to influence the course of events. Some thought the URO was one more Government sponsored agency to soften the resistance of the Tamil people to injustice.

We encountered some lack of confidence concerning the clergy, in particular the members of the Sangha. There were misgivings in the minds of some due to stories concerning the manner in which some members of the Sangha are reported to have related to the events of July 1983. They were not aware that the great majority of the Buddhist monks, specially the Mahanayake Theras unequivocally condemned the July violence and that many Tamil families found refuge in Buddhist temples. Several monks went out on to the streets to calm the people. The Tamil people are now becoming aware that the members of the Sangha are in the forefront of those who want a peaceful solution that ensures justice and security to the all. The numerous URO meetings are helping in this process of communication and confidence building.

Many of those whom we met in Jaffna and Trincomalee expressed that the doctrines of the four religions present in the country and the teachings of their founders and saint-savants were intrinsically supportive of inter-communal peace, understanding and justice. In many there was hope almost against hope, that the URO would succeed in its objective of achieving, through the inter-religious resources available to it, its goals of inter-communal peace and justice. The thought that if the URO failed, nothing else would succeed, gave the deliberations a sense of earnestness and poignancy and an atomosphere of such seriousness and responsibility that irrelevant digressions were avoided and interventions were usually brief and incisive. Many stressed the urgency of the issues.

The point was made that in Sri Lanka four world religions—Buddhism, Hinduism, Islam and Christianity—were genuinely and vitally present. Indeed, it was stated that Sri Lanka, though a small island, is the only country in the world where these four religions were present in their pure and pristine forms. However that maybe, it was undeniable that tremendous responsibility devolved on the four religions and on their leaders to ensure that religious belief and religious practice served the cause of inter-communal peace with justice. If religion could not play a vital role in recalling human beings to the oneness of their essential humanity and to their obligations of respect for one anothers rights and feelings, what use would religion be and what credibility would it have?

At least three solutions to the inter-ethnic problem were identified as being on trial in the country today. There was first *the militant solution* through arms attempted by the youths in the North and increasingly in the East. There was the *military solution* through armed services of the State. The question as to which solution, the militant or the military was attempted first, thereby provoking the other is much less important for the URO than to realize that neither of them accords with what is best and noblest in the religions of the land. Thirdly, there is *the politcal solution*, whereby the sound of guns is muted and human beings concerned for the humanity that binds them together in one human community sit around a table and work out a solution to the problems that exist.

It is precisely the task of the URO—a task to which it has pledged itself and from which for it there can be no return—to create the climate and build countrywide the base for such a lasting, fair, just and equitable political solution.

Herein lies the greatest hope, for the future, that will work to create a plural society based on compassion and tolerance, such as was the Asokan empire.

APPENDIX 5:
SRI LANKA—WHO WANTS A SEPARATE STATE?

(A publication of the Ministry of State, the Government of Sri Lanka; Overseas Information Series, no. 9, 11 November 1983)

The Manifesto of the Tamil United Liberation Front at the General Elections of 1977, sought a mandate from its voters for the creation of "an independent sovereign State of Tamil Eelam." This State was to be constituted of "all the geographically contiguous areas that have been the traditional homeland of the Tamil-speaking people in the country." The boundaries of the State of Eelam were not defined but were identified by the fact that the TULF contested every one of the 14 electorates in the Northern Province, and 8 out of the 10 electorates in the adjoining Eastern Province.[1] This identification has been confirmed by the subsequent general acceptance by the separatists that the Northern and Eastern Provinces constituted the State of Eelam.

The Manifesto proceeded to declare that the following shall be the citizens of Tamil Eelam:

(a) all those people now living in the territory of Tamil Eelam,
(b) Tamil-speaking persons from any part of Sri Lanka seeking citizenship in the State of Tamil Eelam,
(c) Tamil-speaking people of Ceylonese descent living in any part of the world and seeking citizenship in the State of Tamil Eelam.

Leaving aside the invitees under clause (c) (who would have to sacrifice lucrative employment and relatively luxurious conditions of living to accept Tamil Eelam citizenship), clauses (a) and (b) qualify as potential citizens of Eelam an impressive 4 million persons, or more than one quarter of the population of Sri Lanka. This number is made up as follows:

(a) The entire population of the Northern and
Eastern Provinces .... 2.09 million

177

(b) Tamil-speaking persons from other Provinces
    consisting of:

Tamils	0.51 million
Moors	0.69 million
Indian Tamils	<u>0.74</u> million
	<u>4.03</u> million

It is interesting to find out how many people living within the "State of Tamil Eelam" opted to support the TULF in its call for an independent sovereign State and how many Tamil-speaking people outside its boundaries have voiced their support for a separate state.

The Territory of Eelam

The territory of Eelam as identified by the TULF consists of 4 Administrative Districts in the Northern Province and of 3 Administrative Districts in the Eastern Province. The total population of these 7 districts (1981 census) was 2.09 million of which Tamils[2] constituted 1.36 million or 65% of this population. In the Eastern Province, however, the Tamil population consists of a *minority* of less than 41%. In the 3 districts of this Province, Tamils predominate in Batticaloa with 71% but are in a minority in Trincomalee with 34% and a still smaller minority in the Amparai District with only 20%.

The support received by the TULF in its call for a separate State may be gauged by the percentage of votes cast for the TULF in the general election of 1977 in the Northern and Eastern Provinces. The percentages of TULF votes in the 7 districts were as follows:

Jaffna District	71.81%
Mannar District	51.44%
Vavuniya District	58.82%
Mullativu District	52.16%
Trincomalee District	27.18%
Batticaloa District	32.14%
Amparai District	20.25%

Relating these voting percentages to the total population in each District, it can be inferred that only 48% of voters in the Northern and Eastern Provinces pledged support to the TULF in its call for a separate State. Considering that the total population of the Northern and Eastern Provinces is a little more than 2 million, the above percentage suggest that not more than 1 million of the inhabitants of the Northern and Eastern Provinces favour a separate State.

This would leave within the defined boundaries of Tamil Eelam somewhat more than another million who have declined to throw in their lot with this sovereign State. In the Districts of Mannar and Mullativu almost half their population appear to have opted against a separate State.

In the Eastern sector of Tamil Eelam the idea of a separate State appears to have been viewed with even less favour. Tamils constitute 41% of the population of this Province but the TULF received only 26% of the votes cast in the Province. One infers therefore that in the Eastern Province a very large number of Tamils themselves have rejected the idea of a separate State. In the 3 districts constitution this Province, 68% of the population of Batticlaoa District, 73% of the population of Amparai District have voted against the TULF and its proposal for a separate State.

The Tamil-speaking people

The State of Tamil Eelam has also opened its doors to all Tamil-speaking people of Sri Lanka living outside the Northern and Eastern Provinces as well as to expatriate Tamils.

(a) *Tamils*

At the time of the 1981 census 512,340 Tamils lived outside the Northern and Eastern Provinces. Roughly one third of this number (156,000) lived in the District of Colombo, with substantial groups exceeding 30,000 living in the Districts of Kandy, Nuwara Eliya, Puttalam, Badulla and Gampaha.

The bulk of this half million therefore consists of Tamils settled in primarily Sinhala areas, some of them for more than two or three generations, and many of them with no residual links with the Northern or Eastern provinces. The bread winners of these families pursue professions or business vocations or are employed in their areas of residence, and their children pursue their education in these areas. It is difficult to imagine many of these families being able even to eke out an existence if they were to uproot themselves from their present locations to opt for residence in the mythical State of Eelam.

The absence of substantial support for separatism from these members of the Tamil community is indicated by the fact that the TULF (except for the single abortive attempt in the Puttalam electorate in 1977) has not attempted to contest either a District or a Municipal election in these areas. On the other hand the position of most Tamil residents in these areas has been that they have never been supporters of the claim for a separate State.

(b) *Moors*

The Moor community of Sri Lanka numbering over a million and constituting 7.6% of the population has maintained a very clear ethnic and religious identity and has never been associated with the Tamil community in the call for a separate State. Politically this community has identified itself very strongly with right wing political parties in the country and have held distinguished office in every government since Independence.

It is unthinkable that the Moor community which lives in peace and harmony with the majority community in the country, and whose leaders have proclaimed their allegiance to government and expressed their support of an unitary state, will opt for citizenship for the State of Tamil Eelam.

(c) *Indian Tamils*

The only other Tamil-speaking community in Sri Lanka consists of a little over 800,000 Indian Tamils (5.5% of the population) who live mainly in the plantation districts of Nuwara Eliya and Badulla. Their acknowledged leadership, under the banner of a major trade union, the Ceylon Workers Congress, has disassociated itself from the cry for a separate State. The CWC is, in fact, a constituent party of the present government with its leader holding an important cabinet portfolio. The CWC has declared unequivocally both in this country and abroad that should the security of its membership be threatened, it would seek their return to India rather than seek refuge in the state of Eelam.

It is therefore highly unlikely that the invitation of the TULF to all "Tamil-speaking people" outside the State of Tamil Eelam to accept its citizenship will find any substantial response.

(d) *Expatriate Tamils*

The possibility of Sri Lankan Tamils living abroad accepting the offer of citizenship in the State of Tamil Eelam would appear to be even more remote. Many expatriate Tamils have helped to create the terrorist monster in the north of Sri Lanka and supported an intensive propaganda campaign directed at establishing charges of massive violations of human rights amounting to genocide by the majority community. It is easy for these "heroes" who enjoy lucrative employment and live in luxury abroad to acclaim northern terrorists as liberation fighters and to heap scorn and insult on the land of their birth. It would be much less easy for these well-heeled expatriates to give up their affluent life styles in exchange for the inclement climate and the barren soils of the Northern Province of Sri Lanka.

The Demography of Eelam

The realisation of the mythical State of Eelam will produce vast changes in the demographic patterns of Sri Lanka. If only those residents of the Northern and Eastern Provinces who supported the TULF at the last election opt for citizenship in the State of Eelam, more than a million others may opt to leave it. Whether the rest of the Sri Lankan community can accept an influx of a million refugees will not be a matter for debate—it would be a situation impossible to contemplate. At the same time pressure would mount in the rest of the country for the forcible repatriation to Eelam of the half-million Tamil population resident in other parts of Sri Lanka. This is an exercise which could not be carried out without causing massive hardship and human misery far exceeding in volume any hardship alleged to have been inflicted so far on the Tamil community.

If large scale movements of population do not take place—as indeed they cannot—after the establishment of the mythical State, the country would be faced with minority problems far greater than it has ever faced in its history. Besides the problems of a minority of a half million Tamils living outside the State of Eelam (accentuated by the fact that the Sinhala community will find it increasingly difficult to live or function within the new State) the Eelam State itself will be faced with a non-Tamil minority consisting of 35% of its population.

If the pattern of voting in the 1977 General election is repeated at a future election in the State of Tamil Eelam it is quite conceivable that the TULF (which secured only 48% of the votes in this region in 1977) may once again find itself in a minority and the State of Eelam could well come under a government which might oppose the idea of a separate State. More terrorism would then be required to save Eelam from its own Government.

Notes

1. At this election the TULF also presented a candidate for one of the five electorates in the Puttalam District which carries a Tamil population of less than 7%. This contest can hardly be considered a serious claim for the inclusion of this District in the State of Eelam since the TULF secured only 1.7% of the votes cast in this electorate, although the Tamils within the electorate constituted 19.9% of the voters.

2. The word "Tamil" is used here to denote "Sri Lankan Tamils," the indigenous Tamil population of Sri Lanka, as distinct from "Indian Tamils" who are the descendants of more recent immigrees, the plantation workers.

NOTES

Chapter 1

1. Bishop Heber was prompted to write in a poem of the island as a place "where every prospect pleases and only man is vile." The good bishop was only extolling the perfection of nature, but his slur on the imperfect natives ironically begins to take on a reality in the light of recent events.

2. H. A. I. Goonetileke, "July 1983 and the National Question in Sri Lanka; A Bibliographical Guide," in *Sri Lanka, Racism and the Authoritarian State; Race and Class* 26, no. 1 (1984): 159.

3. "In an otherwise excellent news article, 'Recent Fighting in Sri Lanka Dims Hope for Ethnic Peace' (April 22), you state: 'The Sinhalese and Tamils are divided not only by religion but by ethnic background: the Sinhalese are of Aryan stock, the Tamils are of a darker-skinned Dravidian extraction.' This racist nonsense is part of the current mythology of middle-class Sinhalese.

"The Aryans were motley groups of ancient tribes, probably from the Central Asian steppes, that descended onto the Iranian plateau and launched a series of migrations or invasions into Northwest India in the second millennium B.C. Most of the languages of North India, and the language of Sri Lanka, are Indo-European offshoots of the languages of these early settlers.

"However, even during the period of the Buddha, in the sixth century B.C., miscegenation had been complete, and the term Aryan ceased to have any racial connotation. It was simply a descriptive term meaning 'noble.'

"The racial connotations of 'Aryan' were introduced in the late 19th century by Sri Lankan Sinhalese nationalists to differentiate themselves from the Tamils. They were aided by 19th-century European Indologists, who spoke of the Aryan subjugation of dark-skinned peoples (the aboriginal Dravidians)—a hypothesis no longer acceptable to serious historians.

"In reality, there is little difference in the ethnic backgrounds of the Sinhalese and the Tamils. The first colonizers of Sri Lanka were probably North Indians. But according to the chronicles of the Sinhalese, even the first king and his followers married women from South India (Madurai). Thereafter the patterns of royal marriage and mass immigration were wholly from South India, initially from the Tamil country and later (since the 13th century) from Kerala.

183

"As for dark skin, the father of King Dutugemmunu, a great hero of the Sinhalese, was called "Kavan," or crow-colored. There are a few Sinhalese nowadays with fair complexions, but this is probably due to miscegenation with successive waves of European conquerors from the early 16th century onward. Any Aryan complexion comes from the latter-day European descendants of the ancient Aryans." Gananath Obeyesekere, Princeton, N.J., April 24, 1984.

4. See R. Indrapala, "A Brief History of the City of Jaffna," *Commemorative Souvenir, The Jaffna Public Library* (St. Joseph's Press, 1984), pp. 7–11.

5. On these matters, useful recently composed sources are K. Malagoda, *Buddhism in Sinhalese Society, 1760–1900* (Berkeley, Cal.: University of California Press, 1976), and Michael Roberts, *Caste Conflict and Elite Formation: The Rise of a Karāva Elite in Sri Lanka 1500–1931* (Cambridge: Cambridge University Press, 1982). A very useful slightly older authority is Bryce Ryan, *Caste in Modern Ceylon* (New Brunswick, N.J.: Rutgers University Press, 1953).

Chapter 2

1. The riots of 1915 were directed against the Muslims. It appears the chief targets were the "Coast Moors," most of whom were recent migrants from the Malabar Coast of India. As retail traders, they were direct competitors of the low-country Sinhalese traders, who accused their rivals of extending credit on easy terms and charging high prices. The Sinhalese antagonists exploited religious (Buddhist) and racial sentiments, and even the Buddhist revivalist Anagārika Dharmapāla was guilty of this kind of incitement. The British misconstrued the riots as a conspiracy against them and overreacted. They jailed a number of Sinhalese leaders, including the Senanayakes, who were temperance leaders, and A. E. Goonesinha, the leader of the Young Lanka League.

2. K. M. de Silva *A History of Sri Lanka* (Berkeley: University of California Press, 1981), p. 541, surmises that tensions between "generations" became a military conflict on a national scale. The insurrection took place during the Sri Lanka Freedom Party (SLFP) regime of Mrs. Bandaranaike, and de Silva sees it as an action taken by the insurgent Sinhalese youth against the established left, both the populist SLFP and the traditional Marxist parties such as the Lanka Sama Samaj Party (L.S.S.P.) and the Communist Party (C.P.). The public at large did not participate in the rebellion, which was put down by the government police and armed forces "with considerable ruthlessness" (ibid., p. 542). The insurgency—and this is important—showed that a certain amount of widespread underground organization had taken place, led by youth leaders who had a sense of planned strategy and were energized by a revolutionary and millenarian ideology.

3. Eelam is the Tamil name given to the island by these insurgents in preference to the Sinhalese name of Sri Lanka. The insurgents want a separate state in the north and east to be called Eelam; they wish to liberate

Eelam, which was allegedly the area of Tamil rule in pre-British times, from Sinhalese dominance in the rest of the island.

Chapter 3

1. See Professor Virginia Leary, *Ethnic Conflict and Violence in Sri Lanka in July–August 1981 on Behalf of the International Commission of Jurists*, pp. 3–4 (n.p., n.d.). TULF stands for Tamil United Liberation Front.

2. Ibid., pp. 21–25.

3. According to the Census of 1981, about 512,340 Sri Lankan Tamils lived outside the Northern and Eastern Provinces: a third of them were concentrated in the District of Colombo; the rest were distributed in numbers not exceeding 30,000 in the Districts of Gampaha, Puttalam, Kandy, Badulla, and Nuwara Eliya. The Indian Tamils, making up some 800,000, were mainly concentrated in the plantation districts of Nuwara Eliya and Badulla.

4. *The Times* (of London) of 11 August reported that Mr. Douglas Liyanage, a government spokesman, had in an official statement revised the death toll upwards to 350.

5. *The Times* (of London, 5 August 1983) made this allegation: "In Trincomalee, 'mutinous' members of the Navy and Army, with the assistance of the Sinhalese, destroyed and burned down almost 200 Tamil houses and shops. A Hindu temple was damaged."

6. This "standardization" is basically an ethnic quota system. Only thirty percent of the places available in the universities are to be filled on an island-wide merit basis; fifty-five percent are allocated to revenue districts in proportion to their population and filled within each district on a merit basis; the remaining fifteen percent are allocated to revenue districts judged to be educationally underprivileged.

Chapter 4

1. *Final Report for Strengthening of the Development Planning Project*. Submitted by Harvard Institute for International Development to the Deputy Director, Contracts and Procurement Branch, Technical Cooperation for Development (TCD), United Nations, New York, March, 1983.

2. Although the program was in law limited to families with incomes below Rs 3,600 per annum, many others above this minimum were beneficiaries. The estimate is that only about 20% of the island's population was eligible.

3. Gananath Obeyesekere, "Political Violence and the Future of Democracy in Sri Lanka," *Internationales Asienforum, International Quarterly for Asian Studies* 15, no. 1/2 (1984):39–60.

4. Paul Sieghart, *Sri Lanka, A Mounting Tragedy of Errors*. Report of a Mission to Sri Lanka in January 1984 on behalf of the International Commission of Jurists and Its British Section, Justice. (Dorchester: Henry Ling Ltd., The Dorset Press, March 1984), pp. 56–61.

5. The two reports in question, which I shall frequently cite, are:

(1) Professor Virginia Leary, *Ethnic Conflict and Violence in Sri Lanka, Report of a Mission to Sri Lanka in July–August 1981 on Behalf of the International Commission of Jurists.*

(2) Paul Sieghart, *Sri Lanka, A Mounting Tragedy of Errors, Report of a Mission to Sri Lanka in January 1984 on behalf of the International Commission of Jurists and its British Section, Justice.* (Dorchester: Henry Ling Ltd., The Dorset Press, March 1984). Mr. Sieghart is chairman of the Executive Committee of Justice.

6. Leary, *Ethnic Conflict*, pp. 47–48.

7. Sieghart, *Sri Lanka*, p. 63.

8. Ibid., p. 39.

9. Orville H. Schell, former president of the New York City Bar Association, is chairman of the American Watch Committee.

10. Leary, *Ethnic Conflict*, p. 66.

11. Subsequently, Lalith Athulathmudali, appointed minister of internal security, became a close associate and protégé of the president.

12. By another turn of the wheel of fortune, Cyril Mathew was later relieved of his cabinet post for criticizing the president, though in 1985 he still remains an MP and a member of the UNP.

13. Robert N. Kearney and Barbara D. Miller, "Sex-Differential Patterns of Internal Migration in Sri Lanka," *Peasant Studies* 10, no. 4 (1983): 223–50.

14. It is relevant to note that while the urbanized Colombo district has continued to attract a large number of in-migrants, it has also contributed large numbers of out-migrants from the southwest headed to the agriculturally developing regions of the north and east.

15. Kearney and Miller, "Sex-Differential Patterns," p. 227.

16. Colombo district had the highest literacy rate, with 91.1% for males and 84.4% for females; then come, in order, Kalutara, 88.6% for males, 77.7% for females; Galle, 88.1% for males, 77.2% for females; Kurunegala, 88.0% for males, 74.0% for females; Jaffna, 86.3% for males, 79.2% for females; and Matara, 85.6% for males, 71.4% for females.

17. Sieghart, *Sri Lanka*, p. 21.

18. Obeyesekere, "Political Violence," pp. 44–46.

19. Ibid., p. 44.

20. Ibid.

21. Ibid., p. 48.

22. S. W. R. D. Bandaranaike held office as prime minister from 1956 to 1959, and Mrs. Bandaranaike for two periods: 1960–65 and 1970–77.

23. *Key Development Issues for Sri Lanka. Final Technical Report.* Submitted by Harvard Institute for International Development (December 1982), pp. 3–4.

24. See the fascinating account by H. L. Seneviratne and Swarna Wickremaratne, "Bodhipūjā: Collective Representations of Sri Lanka Youth," *American Ethnologist* 7, no. 4 (1980): 734–43.

25. See the illuminating account and interpretation given by Gananath

Obeyesekere, "The Fire-Walkers of Kataragama: The Rise of *Bhakti* Religiosity in Buddhist Sri Lanka," *Journal of Asian Studies* 37 (1978): 457-76.

26. See Gananath Obeyesekere, "Social Change and the Deities: Rise of the Kataragama Cult in Modern Sri Lanka," *Man* 12, nos. 3/4 (1977): 377–96.

27. Don Handelman, "On the Desuetude of Kataragama," *Man* 20, no. 1 (1985): 156–57.

28. Quoted by Handelman, ibid., p. 157.

29. See Cyril Mathew's speech reported in *Hansard* 4 August 1983, pp. 1038–1324.

Chapter 5

1. The following are very useful and standard sources: W. Howard Wriggins, *Dilemmas of a New Nation* (Princeton, N.J.: Princeton University Press, 1960); R. N. Kearney, *Communalism and Language in the Politics of Ceylon* (Durham, N.C.: Duke University Press, 1967); R. N. Kearney, *The Politics of Ceylon (Sri Lanka)* (Ithaca, N.Y.: Cornell University Press, 1973); A. J. Wilson, *Politics in Sri Lanka, 1947–1979* (London: Macmillan, 1979); B. H. Farmer, *Ceylon, A Divided Nation* (London: Oxford University Press, 1963); U. Phadnis, *Religion and Politics in Sri Lanka* (New Delhi: Manohar Book Service, 1976); K. M. de Silva, *A History of Sri Lanka* (Berkeley and Los Angeles: University of California Press, 1981); *History of Ceylon*, vol. 3, University of Ceylon, ed. K. M. de Silva (Colombo: Colombo Apothecaries' Co., 1973).

2. In Sinhalese popular mythology, the disproportionate participation of the Tamils has been exaggerated far more than reality warrants. This is why one is forced to say that this Sinhalese sensitivity is both distorted and overdetermined. I shall address this issue later.

3. The Donoughmore Commission advocated territorial representation and manhood suffrage as essential measures for the achievement of democratic government. The Sinhalese embraced these principles as progressive, and because they would become the chief beneficiaries. The Sinhalese politicians, however, compromised their support of progressive government when they adamantly refused the enfranchisement of the Indian plantation laborers, for that would have eroded their supremacy in the central highlands.

When the Donoughmore Commissioners recommended that the Indian laborers be enfranchised, the politicians espousing the interests of the Kandyan Sinhalese rejected the proposal on the self-interested grounds that Indian labor would dominate the polls in the areas of their maximal concentration. Even the Ceylon National Congress, which led the demand for constitutional progress—and which at this time was dominated by Sinhalese politicians—rejected the proposal for fear that the European planters who employed the laborers might come to exert a tendentious political influence upon them.

4. The Donoughmore Commission rejected provision for "communal" representation and special weightage for the ethnic minorities as pleaded for

by the minority leaders, especially the Tamil leader, Sir Ponnambalam Rama-nathan, and the Muslim leader T. B. Jayah. In the event, when the new constitution was implemented, all the ministers were Sinhalese and the execu-tive committees were dominated by the Sinhalese-elected members. Toward the end of the Donoughmore era, which was dominated by D. B. Jayatilake and D. S. Senanayake, a Tamil member, Arunachalam Mahadeva, was made minister of home affairs. The Soulbury Commission, which sat on the eve of independence, also strongly resisted ethnic and minority demands for consti-tutional protection of minority interests and special representation of minor-ity representatives in the legislature. At this round, G. G. Ponnambalam, leader of the Tamil Congress, led the demand for "50–50" (50% of the seats for the Sinhalese, and the other 50% to be reserved for all the minorities).

5. Heinz Bechert "The Beginnings of Buddhist Historiography: Mahā-vaṃsa and Political Thinking," in Bardwell L. Smith, ed., *Religion and Legitimation of Power in Sri Lanka* (Chambersburg, Pa.: Anima Books 1978), p. 7.

6. Howard Wriggins, *Dilemmas of a New Nation*, p. 226.

7. These tables are taken from an excellent document entitled *Sri Lanka's Ethnic Conflict, Myths and Realities*, Report of the Committee for Rational Development (November 1983). This report is reproduced as appendix 3.

8. The extent of Tamil representation in these professions is difficult to assess. A recent Ministry of State publication entitled *Sri Lanka, the Truth about Discrimination against the Tamils* (Government Press, n.d.) claims these figures for professionals in the public service drawn from the Tamil community. These "propaganda" figures do not correspond with the distribu-tions in the tables I have cited earlier based on official government censuses:

engineers	34.9%
surveyors	29.9%
doctors	35.1%
dentists	24.7%
veterinary surgeons	38.8%
accountants	33.1%
life scientists	41.5%

For the semiprofessional sector of the public service, the figures given are:

medical, dental, veterinary technicians	30.2%
engineering technicians	24.3%
survey draftsmen	27.8%

Chapter 6

1. See Bridget and Raymond Allchin, *The Birth of Indian Civilization, India and Pakistan before 500 B.C.* (Middlesex: Penguin Books, 1968). See also Bridget Allchin, "The Late Stone Age of Ceylon," *Journal of the Royal Anthropological Institute* 88 (1958): 179–201.

2. Allchin and Allchin, *The Birth of Indian Civilization*, p. 227.

3. Susantha Goonatilaka, "The Formation of Sri Lankan Culture: Rein-terpretation of Chronicles and Archaeological Material," in *Ethnicity and*

Social Change in Sri Lanka, Papers presented at a seminar organized by the Social Scientists' Association, December 1979 (Colombo: Karunaratne and Sons, Ltd., 1984), pp. i–xxxiii. See also S. V. Deraniyagala, "A Theoretical Framework for the Study of Sri Lanka's Prehistory," in *Ancient Ceylon, Journal of the Archaeological Survey Department of Sri Lanka* 5 (1984): 81–104.

4. James Rutnam, "Jaffna before the Dawn of History," *Commemorative Souvenir, The Jaffna Public Library* (St. Joseph's Press, 1984), pp. 12–14.

5. Goonatilaka, "The Formation of Sri Lankan Culture," pp. iv–v. The authors he is citing are: S. Paranavitana, *Sinhalayo* (Colombo: Lake House Investments, Ltd., 1967); S. P. F. Senaratne, *Prehistoric Archaeology in Ceylon*, Ceylon National Museums Handbook Series (Department of National Museums, Ceylon, 1969); S. Deraniyagala, *Ancient Ceylon*, no. 2 (Department of Archaeology Colombo, 1972).

6. See John Carswell and Martha E. Prickett, "Mantai 1980: A Preliminary Investigation," *Ancient Ceylon, Journal of the Archaeological Survey of Sri Lanka* no. 5 (1984): 3–68.

7. See Senake Bandaranayake, *Sinhalese Monastic Architecture, The Vihāras of Anurādhapura* (Leiden: E. J. Brill, 1974), pp. 22–23.

8. G. C. Mendis, *The Early History of Ceylon*, p. 17.

9. For a recent evaluation of this activity, see R. A. L. H. Gunawardana's "Irrigation and Hydraulic Society in Early Medieval Ceylon," *Past and Present* 53 (November 1971).

10. Bandaranayake, *Sinhalese Monastic Architecture*, p. 10 This book is volume 4 of Studies in South Asian Culture, ed. J. L. Van Lohuizen-De Leeuw.

11. M. D. Raghavan, *The Karāva of Ceylon, Society and Culture*. (Colombo: K. V. G. de Silva and Sons, 1961), pp. 2–3.

12. See *World Conqueror and World Renouncer: A Study of Buddhism and Polity in Thailand against a Historical Background* (Cambridge: Cambridge University Press 1976), chapters 7 and 8. Also *Culture, Thought and Social Action: An Anthropological Perspective* (Cambridge, Mass.: Harvard University Press, 1985), chapter 7, "The Galactic Polity in Southeast Asia."

13. L. S. Dewaraja, *The Kandyan Kingdom 1707–1760* (Colombo: Lake House Investments, Ltd., 1972).

14. Ibid., p. 27.

15. H. L. Seneviratne, "The Alien King: Nāyakkars on the Throne of Kandy," *The Ceylon Journal of Historical and Social Studies*, n.s., 6, no. 1 (1976): 55–61.

16. Ibid.

17. In a personal communication, Professor H. L. Seneviratne gives this analysis of the signatures of the chiefs who took part in the Kandyan Convention. Signatures in Sinhalese and Tamil scripts are nearly equal in number. Most dramatically, Āhälēpola, the Kandyan chief who was the arch-enemy of the "Tamil King," signed in correct Tamil, as did Ratwatte, the Disāva of Matale. "What is most curious," remarks Seneviratne, "is that the signatures of the two Piḷimatalavves, and of the Disāvas Dūllāve and Millāve seem to consist of *both* Sinhalese and Tamil characters"; in fact, the mixture is roughly

fifty-fifty except in the case of Millåve, who uses predominantly Sinhalese letters.

Seneviratne remarks that from about the thirteenth century the Sinhalese script came to be influenced by the *grantha*, the script of the South Indian languages, and surmises that just as the "Sinhalese" and "Tamils" were interchangeable in Kandyan times, so were the two scripts. All this is further reinforced by the fact that Kandyan Sinhalese "has a very high proportion of Tamil and other South Indian words," many of them being now considered quintessential Sinhalese words. Examples from what is a long list are *pāyanava, adukku, koṭṭal, kodi, uliyakkara, vaṭṭōru, sellam, maṇḍādi, karāva, tuppoṭṭi, ilangam.*

18. Dewaraja, *The Kandyan Kingdom 1707–1760*, chap. 3.

19. Ibid., pp. 47–48.

20. Ibid., p. 48.

21. Ibid., p. 50.

22. Firewalking worship in Draupadi Amman Kōvils and the cult of Kannaki Amman are evidence of the continuance and incorporation of "Hindu" features, which of course were integrated into the amalgam of Sinhalese religion. The latter cult belongs to the same universe as that of Pattini worship, which has been magnificently documented by Gananth Obeyeskere, *The Cult of the Goddess Pattini* (Chicago: University of Chicago Press, 1984).

23. R. L. Stirrat, "Some Preliminary Remarks on Religious and Ethnic Identity in Sri Lanka." Unpublished essay.

24. Nur Yalman, *Under the Bo Tree: Studies in Caste, Kinship, and Marriage in the Interior of Ceylon* (Berkeley and Los Angeles: University of California Press, 1967). In this pathbreaking book, Yalman described the amicable coexistence, bilingualism, and intermarriage between Sinhalese and Tamils in the Pānama region, which lies on the east coast south of Pottuvil. Pānama is a shatter zone that in the 1960s had an "amalgamated social system that is halfway between Sinhalese and Tamil" (p. 310).

25. On the South Indian origins of the Salāgama caste, see Colvin R. de Silva *Ceylon Under the British Occupation*, 2 vols. (Colombo: Apothecaries Co., 1962).

26. A recent work that documents this revival is K. Malalgoda, *Buddhism in Sinhalese Society 1750–1900: A Study of Religious Revival and Change* (Berkeley: University of California Press, 1978).

27. S. Pathmanathan, *The Kingdom of Jaffna*, part 1 (Colombo: Arul M. Rajendram, 1978).

28. On this issue, see H. W. Tambiah, *The Laws and Customs of the Tamils of Jaffna* (Colombo: The Times of Ceylon, n.d.), and Jack Goody and S. J. Tambiah, *Dowry and Bridewealth*, Cambridge Papers in Social Anthropology (Cambridge: Cambridge University Press, 1973).

29. See Arjun Appadurai, *Worship and Conflict under Colonial Rule: A South Indian Case* (Cambridge: Cambridge University Press, 1981); Burton Stein, ed., *South Indian Temples: An Analytical Reconsideration* (New Delhi: Vikas, 1978).

30. R. S. Perimbanayagam, *The Karmic Theater, Self, Society and Astrology in Jaffna* (Amherst: The University of Massachusetts Press, 1982).

31. Ibid., p. 56.

32. K. Kailasapathy, *The Cultural and Linguistic Consciousness of the Tamil Community in Sri Lanka.* Punithavathy Tiruchelvam Memorial Lecture, Tamil Women's Union, Kalalaya (Colombo: New Leela Press, 1982), p. 6.

33. K. M. de Silva, *A History of Sri Lanka* (Berkeley and Los Angeles: University of California Press, 1981), pp. 422–29.

34. See Eugene F. Irschick, *Politics and Social Conflict in South India: The Non-Brahmin Movement and Tamil Separatism, 1916–1929* (Berkeley: University of California Press, 1969); Lloyd I. and Suzanne H. Rudolph, *The Modernity of Tradition: Political Development in India* (Chicago: University of Chicago Press, 1967); Robert L. Hardgrave, Jr., *The Dravidian Movement* (Bombay: Popular Prakashan, 1965); idem, *Essays in the Political Sociology of South India* (New Delhi: Usha Publications, 1979); idem, *The Nadars of Tamilnad: The Political Culture of a Community in Change* (Berkeley: University of California Press, 1969).

Chapter 7

1. Kandyan sensitivities of half a century ago vis-à-vis the low-country Sinhalese are much muted today. A pamphlet entitled *Present Politics and the Rights of Kandyans*, printed in 1920 and authored by J. A. Halangoda, argued that the lawful interests of the Kandyans were being jeopardized by the demands of the low-country Sinhalese leaders for constitutional reform. The pamphlet appealed to the British as guardians and "trustees of Kandyan nationality." The governor, Sir William Manning, skillfully manipulated these internal dissensions in the 1920s to scuttle the aspirations of the Ceylon National Congress for political reform. A Kandyan delegation consisting of J. A. Halangoda, T. B. L. Moonemalle, and G. E. Madawala went to London in 1920 and actually urged "communal" (virtually "ethnic") electorates for the Kandyans because they were a "minority community."

As Kingsley de Silva (*A History of Sri Lanka*, p. 392) explains: "When a high level of education and property qualifications were laid down as conditions for the exercise of the vote under the reforms of 1910–12, the Kandyans had seen the Low-Country Sinhalese and Tamils lead in these spheres converted into the hard reality of political advantage in the electorate (the educated Ceylonese electorate)."

Chapter 8

1. Loki Madan, "Coping with Ethnic Diversity: A South Asian Perspective," in D. Maybury-Lewis, ed., *Prospects for Plural Societies* (American Ethnological Society, 1984).

Chapter 9

1. *Buddhism and the Spirit Cults in North-East Thailand* (Cambridge: Cambridge University Press, 1970).

2. *World Conqueror and World Renouncer: A Study of Buddhism and Polity in Thailand against a Historical Background* (Cambridge: Cambridge University Press, 1976).

3. *The Buddhist Saints of the Forest and the Cult of Amulets: A Study in Charisma, Hagiography, Sectarianism and Millenial Buddhism* (Cambridge: Cambridge University Press, 1984).

4. See the introduction in C. F. Keyes, ed., *Ethnic Adaptation and Identity: The Karen of the Thai Frontier with Burma* (Philadelphia: Ishii, 1979).

INDEX

Government capital expenditures, 159–60

Govikula, 98–99

Goyigama caste, 8, 101, 103, 120, 124

Great Britain, 3, 28, 54, 101, 112, 137; and Bandaranaikes, 132–33; and Kandyan kingdom, 97, 98; and law on confessions, 42; period of colonial rule by, 2, 4, 7–9, 65–68, 78, 82, 140–41; and Senanayake, 129–30; and Sinhalese-Muslim riots, 13, 130; and Tamil caste rivalries, 104

Greater Colombo Economic Commission, 31

Guardian, The, 20, 22, 25

Gunaratnam, K., 23

Gunawardene, Philip, 75

Gunawardene, Vivienne, 41

Gurugalhinna, 90

Hamlyn, Michael, 54

Handelman, Don, 62

Harvard Institute of International Development, 35–37, 56

Hatton, 4

Hindu, The, 20

Hinduism, 103; Kataragama cult in, 59–63; and Śaiva Śiddhānta movement, 107–8; and Sinhalese kingdoms, 81; in Sri Lanka, 4; of Tamils, 5–7

Hirdaramanis, 23

Income levels, 153

India, 17, 35, 124; Aryan-Dravidian division in, 5; fear of intervention by, 23–27, 77–78; national integration in, 127–28; in precolonial period, 81–82; in prehistory, and Sri Lanka, 88–91; and Sinhala origins, 5–7, 92–99; Sri Lankan perception of, 1–2; Tamil Nāṭu of, 77, 105, 110–11; and Tamil origins, 4, 8, 66–67, 102–5; Tamil refuge in, 109–10. *See also* Cōḷa kingdom

Indian Overseas Bank, 24

India Today, 21, 23, 32–33

Indonesia, 2

Indrapala, K., 88

Inflation, 35–37

International Commission of Jurists, 20, 41, 42

International Covenant on Civil and Political Rights, 46–47

International Herald Tribune, 20

International Tamil Conference, 17

Iran, 92

Iron Age, 88–90

Islam. *See* Muslims

Jafferjees, 23

Jaffna, 8–9, 105, 123; ambush of soldiers in, 15, 16; burial sites in, 90; caste structure in, 103–6; kingdom of, 5–8, 102–4; population of, 50; rioting in, 19–20

Jananāthapura, 94

Janatā Vimukti Peramuṇa (JVP), 13–15, 76–77, 122

Jātika Sēvaka Saṅgamaya (JSS), 32–33, 48, 53

Jayasuriya, F. R., 72

Jayawardene, Junius, 17, 18, 71–72, 117; and authoritarianism, 28, 32–33, 39–41; economic policy of, 28, 30–32, 35; faction surrounding, 48; pro-Sinhala agitation by, 73; responses of, to rioting, 20–21, 25, 30, 46; on Tamil "homeland," 109; and Tamil issue, 28–30

JPV. *See* Janatā Vimukti Peramuṇa

JSS. *See* Jātika Sevaka Saṅgamaya

Kailasapathy, K., 107–8

Kalutara, 22, 50

Kandy, 4, 8–9, 66, 120, 124, 191n.1; ethnic distribution in, 11; kingdom of, 7, 8, 59–63, 96–99, 102–3, 189n.17; population of, 50; rioting in, 22

Kandyan Kingdom 1707–1760, The (Dewaraja), 97

Sri Lanka—Who Wants a Separate State?, 123
Śrī Vijaya Rājasiṃha, 97
Śrī Vikrama Rajasiṃha, 98
Standardization policy, 17, 28–30, 80, 185n.6
Stanley, Sir Herbert, 132
Stirrat, R. L., 99
Stone Age, 88–89
Supreme Court (Sri Lanka), 41, 44, 53–54

Tamil Federal Party, 73
Tamil language, 4–5, 131; and Karava, 99; as national language, 29, 73–75, 123
Tamil Nāṭu, 77, 105, 110–11
Tamils, 3–12; in armed forces and police, 15; in colonial period, 65–68; destruction of businesses of, 22–24; diaspora of, 111–13; employment representation of, 78–80; and language issue, 73–77; and political violence, in general, 115–21; and prehistory in Sri Lanka, 91; rioting against, *see* Riots; social profile of, 102–11; and solutions to conflict, 122–28; terrorism by, 15–18, 38, 123
Tamil United Liberation Front (TULF), 16, 19, 29, 109, 123; banning of, 27, 44; defeat of, by UNP, 39; and secession issue, 24, 30, 32, 44–45, 77
Tamotarum Pillai, C. W., 108
Tēcavaḷamai, 102
Terrorism Act of South Africa, 44
Thailand, 1, 2, 137–40
Thiruchelvam, Neelan, 32
Times, The (London), 21, 25, 30, 54
Tipiṭaka, 93
Tirukketisvaram, 92
Tiruvē Bandaṛ, 95–96
Torture, 18, 46–47
Trincomalee: ethnic distribution in,

9–12; population of, 49–51; rioting in, 22, 25, 121
Tri Simhala Peramuna, 73
TULF. *See* Tamil United Liberation Front

Unemployment, 28, 31, 35, 56–57
United Kingdom (U.K.), Prevention of Terrorism Act in, 43–44. *See also* Great Britain
United National Party (UNP), 20, 122, 133, 135; and authoritarianism, 38–47, 53; defeat of, 71, 131–32; economic policy of, 22, 28, 30–32, 35, 54, 83–84; factions within, 48; formation of, 68; pro-Sinhala agitation by, 73, 75; responses to terrorism by, 18, 115, 116; and thuggery, 51–54, 83–84
United States, 3, 26, 30, 112, 137
UNP. *See* United National Party

Vāddas, 88, 89
Vanniyārs, 102–3
Vaṭṭhagamanī, 93–94
Vavuniya, 9, 11–12, 18, 50
Veḷḷāla caste, 8, 103–7, 121
Vijaya, 70
Vijayanagara kingdom, 60–61, 103
Viśākhā Vidyālaya, 76
Viṣṇu, 60, 81
Voltaire, 5

Walave Basin, 90
Week, The, 24
Weeratunge, Lieutenant General, 48
Welikade prison, 16, 24–25
Wickremaratne, Swarna, 59
Wickremasinghe, Ranil, 48
World Conqueror and World Renouncer (Tambiah), 137
Wriggins, W. Howard, 71, 72

Zambia, 3